Emotion in Group Decision and Negotiation

Advances in Group Decision and Negotiation

Volume 7

The book series, Advances in Group Decision and Negotiation—as an extension of the journal, *Group Decision and Negotiation*—is motivated by unifying approaches to group decision and negotiation processes. These processes are purposeful, adaptive, and complex—cybernetic and self-organizing—and involve relation and coordination in multiplayer, multicriteria, ill-structured, evolving dynamic problems in which players (agents) both cooperate and conflict. These processes are purposeful complex adaptive systems.

Group decision and negotiation involves the whole process or flow of activities relevant to group decision and negotiation—such as communication and information sharing, problem definition (representation) and evolution, alternative generation, social–emotional interaction, coordination, leadership, and the resulting action choice.

Areas of application include intra-organizational coordination (as in local/global strategy, operations management and integrated design, production, finance, marketing, and distribution—e.g., as for new products), computer-supported collaborative work, labor-management negotiation, inter-organizational negotiation (business, government, and nonprofits), electronic negotiation and commerce, mobile technology, culture and negotiation, inter-cultural and international relations and negotiation, globalization, terrorism, and environmental negotiation.

More information about this series at http://www.springer.com/series/5587

Bilyana Martinovsky
Editor

Emotion in Group Decision and Negotiation

Springer

Editor
Bilyana Martinovsky
Stockholm University
Stockholm
Sweden

ISSN 1871-935X
Advances in Group Decision and Negotiation
ISBN 978-94-017-7864-0 ISBN 978-94-017-9963-8 (eBook)
DOI 10.1007/978-94-017-9963-8

Springer Dordrecht Heidelberg New York London

Softcover re-print of the Hardcover 1st edition 2015

Printed on acid-free paper

Springer Science+Business Media B.V. Dordrecht is part of Springer Science+Business Media (www.springer.com)

Acknowledgments

I express my gratitude to all authors, reviewers, Stefan Einarson SPRINGER, the Swedish foundation FORTE, and College of Europe for supporting this research project and this publication.

Bilyana Martinovsky

Contents

Introduction

The academic discipline of Group Decision and Negotiation is dedicated to the understanding, the study, and the development of decision taking and negotiation as group activities. Different types of activities are regulated by specific rules, involving different forms of risk evaluation, means for communication, contexts, and stress conditions. Decision taking and negotiation are promoted and studied as rational cognitive and communicative processes, led by Descartes' motto "Cogito ergo sum." Mathematical models, bargain theories, and decision taking systems are the results and the rational means by which the field is developed. Rational measures are taken to estimate the effects of multiple criteria and different forms of utilities. In this context, it is hard to see the role of emotion in such systems and theories, unless it is described in terms of rational reasoning. Since formal approaches to group decision taking and negotiation defined emotion as subjective and nonrational phenomenon, which is hard to rationalize, predict, or give utilities to, they have indeed preferred to eliminate it from their analysis, models, and systems. Yet, empiria show that emotions play an important role in group decision taking and negotiation activities even if they are defined by rigid rules. Since Damasio challenged Descartes with a new view summarized by the motto "Sentio ergo sum," research on emotion started gaining momentum, within neuroscience and cognitive science but also within research on decision taking. In a group context, however, emotion is not anymore only a subjective experience, it becomes an inter-subjective experience and a factor influencing group decision taking and negotiation (GDN). Realizing that we need to explore number of questions such as: How do emotions become inter-subjective? What are the neural conditions and function of emotion in GDN? What are the communicative means for the realization of emotion in GDN? How do emotions influence GDN? How is emotion related to ideology expressed in GDN? What methods could be used for the study of emotion in GDN? In order to answer these questions, this volume examines the nature, realization, effect, and role emotions play in GDN from number of different perspectives such as neuroscience, psychology, linguistics, pragmatics, informatics, sociology, philosophy, and game theory. Each research discipline has own view, study methods, and findings on the matter. Due to the nature of our subject of study, neuroscience and sociology, for example, are increasingly intertwined, creating a space for interdisciplinary enquiry. The same applies also to informatics, sociology, and linguistics.

The volume aims to give the reader a broad view of the state-of-art research on the topic of emotion in group decision and negotiation. Twelve researchers from the USA, Canada, Europe, and Australia contribute to it. We conducted our research independently of each other, yet our chapters show some interesting similarities in focus, findings, and conclusions. In Chap. 1, Iacoboni and Moore explore emotion in GDN from a neuroscience point of view and find that emotional convergence, contagion, and mimicry in a group are supported by a neural resonance, which leads to emergence of group states. The fact that cooperative group states do not emerge when the groups consist of people with neurological disorders, which affect capacity for empathy, indicates the importance of brain connectedness for the establishment of emotive–cognitive group connectedness.

Similarly, Thagard's study (Chap. 3) in political science acknowledges that ideologies influence group conflicts and group discourses and traces the effect of emotion on ideology. It finds that emotional coherence leads to ideologies and disrupts cognitive processes such as inferences. In that sense, person–group problems can be resolved if emotional contagion is understood.

Olekalns and Druckman's Chap. 2 is organized in terms of four themes: moves and exchanges, information processing, social interaction, and the contexts in which negotiation occurs. It also connects findings in social aspects of emotion in GDN with results from neuroscience, which suggest that emotion and cognition are deeply intertwined processes, which can hardly be separated. An interesting insight, derived in part from neuroimaging research, is that "intentional tactics, which may include evading and deceiving, combine elements of thought and feeling in an integrative rather than sequential, competing or additive fashion." However, they report that social and situational context affects emotion in GDN, i.e., the same emotion elicited in different context elicits different brain states. Yet, "emotional inconsistency elicits greater concessions than emotional consistency." With respect to the effect of strategy on emotion in GDN, their chapter suggests that expression of emotion, which is perceived as strategic, reduces trust, whereas authentic emotion elicits lower demands from opponent.

In Chap. 4, Meerts and Vucovic analyze GDN as a psychological process where cognition and emotion are inseparably connected by Theory-of-Mind-based models of self and other. In that sense, stereotyped perceptions of own or other's identity (e.g., national identity), including expected cognitive and emotional attachments and judgments, precede and affect any form of interaction. Negotiations are particularly sensitive to this aspect of communication because they do not need to end up with a particular decision or agreement. The authors' observations of international diplomacy negotiations lead them to the conclusion that they are best described as processes where parties strive to satisfy and enhance the "face" of the negotiator rather than reach particular transactive goals.

The channel of communication, however, has a strong effect on emotion in GDN. The authors of Chap. 5, Griessmair, Hippmann and Gettinger, discuss the impact of emotions in electronic GDN environments. Connectedness of cognitive, emotive, and social processes is found even in electronic-supported decision and negotiation. Yet, rapport building is more difficult through asynchronous than synchronous e-negotiations, the later being characterized as more affective, disinhibited, and competitive than the former. The advantage of e-negotiation/decision systems, which allow more time between interactions, is that they support integration of emotion, inference ability, and goal-oriented behavior. The authors propose a model integrating inter- and intra-personal effects of emotions and how they are influenced by electronically mediated communication and the decision support component of electronic negotiation systems. The interplay between inter- and intra-personal effects is illustrated through the concept of fairness: Unfair concessions offered with positive emotion result in cognitive dissonance, which challenges the possibility for agreement or future cooperation.

Chapter 6 focuses on face-to-face interaction analysis of group decision and negotiation, which explores the discursive realization of variety of emotions occurring naturally in authentic discourse activities. Based on empirical studies, it formulates a model for analysis of emotion in GDN, which allows for both mimicry-based and appraisal-based emotion processes and supports both authentic and strategic realizations of emotion in GDN. In this model, reciprocal adaptation is an influential interactional process supported by neural resonance.

Steven Brams' chapter shows how Theory of Moves explains the choices that players make to extricate themselves from frustrating conflicts. Theory of Moves modifies the rules of play in standard game theory to model how farsighted players think ahead about the consequences of their moves and countermoves. Players' frustration triggers anger that leads them to threaten an adversary, and sometimes carry out the threat or otherwise induce a crisis, that ultimately benefits them. He illustrates Theory of Moves with examples from Aristophanes's *Lysistrata* and Shakespeare's *Macbeth*. Brams' approach differs in his view of inter-subjectivity from the other chapters in this volume as it assumes that players have complete information about the other player's preferences as well as their own but how well or badly one player feels at each outcome or state does not affect how well or badly another player feels, because preferences are assumed given and do not ordinarily change.

All chapters define a need of future study of diversity of emotions as the literature has privileged emotions such as anger, fear, joy, and empathy, but has less insight into emotional states such as shame, surprise, remorse, despair, and certainty. Yet, all authors find that emotional resonance in GDN contexts has the most powerful impact on the activity and its outcome. The validity and potency of this and other insights in this volume can be easily illustrated by the unprecedentedly massive and quick, spontaneous and strongly emotional public reaction in France and elsewhere to the violent attacks of and related to the French newspaper "Charlie Hebdo," which is still going on as I finish this introduction. In this context, it is important to emphasize that the main goal of this book is not only the understanding of GDN processes but also the promotion of GDN as peaceful and ethical means for problem formulation and problem solution.

Bilyana Martinovsky

Chapter 1
Emotions in Interaction: Toward a Supraindividual Study of Empathy

Leonardo Christov-Moore and Marco Iacoboni

Introduction

Our emotions play a central role in daily life, yet our understanding of them remains incomplete. Even though emotions *frame* our thoughts, *color* our experiences, and *motivate* our behavior, conceiving of emotions at all runs into several problems: We cannot grasp and measure an emotion. We cannot examine an emotion with any microscope. Indeed, unlike verbal thoughts, such as descriptions or instructions, emotions can barely be said to be *internal objects*, for we cannot reliably convey them to others. Instead, we must attempt to evoke the appropriate emotion in another. Due to these subjective qualities, our concepts of emotion are rooted in phenomenology, that is to say, in *individual experience.*

Pages upon pages of novels, poems, songs, and treatises have attempted to describe and evoke the rich varieties of sadness, joy, fear, and anger to which the human is subjected. Indeed, it may be due to the compelling nature of emotional experience that we have only recently attempted to examine the *role* of emotions and their reason for being. If one looks beyond the experience of emotion to its context and consequences, one finds the full spectrum of human behavior. Humans have amassed centuries of daily experience, art, philosophy, and science in which emotions and their consequences are ubiquitous. Murder, reproduction, economic behavior, and even the most trivial daily acts are rarely, if ever, divorceable from our emotional states. In short, to understand human behavior, we must understand

L. Christov-Moore (✉)
Ahmanson-Lovelace Brain Mapping Center, Brain Research Institute UCLA (LCM & MI), Los Angeles, USA
e-mail: christovmoore@gmail.com

M. Iacoboni
Department of Psychiatry and Biobehavioral Sciences, Semel Institute for Neuroscience and Human Behavior, David Geffen School of Medicine at UCLA (MI), Los Angeles, USA
e-mail: iacoboni@ucla.edu

B. Martinovsky (ed.), *Emotion in Group Decision and Negotiation*,
Advances in Group Decision and Negotiation 7,
DOI 10.1007/978-94-017-9963-8_1

emotions: relatively hard-wired motivational states that frame our assessments and color our daily experiences, recollections, and predictions.

The study of emotion is still prejudiced by its origin in *individual* experience. However, we are social animals who must constantly perceive and transmit our internal states in order to function within a group. Social interaction is not only an important part of our daily experience, it is also essential to our survival and development. During the first years of life, we rely directly on the care and attention of others to stay alive. We must interact with others, see their faces, touch their skin, hear their voices, and observe their movements in order to develop as healthy, functioning adults. In addition, we must exist within a group and live according to group norms in order to survive and thrive. Indeed, our lives are dominated by the superposition of the different groups to which we belong: our families, fellow sports fans, political affiliations, lifelong cliques, corporation, associations, unions, leagues, causes, the people sharing the elevator with us, whoever may be watching the same show on national television, fellow party guests, etc. In navigating these groups, we move within and between discrete and overlapping sets of norms, moods, goals, and priorities (Barsade 2002; Smith et al. 2007).

Furthermore, our continued survival is intimately tied to our success as flexible, dynamic, and cohesive groups of individuals. The ability of humans to spontaneously and efficiently form coordinated group behaviors necessitates quick, efficient information transfer between group members. Thus, it is not surprising that the internal experience of emotion is accompanied by physiological states that affect our behavior and our appearance, as well as external displays (Ekman 1992; Strack et al. 1988). Furthermore, the neuroscientific study of empathy has found that while we can appraise our emotions and those of others, we can also *share* in the emotions and internal states of others. Neuroscientists have found that rather than possessing distinct mechanisms for perceiving versus experiencing emotion, the two are processed by the same systems, in much the same way. Rather than solely appraising the internal states of others, we may directly experience the emotions and somatic states (pain, nausea, etc.) of others, unconsciously mimic their behavior, and in turn transmit our internal states to others in part via display. Indeed, there is evidence for shared neural representations for perceiving and experiencing *emotion, sensation, and performed behavior* (which we will term *neural resonance* (NR), after Zaki and Ochsner 2012). This suggests that humans in groups are constantly sharing their motivational and affective states, without meaning to and absent conscious awareness. Ourselves may be distributed rather than discrete. This implies that emotions can be examined from the supraindividual perspective. Thus, the central questions become: What is the role of group-level emotions in group behavior, and how do they arise?

We propose that *group states, as the result of shared information among units in interaction, are not reducible to their individual parts*. This central property makes it possible and attractive to *study group emotions as networks and complex systems*, an approach which has been increasingly applied to understanding social systems, group memory, group knowledge, and group beliefs (Kerr and Tindale 2004; Sawyer 2005). In this view, a system can be analyzed in terms of its states as a whole (the network), which arise from its individual components (nodes) and the interactions between them (edges). Indeed, this complex systems' approach is not novel: A limited group of researchers have attempted to analyze social systems as complex systems, by examining the way groups are formed and coordinated and the ways they develop. The implication of this view is that to adequately comprehend group emotions, we must understand the behavior of the group emotion as a single construct, the properties of the individuals that can give rise to different group emotions, and the manner in which emotional information is conveyed between individuals. The latter component remains the least well understood and stands to benefit most from the novel findings supplied by neuroscience.

In this chapter, we will review the contemporary study of emotion and emotional contagion, their role in decision-making and group behavior, and current neuroscientific findings on shared neural representations for the perception and experience of emotion. We will conclude by discussing evidence from our group, which suggests that our neural mechanisms for decision-making and other cognitive functions exist in interaction with others used in NR.

Group States

We will structure our review of group emotions through analogy with the structure of a network (as formalized by graph theory). A *network* possesses its own properties as a whole, but also a structure defined by *nodes*, or units, within it, and *edges*, the links between nodes, which describe the transfer of information between them. The complex systems/graph approach has also been applied to group memory and knowledge, in the context of the "group mind." Indeed, Wegner (1987), in speaking of "transactive memory systems" proposed a group-level system which is "therefore not traceable to any of the individuals alone, nor can it be found somewhere "between individuals." Rather, it is a property of a group" (Wegner 1987), built up over time, which derives from individuals to form an information-processing system that eventually may return to have a profound influence upon its individual participants. We will examine the properties of individual affective states (nodes), patterns of group emotion and behavior (network states), and the properties of affective sharing between individuals (edges). This last component will be the main focus of this chapter, as it is the least well understood. We will also look at how information transfer between individuals causes their individual states to coalesce, allowing group states to *emerge*. Before we continue, let us quickly review the main concepts, which underlie our approach.

Scientific intuition in new domains proceeds best through analogy with prior ideas. To introduce the notion of group states, we propose the use of two concepts taken from physics and mathematics: *coalescence* and *emergence.*

One way to think about coalescence is through analogy with the Einstein–Bose condensate, a form of matter that exists when atoms in a substance are cooled to near absolute zero. At that temperature, the individual atoms' energies decrease to a point where their individual quantum states *coalesce* into a single quantum state, meaning that the properties of single atoms are no longer independent (information about a "single atom" is informative of the whole). In a similar fashion, humans experience a phenomenon known as *mood convergence* (also called *self-other merging* at the level of dyadic interaction) (Barsade 2002; Smith et al. 2007), which at its extreme results in extremely cohesive, coordinated mood and resultant judgment, beliefs, and behavior. However, simple convergence does not inevitably produce coordinated, optimal behavior. Nor does it imply strict affective homogeneity between group members (indeed, as we will discuss further on, homogeneity may produce negative consequences), simply that information about their internal states is less independent (in the statistical sense). Hence, we will refer to the degrees of *coalescence* in group states as a marker of a group's capacity to act as a single organism, allowing new *group* states to emerge (which can take many forms, both positive and negative). This leads us to another important property, *emergence.*

Whenever you have a multitude of individuals interacting with one another, there often comes a moment when disorder gives way to order and something new emerges: "a pattern, a decision, a structure, or a change in direction" (Miller 2010). Social beings in interaction may produce an overall state which no individual member is consciously aware of but which affects all members of the group. You might say that the group state *emerges* from the interactions between its members. This is a common phenomenon in nature. The ant colony is a quintessential example of emergence. The queen does not give direct orders and does not tell the colony what to do. Instead, each ant reacts to stimuli in the form of chemical scent from larvae, other ants, intruders, food, and buildup of waste and leaves behind a chemical trail, which, in turn, provides a stimulus to other ants. Here each ant is an autonomous unit that reacts in accordance with genetically encoded rules and its local environment. Despite lacking centralized decision-making, ant colonies exhibit complex behavior and have demonstrated the ability to optimize transportation and distribution of resources. Groups of human beings in which individuals are free to regulate themselves tend to produce spontaneous ordered behavior. A classic traffic circle is a good example, with cars moving in and out with such effective organization that one modern city (Palo Alto) has begun replacing stoplights at problem intersections with traffic circles and getting better results (see a full report at http://www.terrain.org/articles/2/siegman.htm). Open-sourced projects also form a compelling illustration of emergent organization and self-monitoring. Chaos theory arose in part to explain the ubiquitous yet puzzling phenomena of spontaneous self--organizing group behavior, now called *emergent behavior*. Biology could be viewed as an emergent property of the laws of chemistry. Similarly, *psychology can be understood as an emergent property of neurobiological laws*. We propose additionally that *group behavior should be understood as an emergent property of neural processes, which have historically been studied from the individual perspective*. Group behavior in humans clearly demonstrates *emergence.*

The emergence of group states facilitates group cognition, which can result in better decisions and more coordinated behavior (Wegner 1987). On the whole, simple majority processes tend to allow groups to perform better than individuals (reach more optimal solutions, make fewer errors, etc.) typically because most individuals will more often favor the correct or better alternative. If all of the members of a group know something, it probably does have more validity than something that is only known by one member. Furthermore, in a group endeavor with a common goal, gaps in each member's individual knowledge and memory can be supplanted by the other members, as in, for example, a musical group rehearsing a new song. By synching with other members affectively and behaviorally, musical cues are quickly transmitted from knowledgeable members to others, bringing up overall performance. Furthermore, as demonstrated by teams (in sports, warfare or otherwise), political groups, corporations, and other forms of purposeful collectives, groups with coordinated motivations and behavior can vastly outperform loose groups of unaffiliated individuals. However, group behavior bears a complex relationship to group characteristics. As the previous examples also demonstrate, suboptimal or dangerous outcomes (like groupthink, mass hysteria, or the "observer phenomenon") can arise when there is too much coalescence within a group.

In short, we know that human beings in groups exhibit spontaneous, coherent, apparently intentional behavior. However, all complex systems are not created equally. Interactions alone do not produce coherent, organized behavior of the kind that has led to our success as a species. Therefore, what determines how "coherent" emergent behavior is? One might reason that on one extreme, if individuals not interact at all, there cannot be emergent behavior. However, as complexity theorists have argued, more interactions do not equal more coherent emergence. Indeed, excessive interactions can actually pump "noise" into the system, drowning out the emergent "signal." There must be a constraining factor present that causes individuals to "synch" with the emergent behavior. We propose that the degree of *emergence* of coordinated group behavior requires *coalescence* within it. However, too much coalescence, as we will see later, is not optimal either. Rather, as complexity theorists have observed in many self-stabilizing systems ranging from piles of sand to the human brain itself, a broad dynamic range of possible emergent states requires that the system remains in the "sweet spot" between complete anarchy and complete coalescence. As we will see, the dynamic and nonlinear nature of our neural mechanisms for affect sharing (or emotional contagion) provides an excellent foundation for a system of this kind. Hence, the neural mechanisms that facilitate emotional sharing and coordination in dyads can be reframed as promoters of dynamic coalescence, emergence, and thus *group entitativity* (the property of a group acting as a single entity). Indeed, emergent properties are highly plausible subjects of evolutionary pressure (Corning 2002) and may in fact be an underlying property of all biology (Prindle and Hasty 2010). This expands our view of empathy from the individual and dyadic to the supraindividual.

Nodes: Individual Emotions and Decision-Making

We will define emotions as physiological and motivational states that are precognitive, and of long duration relative to immediate thoughts, perceptions, and impulses. They form a repertoire of responses to the internal and external environment, which have resulted from eons of evolution, and which exist prior to the conscious experience of emotions, which we call "feelings". This distinction is important, since we are not examining the sharing of feelings, or group feelings, but the underlying motivational states (which can arise from phenomena like pain, nausea, and motor behavior not typically associated with the colloquial usage of emotion,). Emotions arise from physiological and neural changes and result in changes in appearance (an integral part of their function in social animals) and behavior. Indeed, though we can experience emotions in isolation, it requires great effort to suppress their accompanying outward expression, which hints at old, deep links between experience and display. Furthermore, emotional display can in turn activate shared representations for perception and experience in others, evoking analogous emotional states in observers and bystanders. Hence, it is reasonable to think of them as interaction constructs or supraindividual. Before we proceed with the role of emotions in group behavior, we want to briefly review the studies of the role and biological basis of emotion up to the present day.

Emotion is difficult to define among psychologists, more than a hundred years after the James–Lange theory of emotion was first introduced, although four components are generally taken into account in its consideration: emotional experience, physiological arousal, expressive reactions, and emotion-related instrumental activities (e.g., adaptation and goal pursuit) (Kleinginna and Kleinginna 1981) (Reisenzein 1983). Emotional experience is ubiquitous in human culture. The scientific study of emotion, however, had its origin in physiology, due largely to the techniques available at the time.

Theories of Emotion

The James–Langue theory of emotion (1884), from the related ideas of American psychologist and philosopher William James and of Danish psychologist Carl Lange, is the best-known physiological theory of emotion. According to James and Langue, we experience conscious emotion in response to physiological changes in our body. This runs counter to the common conception at the time, that a consciously perceived emotion is evoked by a situation and the body changes in response to the emotion.

American physiologist Walter Cannon proposed that emotional experience can occur independently of emotional expression. His theory, modified by Philip Bard, was called the Cannon–Bard theory of emotion (1927). Cannon cited animal and human cases in which a transected spinal cord, which was supposed to eliminate sensation, did not seem to diminish emotion. Cannon also made the observation that there was a lack of a reliable correlation between emotional experience and the physiological state of the body: Some of the same physiological changes that characterize fear can also accompany other emotions such as anger or nonemotional conditions such as fever (Bear et al. 2007).

Recent research suggests that sensory input can have emotional effects on the brain without our being aware of the stimuli. Arne Ohman, Ray Dolan, and their colleagues showed that subjects who underwent aversive conditioning to angry faces had an autonomic response of increased skin conductance (sweaty palms) when shown these angry faces briefly, followed by a masking stimulus. Although the masking stimulus made the subjects perceptually unaware of the angry faces, they still had an emotional response to them (an *unconscious emotion*). In a similar experiment, amygdala activation shown with PET imaging occurred only when an angry face preceded the masking stimulus (Bear et al. 2007).

Emotions in the Brain

Recent experimental work suggests that the hypothalamus, amygdala, and parts of the prefrontal cortex are important structures in the processing of emotions, though a single system of emotion may not exist and use of the term "limbic system," although common, is controversial. Additionally, some components of the Papez circuit are no longer considered important for the expression of emotion, such as the hippocampus (Bear et al. 2007).

In addition, a network of prefrontal structures is increasingly viewed as essential for the control of emotion as well as its incorporation into decision-making (Fehr and Camerer 2007; Frith and Singer 2008). These include the ventromedial prefrontal cortex and dorsolateral prefrontal cortex.

Decision-Making

Insights from experimental economics, business, behavioral biology, cognitive psychology, and neuroscience suggest that emotions play a vital role in decision-making (Reimann and Bechara 2010). Reimann and Bechara (2010) recently reviewed the somatic marker framework, originally proposed by Damasio et al. (1996), as a neurological theory of decision-making. The somatic marker hypothesis holds that somatic markers, or emotion-related signals that are "indexed changes in the visceral state," influence cognitive processes in human reasoning and decision implementation. Changes in the visceral state include changes in heart rate, blood pressure, gut motility, and glandular secretion. Particularly, the consequences of possible choices are coded affectively by the decision-maker (Reimann and Bechara 2010). In this way, decision-making involves mechanisms not limited to those for conditioning or cognition alone (Damasio et al. 1996). Somatic markers can be nonconscious by biasing behavior when a person is not aware of them (Reimann and Bechara 2010), or conscious, e.g., by "qualifying" certain option-outcome scenarios as dangerous or advantageous.

Blanchette and Richards (2010) examined the influence of affect on higher-level cognition, including interpretation, judgment, decision-making, and reasoning. Complex effects of emotion were found on decision-making and reasoning, and emotion could both hinder and promote normatively correct thinking. Emotion also affected reasoning style (Blanchette and Richards 2010).

Although decisions are ideally made when an individual is calm and collected, many are commonly made in emotionally taxing conditions, such as when one is laid off from a job or becomes divorced from his or her spouse. Therefore, it is important to understand how affective states influence people's decision-making (Raghunathan and Pham 1999). Raghunathan and Pham (1999) compared the decision-making of anxious and sad individuals to show that emotions of equal valence can yield distinct and predictable biases; in the case of their study, these were biases in favor of either low-risk/low-reward or high-risk/high-reward options. They argue that this is because anxiety primes an implicit goal of uncertainty reduction, whereas sadness primes the implicit goal of reward replacement (Raghunathan and Pham 1999). This pattern was evident when the decision applied to the self and not when participants chose on behalf of someone else (Blanchette and Richards 2010).

Generally, anxiety leads to risk aversion for both trait anxiety and induced anxious moods. Risk aversion is not characteristic of all negative affective states and seems to be at least partly specific to anxiety. People in positive moods can be risk averse. For example, Isen and colleagues (1983, 1987) showed that in a game of roulette, subjects in a positive mood are more risk averse than controls when the odds of losing are high. In low-risk situations, however, these individuals are more risk seeking. This may be accounted for by the concept of perceived utility. Decision-making involves both estimating the likelihood of events (judgment) and the perceived utility of the reward or outcome. Positive moods affect the perceived utility of negative outcomes in that losses are perceived more negatively by positive participants than controls. Risk aversion in positive individuals may therefore stem not from an increase in the perceived likelihood of negative outcomes, but from losses being perceived as more consequential (Blanchette and Richards 2010). Fear seems to increase both the perceived consequentiality of negative outcomes and their likelihood, though the evidence for this is mixed. In summary, the research on incidental affects shows that anxious states and positive states increase risk aversion, while sadness increases risk tolerance or even risks seeking (Blanchette and Richards 2010).

Traditionally, the concepts of emotion and reason have been held distinct, and it is likely because of this that higher cognitive processes were until recently studied separately from affect. However, the widely held notion that regions of the brain can be conceptualized as either affective or cognitive is undergoing resistance on the basis that complex cognitive–emotional behaviors involve a high degree of connectivity between regions and dynamic brain network interactions (Pessoa 2008). Viewing emotion as a type of cognition will likely lead to novel insights regarding its definition (Cunningham and Kirkland 2012; Haidt 2001).

Networks: Group Emotions and Decision-Making

Moods, judgments, and behavior have been shown to converge among individuals in a group. This finding comes predominantly from management science, with the study of work groups. Mood convergence has also been found in many types of teams (accountants, nurses, cricket players). Indeed, evidence suggests that moods in a group are related even after controlling for individual circumstances or status. The mood can be observed and measured by internal and external observers, and there is a positive relationship between this convergence and stable membership, norms about mood regulation, and task and social interdependence (Smith et al. 2007). This suggests that coordinated group behavior may be greatly enhanced by affect sharing between group members (Smith et al. 2007). Greater group cohesion can make it more likely that group members will interpret and respond to future emotional events in similar ways. "Thus, an event that prompts shared group pride (emotion) might promote greater interaction, cohesiveness, and influence (behavior) in a way that makes interpretation of a future event (appraisal) even more likely to result in group pride (emotion), and so forth" (Smith et al. 2007).

The study of group emotions has followed two central approaches, top-down and bottom-up (Barsäde and Gibson 1998). The top-down approach considers group emotions as distinct from individual emotions, i.e., as a supraindividual or emergent phenomenon. It focuses on the overall patterns of behavior of the social network. The bottom-up approach typically analyzes group emotional states in terms of the properties of the group's members. This approach is interesting in that it considers individual differences. The two approaches, as we will see, are complementary. Indeed, the composition of groups is important to consider, even if the group state is not reducible to the units. An understanding of pertinent individual properties (nodes) enhances our understanding of how these properties, in interaction (edges), determine emergent group states (networks).

Intergroup emotions theory (Smith et al. 2007) holds that intergroup emotions are experienced by individuals when they identify with a social group, making the group part of the psychological self. What differentiates such group-level emotions from emotions that occur purely at the individual level? The authors argue that 4 key criteria define group-level emotions:

1. Group-level emotions are distinct from the same person's individual-level emotions.
2. Group-level emotions depend on the person's level of group identification.

3. Group-level emotions are socially shared within a group.
4. Group-level emotions contribute to motivating and regulating intragroup and intergroup attitudes and behavior.

Group-level emotions have the same basic functions for a group as emotions have for the individual (Smith et al. 2007). They allow for regulation of judgment and behavior. They influence individual group outcomes by providing information about group welfare, directing group appraisal of events, enforcing group cohesion (e.g., smiling as semiotic for acceptance, approval, bonding) and promoting group survival (displays of fear, alert, attack, or nausea). Group moods also have an impact on group dynamics: Group anger can motivate a directed attack, group pride can enforce in-group/out-group distinctions and promote affiliation, and group happiness and sadness enhance group cohesion and prosociality, while contempt and fear can homogenize a group's individual and collective behavior toward a defined object or class of objects. Indeed, group-level emotions also relate to action tendencies, particularly for collective actions (just as individual emotions motivate individual actions). Thus, group emotions should be "important causes of people's participation in political campaigns, social movements, strikes, demonstrations, and other collective acts—and therefore, in turn, be important causes of large-scale social change" (Barsade 2002).

Edges: Emotional Convergence, Emotional Contagion, and Mimicry

While recent studies in social psychology and management studies have come a long way in defining and characterizing patterns of group emotions as a whole, and the relevant properties of individuals within a group, or the nodes and networks, the study of the transmission of emotions (the edges) and internal states within groups remains incomplete. We propose that the best area to begin addressing this gap lies in the study of *shared emotions* and *empathy*.

This basic phenomenon of emotional convergence is an intriguing metric for examining sharing and transmission of emotion between individuals in a group, as convergence increases the potential for coalescence and subsequent emergence of optimal group behavior. Indeed, as we will discuss later, similar factors seem to promote convergence as well as the low-level mechanisms of empathy explored by cognitive neuroscientists in recent years, suggesting that they share common mechanisms.

A number of factors have been posited to explain why group members tend to share emotions (Brief and Weiss 2002):

1. Common socialization experiences and common social influences,
2. Similarity of tasks and high task interdependence,
3. Membership stability,

4. Mood regulation norms and rules,
5. Emotional contagion.

Of these five, emotional contagion has the most immediate link to our focus, as it is the factor most directly linked to emotion *transmission,* and arguably the poorest understood of the five. However, this should not be taken to mean that we are overlooking a–d. Rather, a better understanding of emotional contagion and its neural basis may make their role clearer.

Emotional Contagion

Emotion has been considered an individual phenomenon, bearing on an individual's own "goals, desires, concerns and experience" (Smith et al. 2007). However, factors that weigh on the individual (1–4 in the section above) do not fully explain group emotional convergence. There may be an additional powerful layer of preconscious, automatic processing which causes us to immediately share in the internal states of others. This brings us to the concept of emotional contagion. Emotional contagion in social psychology has typically been examined as a low-level form of empathy, studied in dyadic interactions, a tendency which obscures its role in group states. In the group context, emotional contagion can be defined as a process by which people tend to take on the emotions displayed by fellow in-group members with whom they interact. The term interaction is used loosely here and encompasses dyadic, face to face interactions as well as cohabitation (people sharing a common space can experience emotional contagion even if they are not directly interacting or fixating on each other) and instances in which leaders or members are portrayed in the media or in a larger setting (like a gathering or political rally), causing emotional contagion within observing group members. That is to say emotional contagion may spread in many fashions, such from node to node within a social network, or from a single node to all others. Furthermore, contagion is not always a case of direct matching between affective states. Indeed, optimal group behavior, while cohesive, seems to require coordination rather than direct matching. This key property may be partly responsible for the complexity observed in patterns of group behavior, in which members' behavior is heterogeneous yet coordinated (such as in carrying a heavy object, where some individual must pull while others must push). We will examine looks at how emotions are transmitted via facial expressions and body language, and the factors that modulate the degree to which this occurs.

Imagine that a subject is told that his physiological state will be assessed while observing another person experiences different stimuli. If the other subject plunges his hand into cold water and winces with pain, the observer will probably twinge with pain, and when the other subject smiles with pleasure in response to an unknown stimulus, the observer will likely express a more positive mood. The subject has experienced emotional contagion—that is, emotion caused by the observable feelings of another person. Research dating back to the 1960s has shown that humans, starting in infancy, show evidence of emotional contagion: automatic physiological and emotional responses to the pain, distress, and pleasure of others (Druckman and Bjork 1994).

Emotional contagion classically refers to a process in which a person or group influences the emotions or behavior of others through conscious or unconscious induction of emotional states, intentions, foci of attention, and behavioral attitudes. In this way, it is similar to cognitive contagion (the transmission of ideas and beliefs), but it does not share the content or the processes by which it is "caught." What is interesting about emotional contagion is that while the affective states it induces are similar to those based on our own experiences and feelings, its subtlety and the variety of ways in which it can be induced make it a unique way to influence behavior. Emotional contagion contains some purposeful processing, like evaluation, interpretation, and expectation, yet emotional contagion occurs most often at a less conscious level based on automatic processes and physiological responses (Barsade 2002). For this reason, affect induced via contagion is likely to play a larger role in social situations, such as when a small group is attempting to complete a task, play a competitive team sport, or participate in a training regimen or political rally. Furthermore, since contagion most likely functions via pre-conscious, implicit mechanisms, its effect may be more easily attributed to the situation, and its source may be obscured. This may in turn increase the framing effect of the emotional state, since the cause of the affective state is less clear (Druckman and Bjork 1994). Indeed, emotional contagion was initially studied in the context of social learning. A central feature of social learning is the ability of an observed person's affective response to an object to influence an onlooker's affective response to the same object (such as an aversion to an ingested root which has just caused pain and vomiting in a conspecific) (Druckman and Bjork 1994).

It is critical to note that since an observer's situation is necessarily different from a model's, a perfect match in emotion cannot be expected (some researchers prefer the term "socially induced affect," for this reason). Indeed, experiments on emotional contagion have demonstrated both concordant (similar affect) and discordant (opposing affect) affect (Druckman and Bjork 1994). Concordant induction is the transmission of affect in the same direction—either positive or negative—as in the experiment described above. Discordant induction is the transmission of the opposite affect: For example, when a performer's achievement produces envy in an observer or when a disliked person's failure produces happiness in the observer, four possibilities are then defined by the direction of the model's affect (positive or negative) and the observer's affect (positive or negative). Negative—negative induction seems to be the most prevalent in the literature (which makes sense, since rapidly coordinating behavior in response to distress is important for social animals).

It is clear that emotional contagion is not a case of direct matching alone. Indeed, it is hard to conceive of a variety group states emerging from simple homogeneity of affect. Coordinated and dynamic group behavior probably requires a variety of modes of affect sharing to accommodate different social relationships. Thus, it is not surprising that emotional contagion, or "socially induced affect" (Druckman and Bjork 1994), shows a great deal of modulation in response to context.

Individual and interpersonal factors can moderate socially induced affect. First, individuals vary in their ability to pick up on and respond to nonverbal affective cues, as well as in their emotional expressiveness. Thus, it is likely that more sensitive individuals will be more sensitive to emotional contagion, and more expressive individuals will be more likely to induce affect in others. Furthermore, studies have found greater evidence of contagion when subjects believed they were similar to the model and when they liked the model. There are, of course, cultural influences on socially induced affect, such as collectivist tendencies, or a greater or lesser tendency to exhibit emotions. Thus, it is necessary to keep intra- and interpersonal factors as well as cultural factors in mind when studying emotional contagion and group behavior. This is consistent with the notion that emotional contagion, like NR, is subject of implicit forms of modulation, not necessarily relying on immediate cognitive appraisal, but perhaps the result of past experience or past appraisals (such as another's past behavior influencing immediate reactions to their pain and distress). Indeed, group affiliation, status, attractiveness, ease of mimicry, and perceived moral character of the "other" have been shown to modulate physiological, behavioral, and neural correlates of emotional contagion (Druckman and Bjork 1994).

One proposed mechanism of emotional contagion is mimicry of a model. Imitation of expressions is a phylogenetically ancient and basic form of intraspecies communication found in many vertebrate species. If mimicry is such a basic phenomenon, then the cognitive resources necessary for mimicry may be minimal. Indeed, early research on mimicry has been instrumental in the development of current neuroscientific theories of contagion.

Electromyograph (EMG) recordings of subjects who were watching videotapes of arm wrestling and stuttering found greater EMG activity in the muscles that corresponded to the muscles being used by the observed models than in muscles that did not correspond to the muscles being used by the models (Berger and Hadley 1975). Dimberg's (1982, 1988) studies of facial reactions to facial expressions found that 8-second presentations of slides of angry and happy faces elicited facial EMG responses in the subjects' muscles consistent with the posed expression. Specifically, activity in the muscles used to pull cheeks back in a smile was higher when subjects viewed a happy face and higher in the muscle used to wrinkle the brows when subjects viewed an angry face.

Mimicry of nonstatic faces has been demonstrated in several studies. Vaughan and Lanzett (1980, 1981) reported that a model's facial display of pain instigated congruent facial activation in an observer. Mimicry of positive expressions has been found by Bush et al. (1989), who tested facial reactions of individuals watching a videotaped comedy routine. Subjects saw two target comedy routines, one of which had smiling faces dubbed into the presentation during sound track laughter. Half the subjects had been told to inhibit their facial expressions. The half whose expressions were spontaneous displayed greater zygomatic and orbicularis oculi activity (narrow eyes, as when smiling, but also evident in pain grimace) during the dubbed segments than during the segments without smiling faces.

When subjects were shown a videotape of a model displaying periodic pain expressions, they found that observers who were instructed to pose an expression of pain while the model was expressing pain experienced greater changes in skin conductance and heart rates than observers instructed to either behave naturally or inhibit their facial actions. Conversely, other researchers showed subjects videotapes of comedy routines, with smiling faces dubbed into one performance during sound track laughter and not into the other. Half of the subjects had been told to inhibit their facial activity. Those in the spontaneous condition reported greater amusement during the dubbed condition and greater amusement than those told to inhibit their expression; these findings support the perspective that mimicry of others' facial expressions can produce or enhance affective responses (reviewed in Druckman and Bjork 1994).

A large body of research exists, suggesting that mimicry is a mechanism by which affect might be quickly and automatically induced between individuals (Chartrand and Bargh 1999; McIntosh 2006). Indeed, mimicry may be a manner not only of internally evoking the motor pattern being observed, but also of enhancing the resultant emotional experience via facial feedback. The underlying mechanism by which this occurs was unclear until the recent advent of neuroscientific work on the neural substrate of mimicry and empathy: an intriguing phenomenon known as *mirroring*, or *NR*.

Neural Resonance

Broadly speaking, NR refers to a theory that holds that when we observe others in pain, experiencing emotions or nausea, or engaging in motor behavior, our brain may process the experience as it would if the experience were happening to us. This is based on a growing body of evidence showing that a similar network of brain areas is active whether we are experiencing ourselves or perceiving the internal states of others. Not surprisingly, this property has led many theorists to consider NR a core process in empathy (Zaki and Ochsner 2012).

Often, new information on a single subject can change the way we categorize that subject. Physicists' work on electrons, which originally occurred in the context of the internal structure of matter, led to the understanding that electrical energy and magnetism were one and the same and that matter and energy are simply two sides of the same coin. The study of matter led to insights into the nature of energy. In a similar fashion, NR was first studied within the context of motor behavior and has since changed our understanding of how human beings share every aspect of internal experience, from behavior to emotion and somatosensation (pain, touch, and visceral sensations like disgust).

The study of NR began in a primate laboratory; a group of Italian scientists at the University of Parma were studying the responses of motor cells in a macaque brain while it performed grasping actions. At some point, the scientists realized that something odd consistently happened when the monkey *saw* one of the experimenters grasping an object. A cell fired in the monkey's motor cortex that had previously been recorded firing when the monkey itself *grasped* the peanut. This was the first report of what are now called *mirror neurons* (Di Pellegrino et al. 1992). Mirror neuron research is now a burgeoning field, and the original finding that prompted it has been widely replicated in numerous ways. The idea of a common coding for perception and execution of action is almost banal, not even two decades later. However, at the time this finding was a radical departure from prior assumptions about a separation in the brain between perception and execution. Indeed, one could call this moment the point of departure for a revolution in the science of sensorimotor integration and cognition. Coupled with an increased emphasis on integrated, network views of the brain, we are in an age when the idea of cleanly separate systems for perception, cognition, behavior, and emotion is becoming increasingly untenable.

Since that historic day in Parma, the study of common-coding, perception-action matching, mirroring, or *resonance* (to use several popular synonyms) has proceeded quickly, demonstrating that this phenomenon extends far beyond motor behavior in macaques.

In 1995, Fadiga and colleagues examined the excitability of motor cortex while human subjects observed different hand and arm actions. They found that when subjects watched a particular motion, the parts of subjects' motor cortex corresponding to the muscles being used in the observed action *and not others* became more active. In a sense, the subjects' motor areas were becoming active as if *they were performing the action themselves.* A number of groups have found a similar pattern when subjects observe other people being touched or experiencing painful stimuli. The parts of the brain that encode the sensory and affective components of pain and touch also seem to become active when we observe another person in pain or being touched. Researchers have since found similar results for the perception and experience of disgust. Of most interest to our discussion here, there is ample evidence that our emotional centers become active when we observe others experiencing emotions (for a review of these findings, see Keysers and Fadiga 2008).

Previously, herein, we emphasized the role of display in emotion and mimicry in emotional contagion. Aside from the obvious example of motor behavior, all of our internal states have external correlates, not all of which are necessary for the state itself. We change our bodily posture, we make facial expressions, and we make characteristic bodily gestures. This is important to note because, though we are postulating that humans are walking mind-readers and state-sharers of a sort, this does not occur through telepathy or magic. Rather, it is thought that we initially process the external motor manifestations of internal states like emotions, and this information in turn activates the corresponding affective response.

Interestingly, we also seem to activate emotional areas when we try to guess or imagine what others are feeling (Zaki et al. 2009). This has two powerful implications: First, we process the internal states of others as if they were happening to us, whether we are observing them or just imagining them. Second, the distinction between self and other in the brain is less sharp than previously thought. Indeed, early in life, when we are infants, there can scarcely be said to be a distinction between ourselves and others. We imitate others compulsively and share their emotions.

Just as this automatic sharing is developmentally early, it is also thought to be phylogenetically early and essential for social interaction (Meltzoff 1990). Preston and De Waal (2002) discussed evidence that perception-action matching exists in many less-advanced forms of life and may be a quick way for social animals to "comprehend" the internal states of others, allowing them to attend to their wounded, counter aggression, move as a group, or respond to a common threat. Many theorists now consider perception-action matching, or NR, as we are calling it, a cornerstone of our remarkable ability to understand and share in the internal states of others (Gallese 2007; Preston and De Waal 2002; Zaki and Ochsner 2012). Indeed, NR of every kind seems to correlate with self-reported measures of empathy (Avenanti et al. 2009; Chartrand and Bargh 1999; Jabbi 2007; Pfeifer et al. 2008). The more empathetic you are, the stronger your internal representation of the states of others seems to be, and the more likely you are to unconsciously mimic the behavior of others.

However, this phenomenon raises a very important question. If the internal states and behavior of others are coded the same way as our own, how do we come to know what is us and what is not us? This question may seem easy, or obvious, but in fact we have a very sophisticated system for visuospatial attention in our parietal lobe that, among other things, allows us to distinguish between self and other and keeps our body image stable and localized (Trimble 2007). Temporarily disrupting the functioning of this area has been shown to decrease the accuracy with which we distinguish between our own face and that of a friend. Stimulation of this area can cause out-of-body experiences, in which the subject feels detached from his own body. Schizophrenics' hallucinations and beliefs in external telepathic intrusion are now thought to be at least partially due to a dysfunction in the systems responsible for determining what is self and what is other (Farrer et al. 2004; Perlstein et al. 2001; Waters and Badcock 2010). Our inner verbalizations or the clips of music we recall without intending to may, to the schizophrenic, seem externally generated, the ramblings of an evil spirit or telegraphed messages from the oval office.

While we cannot simply call this the "self or other" system, it is clear that our brain devotes considerable energy to establishing where "I" am with regard to "everything else" and establishing what is happening to me versus what is happening to other people. A second question, which we will soon see is closely related, is the following: If we are constantly processing the internal states and actions of those around us, why do not we constantly mimic the behavior of others, and feel everything that we observe them to feel? This may seem obvious unless one consider the following: lesions to a part of the brain called the prefrontal lobe, which is involved in controlling and monitoring our behavior, decision-making, and other complex, high-level processes, can cause subjects to compulsively imitate the behavior of others, even when the behavior is absurd or impractical (such as putting a pair of spectacles on top of another already on the face) (De Renzi et al. 1996). Next, consider the case of "mirror-touch synesthesia," a recently discovered condition in which a person can actually feel the sensations of others *exactly as if it was happening to them on their own body*. A more recent study of this phenomenon found that mirror-touch synesthetes are more empathetic (Banissy and Ward 2007), further suggesting that empathy involves a degree of self-other merging.

All of these cases share a common theme: Our sense of self may not be a given. Indeed, we require control systems, both to help us distinguish what is happening to whom and to keep us from constantly "merging" with others or mimicking them. In fact, humans show no evidence of awareness that others have distinct beliefs from them until they are several years old (Meltzoff 1990). Interestingly, many of the brain areas we know to be involved in the control of emotion, pain, imitation, etc., are also implicated in theory of mind, perspective-taking, and other "cognitive" forms of empathy, which, rather than allowing us to share the states of others, allow us to imagine and understand the states of others (Miller and Cohen 2001; Pineda 2008; Schulte-Rüther et al. 2007; Spengler et al. 2010; Zaki et al. 2009, Zaki and Ochsner 2012). Why might this be? Possibly, the ability to understand other minds, their beliefs, intentions, and feelings requires us first to understand that *they are different from our own*. In a sense, we must close ourselves off from others and our own sensations in order to make a space in which to detachedly examine them, much in the same way we have to close the windows and turn off the lights in order to see a movie clearly and not have the images and audio get muddled with sounds from the outer world. Not only that, but there is a close relationship between our behavior toward others and our degree of *resonance* with them.

Those whom you love and trust in extremes almost become a part of you. You feel their pain and their joy, which should logically impel you to act on their behalf, or *as you would have them act unto you*. On the other hand, those you truly hate and distrust are separate, different. Their pain moves you less (and can even give you some pleasure), and their joy can be angering. We as humans are clearly capable of modulating (consciously and unconsciously) the degree to which we *resonate* with others. We are also capable of evoking in ourselves the emotions, behavior, and sensations of an absent other, or even of ourselves at another time, past or present. Thus, we seem to be able to selectively inhibit our automatic responses to others and our own emotional states, and evoke our own responses voluntarily in their absence, or despite their presence. Indeed, what we propose is that these two broad systems, for *neural resonance* (which we will call the NR system), and the other, for *cognitive control/theory of mind*, (which we will jointly call the top-down system, for short), are tightly connected.

While we now associate the top-down system with decision-making, musing about others, etc., this system may have arisen in part as a form of contextual control for the NR system. This is not unlikely, considering the fact that both the cognitive functions the top-down system encapsulates and the corresponding brain areas, the temporal and prefrontal cortices, both developed late in our evolution and is the last to mature during our development. Whether considering the evolution of man, or the development of a single human, one can conceive of a being who begins with no coherent self, simply reacting to the environment, and in a sense, being its environment. Slowly, it begins to form a sense of what is self and what pertains to the other, allowing it to more selectively respond to its own needs and to the behavior of others. Eventually, this context and data-driven system allow for refined patterns of inhibition as well as disinhibition, allowing the organism to simulate its own states for the purpose of revisiting past experiences, as well as imagine future ones, to imagine the outcomes of different paths of behavior, their consequences to itself as well as others, and to selectively synchronize its behavior with other organisms and quickly share in their internal states.

Indeed, in our laboratory, we have recently been conducting experiments to test a model in which NR systems and top-down systems exist in interaction, regardless of the task. In this model, rather than just using the NR system when we view others in pain, feeling emotion, or performing behavior, and using the top-down system when we need to consciously make decisions in a social setting, or guess the beliefs and intentions of others, or take another person's perspective, we use both, in different capacities. During "NR tasks," top-down systems allow for a quick yet flexible modulation in response to context, allowing us to selectively inhibit or disinhibit our vicarious responses to others (a process which likely occurs both consciously and unconsciously) and hence resonate with them or not. Numerous studies have shown that NR, much like emotional convergence, is modulated by contextual appraisal and attention (Gu and Han 2007; Guo et al. 2012; Lamm et al. 2007; Liew et al., 2011; Loggia et al. 2008; Singer et al. 2004).

Conversely, some authors propose that top-down empathy processes such as mentalizing and perspective-taking can, in some contexts, employ information derived from NR (Obhi 2012; Zaki et al. 2009). There is also evidence that our immediate affective responses to others' pain and distress (probably driven by NR) can influence our conscious, deliberative behavior toward others (a top-down process), causing us to behave in a more prosocial fashion (Hein et al. 2010; Masten et al. 2011; Ma et al. 2011; Smith 2006). Recent studies suggest that a large portion of the reading of intentions can derive from low-level mechanisms for reading biological motion (Obhi 2012), and the recently resuscitated field of empathic accuracy has shown that accurately discerning the internal states of others as well as inferring intentions from observed behavior relies on the interaction between NR and top-down systems (Liew et al. 2011; Zaki and Ochsner 2012). Indeed, without this interaction, and without the participation of both systems, we would be utterly helpless in a social interaction at best and dangerous at worst. Perhaps it is due to the need for a widespread network of systems for social cognition that it takes us so long to perfect and is the one of the primary areas of dysfunction for nearly every major psychiatric disorder.

Direct evidence for an integrated view of NR and top-down systems is still lacking. However, recent work from our group (Christov-Moore et al., under review) suggests that these two systems are not only integrated, but that the nature of their interaction is stable across tasks that are thought to engage only one or the other. This means that the way the two systems interact during NR tasks is indicative of their interaction during top-down tasks as well. To test this idea, we had subjects perform two classic stimulus-driven NR tasks inside an MRI scanner: observation and imitation of emotional facial expressions (emotion imitation or EI) and observation of a human hand being pierced by a needle (needle test or NT) (Bufalari et al. 2007). Next, we had the subjects play a classic top-down task, the Dictator Game (Engel 2011), in which they decide how to share a sum of money ($10 per trial) between themselves and a series of profiles which represented people in the local community. Subjects were made aware that the money they decided to give would actually be given to the people the profiles corresponded to. Also, to remove as much social pressure from their decisions as possible, we had them perform the task alone, unobserved, and their responses were kept completely anonymous from the experimenter as well as the people with whom they were sharing the money. In addition, we introduced a contextual variable: The profiles also displayed the player's incomes, which could vary between low ($18–30,000/yr) and high ($80–200,000/yr) incomes. We hypothesized the following:

a. Given that NR and prosocial/generous behavior are both correlated with empathy, we predicted that subjects' activation in NR systems during the tasks (emotion-related areas for emotion imitation and pain-related areas for the needle test) would be positively correlated with their generosity.
b. Since we are assuming an inhibitory role over NR for top-down systems, we predicted that subjects' activation in top-down systems would be *negatively* correlated with their generosity.
c. Given that we are assuming that top-down systems generally interact in a stable fashion but have roles which depend on the task, we predicted that activation in top-down areas during the NR tasks would be correlated with markers of contextual processing in the DG, namely subjects' tendency to *modulate* their generosity (or prosocial inclinations) in response to context (income).
d. Last, since we are assuming that this pattern arises from a stable interaction, and not simply the independent functioning of two systems, we predicted that NR and top-down systems would show a functional interaction during the NR tasks and that this interaction would also predict subjects' offers in the Dictator Game.

Our hypotheses were robustly confirmed by our results (see Fig. 1.1). Visuospatial, sensory, and emotional systems known to be involved in NR for *both tasks* (Carr et al. 2003; Pfeifer et al. 2008; Lloyd et al. 2006; Naito et al. 2008) and corresponding top-down systems (Miller and Cohen 2001) exhibited the predicted pattern of correlations as well as a robust functional interaction, the strength of which was negatively correlated with subjects' generosity.

The above diagram illustrates the results of our experiment, in which we correlated activation during two distinct fMRI tasks with subjects' generosity in the Dictator Game, an economic scenario in which the subject divides up a sum of money between themselves and virtual players. Each row represents results from one fMRI task, listed on the left side, while each column displays areas where activation is positively (left column) or negatively (right column) correlated with

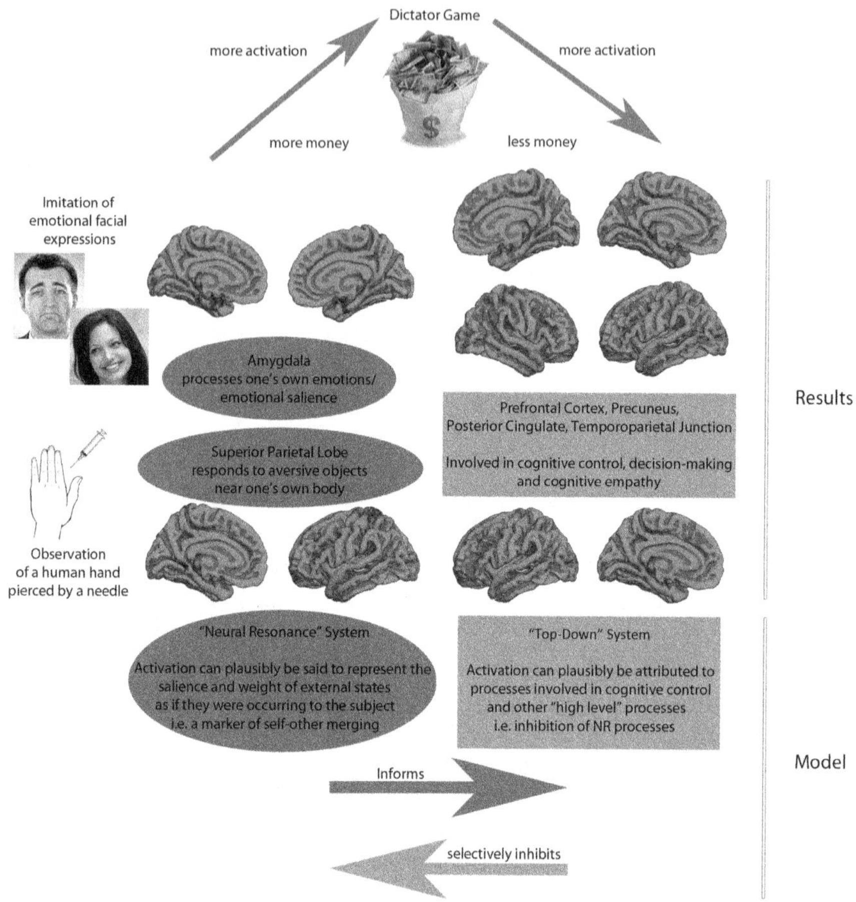

Fig. 1.1 Overview of model and results

subject's generosity in the Dictator game. The first row of colored text boxes lists the primary brain structures displayed as well as their proposed function. The bottom row of colored text boxes and arrows displays a simplified version of our model, in which NR systems and top-down systems interact in a characteristic and stable manner.

Modern, network-oriented models of brain function have become increasingly accepted in recent years, supporting the idea that the brain is highly interconnected and that brain functions are widely distributed rather than modular (Fox and Friston 2012; McIntosh 2000). This notion makes it highly implausible that systems involved in NR and high-level systems involved in top-down processes such as theory of mind and empathic decision-making do not develop and function in interaction, even in tasks which seemingly engage only one type of system/process.

Having reviewed NR, we return to its role in group states. We hypothesize that emotional convergence (coalescence) and emergent behavior are reliant on mechanisms of NR. If our hypothesis is correct, we should see some correspondence between factors associated with both modulation of emotional contagion and modulation of NR. In addition, there should be a similar correspondence between factors classically associated with emotional convergence in groups and conditions that favor NR in individuals. This is because emotional convergence is studied in groups, while NR is (thus far) studied as an individual or dyadic phenomenon. Finding such overlaps would add weight to our thesis that NR is a key metric for expanding the study of emotional contagion and group states.

Indeed, an initial review finds that common socialization experiences and common social influences are keys to defining in-group affiliation and a perception of increased self-other similarity, which has been shown to be a modulator of NR (Cheng et al. 2010; Hein et al. 2010). Second, similarity of tasks and high task interdependence should enhance NR for a number of reasons: First, physical similarity of behavior should enhance rapport and self-other identification, and task interdependence requires the engagement of basic NR mechanisms involved in comprehending the actions of others as well as the intent of their actions or their goals (Iacoboni et al. 2005; Van Baaren et al. 2009). Membership stability, at the level of the individual, merely means that the individual will encounter the same group of individuals more often and be exposed to situations of face-to-face interaction, task interdependence, and being the donor and recipient in instances of prosocial behavior (which are typically increased inside groups).

Group States as Complex Systems

It is beyond the scope of this chapter to exhaustively review group behavior and decision-making. However, we propose that affect sharing among individuals is essential for coherent group states to emerge. Several studies have found that mood influences performance of certain tasks. Overall, negative affect appears to reduce visuospatial and cognitive performance, while positive affect seems to enhance performance in individuals. This has implications for group performance in response to affect spread as the result of contagion (Druckman and Bjork 1994). Since affect has an effect on performance, contagion can propagate behavioral effects within a group. In an example taken from Druckman and Bjork (1994), "a person watching a radar screen for possible enemy incursions may be somewhat distracted if he or she is angry at being selected for this duty. A second person sitting next to the first, angry, person may be more distracted, however, if she or he is experiencing negative affect socially induced from the first person. The second person may have to exert effort to both deal with the negative affect and to discover the cause of the negative affect. That person, who is experiencing socially induced affect, might suffer a greater decrement in performance—responding as quickly as possible to signs of danger from the screen—than the first person."

Here are a few speculative examples of our own:

Paleolithic James splits a coconut with a rock producing a positive emotional response in the individuals of the group. The positive affect, which promotes more cooperative behavior (Barsade 2002), facilitates greater coalescence and mass mimicry of the same behavior, resulting in a small cultural advance.

Jill reveals or indicates that she belongs to same group/team/tribe as her interlocutors, this contextual information modulates attention to her and facilitates NR, and now her emotions and states are shared with group effects (conflict or cooperation, for example).

In addition, there is a fair amount of research that indicates that affective states that arise from empathy can cause prosocial or altruistic behavior (Batson and Shaw 1991; Preston and De Waal 2002; Smith 2006). When one feels what another in distress is feeling, one may be more likely to help that person, although this may occur simply to alleviate one's own distress. If liking another person increases socially induced affect, members of groups that like each other may be more likely to help one another, increasing cooperative behavior and likely improving the chances of a group's survival.

Thus far, we have only considered group properties that arise from coordination among members. However, a single individual or group of individual can and often does deliberately hijack these mechanisms to coordinate group behavior toward a goal. Indeed, deliberate emotional contagion is a common feature of organizational culture, socialization, and leadership processes. Leaders in general, especially charismatic or transformational leaders, make explicit and strong use of emotions (Smith et al. 2007) to influence group coherence and create or destroy affiliations between members of groups. An easily mimicked leader may be better able than a less easily mimicked one to make their audience feel what he or she is feeling about the topic. Beyond that, a speaker may be able to influence the observers' attitudes toward specific topics via inadvertent emotional contagion. For example, if an instructor frowns or smiles during the discussion of a particular topic, the students may experience concordant or discordant affect (depending on contextual aspects of the speaker), resulting in unintended affective associations with the subject matter that are not inherent to the subject itself.

Furthermore, a speaker who is liked may be more likely to persuade individuals to follow an unsupported objective than one who is disliked (Druckman and Bjork 1994). Perhaps this is why emotional, charismatic, and rhetoric-laden speech and cults of personality are more prevalent when the substance of a message is incoherent, inaccurate, or contrary to the audience's interests. This is an example of why it is important to be aware of variables that moderate or interact with socially induced affect.

The relationship between coalescence and *successful group behavior* is complex. Constructs that typically are seen as positive aspects of groups (cohesiveness, coalescence, etc.) do not invariably lead to improved group outcomes (Kerr and Tindale 2004). Thus, it is important to understand how affect is shared between group members. The practical outcome of this model is that since contagion is unconscious and involuntary, yet powerful, members may not be aware of its effect, leading to outcomes such as unrealistic confidence and dangerous feelings of invulnerability due to one member's inciting euphoria (which spreads quickly), or the inverse, a "negative Nancy" reducing group cohesion and effectiveness. Thus, group members need to be aware of contagion and its ramifications for their group dynamics and decision-making (Barsade 2002). Indeed, groupthink, a phenomenon in which there is a high or complete homogeneity between the beliefs and motivational states of members, has been shown to be detrimental (in most cases) to group behavior, counteracting the benefits of group decision-making (Packer 2009). Groupthink can have many negative outcomes, from both the performance and ethical perspective. For example, it can allow for group behavior that would be aberrant to the individual (as in the recent case of abuses at Abu Ghraib), as well as suboptimal decision-making (Post and Panis 2011). Another example of a suboptimal group state that can arise from excessive coalescence is mass panic. Panic is a state that is detrimental to the performance of any task, particularly a group task under potentially dangerous conditions when order is essential to performance, as it can impair concentration and coordination, and affect decision-making. Panic often occurs in group situations and can spread quickly. Yet another, related, example is mass hysteria. Research on mass hysteria suggests that relationships among people are an important determinant of who experiences the hysterical symptoms. An individual is more likely to exhibit symptoms if a friend experiences symptoms. Like the finding on panic in a group, this finding suggests that the emotional state of one's friends is likely to have a strong influence on one's own emotional state. Within a large group, it may be pockets of friends that panic first. This further supports a role for emotional contagion (and its modulation based on factors like liking, affiliation, status) in patterns of group affective states.

Our model of dynamic interaction between bottom-up and top-down neural processes can additionally apply at a supraindividual level, in which coalescence among members is unconscious and involuntary, but since NR is modulated by factors that can be contextual and cognitively attained or enforced or appraised (like group identity or allegiance), these deliberative processes have an effect on the transmission of emotion and are in turn influenced by the resulting group emotion. In essence, individual and supraindividual affect may interact in the same way NR and top-down systems interact at the individual level. This hierarchical superposition of dynamic feedback systems may allow for the complexity of group affective states observed in the social world.

Further Research

We have examined how NR—which is generally conceived in neuroscience as playing a major role in one to one interactions—may play out on the group level, to quickly facilitate group affective and motivational states. However, as will be recalled from the above paragraphs, NR is modulated by context, intrapersonal factors, and attention. What occurs when we take this consideration to the level of the group? If greater resonance equals greater group integration, then we can postulate that individual differences in the NR/top-down interaction and context can change the degree to which an individual coalesces with the group, is loyal to affiliation, or modulates affiliation in response to context. This may be why studies of empathy have revealed metrics that predict different strategies of individuals within a group, e.g., psychopaths (Blair 2003; Fecteau 2008).

The call for a supraindividual study of social cognition was recently voiced by Schilbach et al. (2013). Along the same lines, we conclude this chapter with some questions that this chapter implies and some ideas of how to answer them.

1. Do individual neural metrics of empathy follow the shifting of group allegiance?

Brain activity in regions involved with NR as well as behavioral metrics which imply self-other merging (such as involuntary mimicry) has been associated with greater dispositional empathy, prosocial behavior, cooperative behavior, positive rapport, and other individual/dyadic qualities(Chartrand and Bargh 1999; Lakin and Chartrand 2003; Van Baaren et al. 2009). We propose that *these measures are also predictive of coalescence in groups*. Using massive hyperscanning (Montague 2002), (multiple linked MRI or EEG apparatuses) and a virtual environment in which groups of subjects could band together in different configurations while performing a group task, as well as stimuli which allowed for repeated exposure to other players, this hypothesis could be neatly tested. Consider a scenario in which 7 subjects are tasked with a purposeful, rewarding objective (such as building an optimally large tower using a finite set of pieces), in which their decisions were constrained in such a way that their initial choice (which would not be overly consequential to overall outcome or too clear a choice) would divide the group into two. Following this decision, the rest of the scenario could proceed automatically. All subjects could observe both towers' progress and would be exposed to photographs of all other subjects, in random order, multiple times (for the sake of averaging). Subjects could, in every round, choose to change "teams." One could then examine how their NR was modulated in response to the affiliation of other subjects, how it changed in response to a new teammate, and how it responded to a defector or member of the other team. Furthermore, one could examine correlations among teams, and whether this increased, and examine how activity correlated with persistent allegiance. Finally, one could examine the propensity to prefer allegiance over reward (persisting in a "losing" team) and vice versa and examine the emergence of leaders. This design is obviously imperfect and would require very long scenarios with many iterations of allegiance shifting and NR measuring, but the basic idea appears valid.

2. Does NR increase with task interdependence, and not simply during mimicry?

Using a similar hyperscan setup as above (as most of these designs would require), one could examine whether NR and its modulation mapped as well onto convergence as we are here proposing. Namely, by comparing whether NR is sensitive to the actual sensory properties of individual behavior (same or different behavior) or coalescence (same or different objective).

3. Can "bottom-up" interventions based on NR influence the study of conflict mediation in groups and help mediate the effects of negative propaganda?

Interventions based on stimulating NR through imitation, gaze-following, and perspective-taking have already been used at the individual level to enhance social cognition in psychiatric populations (Ingersoll 2008, 2010, 2012). In healthy individuals, mimicry has been shown to increase trust and positive rapport (which are themselves correlated with spontaneous mimicry among individual) (Chartrand and Bargh 1999; Van Baaren et al. 2009). Perhaps similar techniques could be used to enhance conflict mediation between members of opposing groups, when interventions directed at conscious, cognitive processes are insufficient.

Intriguingly, research suggests shown that increasing task interdependence can improve cooperation between individuals in a group. Aside from the philosophical notion of a "common goal," this finding may point to the importance of NR and emotional convergence for conflict mediation. As may be recalled from earlier points in the chapter, task interdependence is a key factor in enhancing emotional convergence.

4. Can the parallel and interacting processes of deliberative cognition and NR as we propose be modeled at the group level in a network schema?

Our model provides a simple, tractable approach to the study of interactions between NR and mechanisms for decision-making and cognitive control. Conceivably, a group implementation of this model in the modeling of affective information transmission between nodes in a social network could improve the modeling and analysis of emergent social behavior.

Conclusions

Humans are "walking mood inductors" continuously influencing, and influenced by, the moods, judgment, and behavior of others. We propose that this quality is not simply advantageous to individuals by allowing them to understand and mimic others. Rather it also has group-level benefits by facilitating the rapid transfer of emotional states, allowing for more cohesive, dynamic, and coordinated group behavior.

It is beyond the scope of this chapter to review all the factors that can make for more efficient or successful groups (i.e., groups that reap the benefits of group behavior). All we are proposing is that these group states owe their emergence to a phenomenon (empathy/neural resonance) of information transfer that is historically studied from an individual perspective. These mechanisms may be necessary but not sufficient to produce successful group states and group behavior. This rests on the axiom that NR and empathy are necessary for interaction within a group, a proposal with some support in clinical literature: Psychiatric and neurological disorders which affect empathy and social cognition also tend to impair behavior within the group. Indeed, it is difficult to conceive of a coordinated group composed of individuals with impaired recognition and prediction of others' internal states.

Hence, as complexity theorists argue, the unit for analysis needs to shift from individual cognition to distributed cognition in complex systems. The complex systems' approach has been applied to group behavior in a number of ways, from theories of small group formation, coordination, development, and adaptation, to work utilizing this theory to study how clusters of social influence, in which everyone holds similar opinions, vary according to the available communication channels. Evolutionary principles and models have also been used to explore the adaptiveness of various forms of group decision-making. For example, some scholars have argued that the popularity of majority rules based on shared preferences may stem from their adaptive value. Such decision processes can help constrain self-interested behavior to the advantage of group fitness and provide quick and easy heuristics in decision environments (allowing for more optimal solutions and fewer errors, with minimal extra effort). The tools of modern information technology have helped us pose questions that might never arise in the usual contexts of face-to-face groups. New methods such as using virtual reality to create and analyze group processes, combined with implicit behavioral, physiological, and neural measures, can further explore how group states emerge and evolve (Kerr and Tindale 2004).

This approach has already borne fruits in management sciences in the clinical setting, where ethical as well as clinical decisions in acute care are generally arrived at in a team context and are often informed by experience of one or more key team members. By shifting the focus from individual cognition to distributed cognition, scientists in the clinical setting have begun to develop multiperson simulation techniques to enhance group learning and performance and reduce groupthink, by focusing on team and system failures rather than individual errors (Snelgrove et al. 2011). The group approach to understanding group behavior is borne out in such studies, where by changing the interactions among members of the group, the group's performance can increase, resulting in the already understood group advantage in problem solving.

However, the study of group emotional states and group behavior, already decades old, has lacked a complete understanding of how emotional and intentional information is transmitted among individuals since it has focused on conscious, deliberative forms of appraisal. Theorists have already considered that appraisal cannot be the only explanation for the emotional convergence and quick coordination observed in groups and that emotional contagion must play a role (Smith et al. 2007). However, study of emotional contagion, until recently, was limited to observed behavior and physiology. Now, recent studies in neuroscience have provided a plausible neural basis for emotional contagion in NR. This field of study has in turn greatly expanded our notion of what humans can directly transmit to one another. In addition to emotions, humans seem open to the contagion of somatosensation, intention, and even motor behavior. Furthermore, humans are not indiscriminate sponges, even if much of our assimilation of others' internal states is preconscious. Like ants, the extent to which we "resonate" with others and hence form groups (however temporary) is modulated by context and predisposition. Within this context, the mechanisms of appraisal, identification, and cognitive contagion, already well researched, can find their link to more recent studies on the neural mechanisms underlying empathy.

Humans have survived, in part, because we can form more nuanced, intelligent collectives than other species. Perhaps selection of group behavior is a fruitful approach to understanding how mechanisms for emotional contagion evolved. By integrating neuroscientific data collected on group states, coupled with novel models and methods for interpreting said data, we may greatly enhance our understanding of every component in this puzzle, from the evolutionary and developmental role of individual affect and empathy to the evolution and optimization of group states and behavior.

Increasing awareness of the connectedness of the human brain has led to similar awareness of the connectedness of cognition and emotion. We propose that this property extends to the study of individuals and groups. Increasingly improved transmission of information between humans in the information age makes this study highly relevant, as we carry on the macroequivalent of the transition from multicellular to pluricellular organisms in our transition from scattered groups to ever more integrated, massive societies. By linking the individual study of empathy at the level of brain function to group entitativity and behavior, we may lay down the foundations and raison d'etre for a supraindividual study of emotion.

Acknowledgments The authors wish to thank Nikita Crofton for her help in preparing this manuscript, as well as Scott Huettel for his help in designing the modified Dictator Game used here. This work was supported by NIH grant 1R21MH097178 and the NSF Graduate Research Fellowship #DGE-1144087. For generous support, the authors also wish to thank The Staglin Center for Cognitive Neuroscience, the Brain Mapping Medical Research Organization, Brain Mapping Support Foundation, Pierson-Lovelace Foundation, The Ahmanson Foundation, William M. and Linda R. Dietel Philanthropic Fund at the Northern Piedmont Community Foundation, Tamkin Foundation, Jennifer Jones-Simon Foundation, Capital Group Companies Charitable Foundation, Robson Family and Northstar Fund.

References

Avenanti, A., Minio-Paluello, I., Bufalari, I., & Aglioti, S. M. (2009). The pain of a model in the personality of an onlooker: Influence of state-reactivity and personality traits on embodied empathy for pain. *NeuroImage, 44*(1), 275–283.

Banissy, M. J., & Ward, J. (2007). Mirror-touch synesthesia is linked with empathy. *Nature Neuroscience, 10*(7), 815–816.

Barsade, S. (2002). The ripple effect: Emotional contagion and its influence on group behavior. *Administrative Science Quarterly, 47*(4), 644–675.

Barsäde, S., & Gibson, D. (1998). Group emotion: A view from top and bottom. *Research on Managing Groups and Teams, 1*(82), 81–102.

Batson, C., & Shaw, L. (1991). Evidence for altruism: Towards a pluralism of prosocial motives. *Psychological Inquiry, 2*(2), 107–122.

Bear, M. F., Connors, B. W., & Paradiso, M. A. (2007). *Neuroscience: Exploring the brain* (3rd ed.). Philadelphia: Lippincott Williams and Wilkins.

Berger, S. M., & Hadley, S. W. (1975). Some effects of a model's performance on an observer's electromyographic activity. *American Journal of Psychology, 88*, 263–276.

Blair, R. J. R. (2003). Neurobiological basis of psychopathy. *The British Journal of Psychiatry, 182*(1), 5–7.

Blanchette, I., & Richards, A. (2010). The influence of affect on higher level cognition: A review of research on interpretation, judgment, decision making and reasoning. *Cognition and Emotion, 24*(4), 561–595.

Brief, A., & Weis, H. (2002). Organizational behavior : Affect in the workplace. *Annual Review of Psychology, 5*, 279–307.

Bufalari, I., Aprile, T., Avenanti, A., Di Russo, F., & Aglioti, S. M. (2007). Empathy for pain and touch in the human somatosensory cortex. *Cerebral Cortex, 17*(11), 2553–2561. (New York, N.Y. : 1991).

Bush, L. K., Barr, C. L., McHugo, G. J., & Lanzetta, J. T. (1989). The effects of facial control and facial mimicry on subjective reactions to comedy routines. *Motivation and Emotion, 13*, 31–52.

Bush, L. K., McHugo, G. J., & Lanzetta, J. T. (1986). The effects of sex and prior attitude on emotional reactions to expressive displays of political leaders. *Psychophysiology, 23*, 427.

Carr, L., Iacoboni, M., Dubeau, M.-C., Mazziotta, J. C., & Lenzi, G. L. (2003). Neural mechanisms of empathy in humans: A relay from neural systems for imitation to limbic areas. *Proceedings of the National Academy of Sciences of the United States of America, 100*(9), 5497–5502.

Chartrand, T., & Bargh, J. (1999). The chameleon effect: The perception–behavior link and social interaction. *Journal of Personality and Social Psychology, 76*(6), 893.

Cheng, Y., Chen, C., Lin, C.-P., Chou, K.-H., & Decety, J. (2010). Love hurts: An fMRI study. *NeuroImage, 51*(2), 923–929.

Corning, P. A. (2002). The re-emergence of "emergence": A venerable concept in search of a theory. *Complexity, 7*(6), 18–30. doi:10.1002/cplx.10043.

Cunningham, W. A., & Kirkland, T. (2012). Emotion, cognition, and the classical elements of mind. *Emotion Review, 4*(4), 369–370.

Damasio, A. R., Everitt, B. J., & Bishop, D. (1996). The somatic marker hypothesis and the possible functions of the prefrontal cortex [and discussion]. *Philosophical Transactions of the Royal Society of London. Series B, Biological Sciences, 351*(1346), 1413–1420.

Di Pellegrino, G., Fadiga, L., Fogassi, L., Gallese, V., & Rizzolatti, G. (1992). Understanding motor events: A neurophysiological study. *Experimental Brain Research, 91*, 176–180.

Dimberg, U. (1982). Facial reactions to facial expressions. Psychophysiology 19:643–647. 1988 Facial electromyography and the experience of emotion. *Journal of Psychophysiology, 2*, 277–282.

Dimberg, U., Thunberg, M., & Elmehed, K. (2000). Unconscious facial reactions to emotional facial expressions. *Psychological Science, 11*(1), 86–89.

Druckman, D., & Bjork, R. A. (1994). *Learning, remembering, believing: Enhancing human performance (p. 395).* Washington DC: National Academies Press.

Ekman, P. (1992). An argument for basic emotions. *Cognition and Emotion, 6*, 169–200.

Engel, C. (2011). Dictator games: A meta study. *Experimental Economics, 14*(4), 583–610. doi:10.1007/s10683-011-9283-7.

Farrer, C., Franck, N., Frith, C. D., Decety, J., & Georgieff, N. (2004). Neural correlates of action attribution in schizophrenia, *131*, 31–44.

Fecteau, S. (2008). Psychopathy and the mirror neuron system: Preliminary findings from a non-psychiatric sample. *Psychiatry Research, 160*, 137–144.

Fehr, E., & Camerer, C. F. (2007). Social neuroeconomics: The neural circuitry of social preferences. *Trends in Cognitive Sciences, 11*(10), 419–427.

Fox, P. T., & Friston, K. J. (2012). Distributed processing; Distributed functions? *NeuroImage, 61*(2), 407–426.

Frith, C. D., & Singer, T. (2008). The role of social cognition in decision-making. *Philosophical Transactions of the Royal Society of London. Series B, Biological Sciences, 363*(1511), 3875–3886.

Gallese, V. (2007). Before and below "theory of mind": embodied simulation and the neural correlates of social cognition. *Philosophical Transactions of the Royal Society of London. Series B, Biological Sciences, 362*(1480), 659–669.

Gu, X., & Han, S. (2007). Attention and reality constraints on the neural processes of empathy for pain. *NeuroImage, 36*(1), 256–267.

Guo, X., Zheng, L., Zhang, W., Zhu, L., Li, J., Wang, Q., et al. (2012). Empathic neural responses to others' pain depend on monetary reward. *Social Cognitive and Affective Neuroscience, 7*(5), 535–541.

Haidt, J. (2001). The emotional dog and its rational tail: A social intuitionist approach to moral judgment. *Psychological Review, 108*(4), 814–834.

Hein, G., Silani, G., Preuschoff, K., Batson, C. D., & Singer, T. (2010). Neural responses to ingroup and outgroup members' suffering predict individual differences in costly helping. *Neuron, 68*(1), 149–160.

Iacoboni, M. (2009). Imitation, empathy, and mirror neurons. *Annual Review of Psychology, 60*, 653–670.

Iacoboni, M., Molnar-Szakacs, I., Gallese, V., Buccino, G., Mazziotta, J. C., & Rizzolatti, G. (2005). Grasping the intentions of others with one's own mirror neuron system. *PLoS Biology, 3*(3), e79.

Ingersoll, B. (2008). The social role of imitation in autism: Implications for the treatment of imitation deficits. *Infants and Young Children, 21*(2), 107–119.

Ingersoll, B. (2010). Pilot randomized controlled trial of reciprocal imitation training for teaching elicited and spontaneous imitation to children with autism. *Journal of Autism and Developmental Disorders, 40*(9), 1154–1160.

Ingersoll, B. (2012). Brief report: Effect of a focused imitation intervention on social functioning in children with autism. *Journal of Autism and Developmental Disorders, 42*(8), 1768–1773.

Jabbi, M. (2007). Empathy for positive and negative emotions in the gustatory cortex. *Neuroimage, 34*, 1744–1753.

Kerr, N. L., & Tindale, R. S. (2004). Group performance and decision making. *Annual Review of Psychology, 55*, 623–655. doi:10.1146/annurev.psych.55.090902.14200.

Keysers, C., & Fadiga, L. (2008). The mirror neuron system : New frontiers. *System, 3*, 193–198. doi:10.1080/17470910802408513.

Kleinginna, P. R, Jr, & Kleinginna, A. M. (1981). A categorized list of emotion definitions, with suggestions for a consensual definition. *Motivation and Emotion, 5*(4), 345–379.

Lakin, J. L., & Chartrand, T. L. (2003). Using nonconscious behavioral mimicry to create affiliation and rapport. *Psychological Science, 14*, 334–339.

Lamm, C., Nusbaum, H. C., Meltzoff, A. N., & Decety, J. (2007). What are you feeling? Using functional magnetic resonance imaging to assess the modulation of sensory and affective responses during empathy for pain. *PLoS ONE, 2*(12), e1292.

Liew, S.-L., Han, S., & Aziz-Zadeh, L. (2011). Familiarity modulates mirror neuron and mentalizing regions during intention understanding. *Human Brain Mapping, 32*(11), 1986–1997.

Lloyd, D., Morrison, I., & Roberts, N. (2006). Role for human posterior parietal cortex in visual processing of aversive objects in peripersonal space. *Journal of Neurophysiology, 95*(1), 205–214.

Loggia, M. L., Mogil, J. S., & Bushnell, M. C. (2008). Empathy hurts: Compassion for another increases both sensory and affective components of pain perception. *Pain, 136*(1–2), 168–176.

Ma, Y., Wang, C., & Han, S. (2011). Neural responses to perceived pain in others predict real-life monetary donations in different socioeconomic contexts. *NeuroImage, 57*(3), 1273–1280.

Masten, C. L., Morelli, S. A., & Eisenberger, N. I. (2011). An fmri investigation of empathy for 'social pain' and subsequent prosocial behavior. *NeuroImage, 55*(1), 381–388. doi:10.1016/j.neuroimage.2010.11.060.

McIntosh, A. R. (2000). Towards a network theory of cognition. *Neural Networks : The Official Journal of the International Neural Network Society, 13*(8–9), 861–870.

McIntosh, D. N. (2006). Spontaneous facial mimicry, liking and emotional contagion. *Polish Psychological Bulletin, 37*(1), 31. Retrieved from Google Scholar.

Meltzoff, A. (1990). Foundations for developing a concept of self: The role of imitation in relating self to other and the value of social mirroring, social modeling, and self-practice in infancy. In D. Cicchetti & M. Beeghly (Eds.), *The self in transition* (pp. 139–164). Chicago: University of Chicago Press.

Miller, P. (2010). *The smart swarm: How understanding flocks, schools, and colonies can make us better at communicating, decision making, and getting things done*. New York: Avery.

Miller, E. K., & Cohen, J. D. (2001). An integrative theory of prefrontal cortex function. *Annual Review of Neuroscience, 24*, 167–202.

Montague, P. (2002). Hyperscanning: Simultaneous fMRI during linked social interactions. *NeuroImage, 16*(4), 1159–1164.

Naito, E., Scheperjans, F., Eickhoff, S. B., Amunts, K., Roland, P. E., Zilles, K., et al. (2008). Human superior parietal lobule is involved in somatic perception of bimanual interaction with an external object. *Journal of Neurophysiology, 99*(2), 695–703.

Obhi, S. S. (2012). The amazing capacity to read intentions from movement kinematics. *Frontiers in Human Neuroscience, 6*, 162. doi:10.3389/fnhum.2012.00162.

Packer, D. J. (2009). Avoiding groupthink: Whereas weakly identified members remain silent, strongly identified members dissent about collective problems. *Psychological Science, 20*(5), 546–548. doi:10.1111/j.1467-9280.2009.02333.x.

Perlstein, W. M., Carter, C. S., Noll, D. C., & Cohen, J. D. (2001). Relation of prefrontal cortex dysfunction to working memory and symptoms in schizophrenia. *The American Journal of Psychiatry, 158*(7), 1105–1113.

Pessoa, L. (2008). On the relationship between emotion and cognition. *Nature Reviews Neuroscience, 9*(2), 148–158.

Pfeifer, J. H., Iacoboni, M., Mazziotta, J. C., & Dapretto, M. (2008). Mirroring others' emotions relates to empathy and interpersonal competence in children. *NeuroImage, 39*(4), 2076–2085.

Pineda, J. A. (2008). Sensorimotor cortex as a critical component of an "extended" mirror neuron system: Does it solve the development, correspondence, and control problems in mirroring? *Behavioral and Brain Functions (BBF), 4*, 47.

Post, J. M., & Panis, L. K. (2011). Crimes of obedience:"Groupthink" at abu ghraib. *International Journal of Group Psychotherapy, 61*(1), 48–66. Retrieved from Google Scholar.

Preston, S. D., & De Waal, F. (2002). Empathy: Its ultimate and proximate bases. *The Behavioral and Brain Sciences, 25*(1), 1–20. discussion 20–71.

Prindle, A., & Hasty, J. (2010). Biochemistry. Stochastic emergence of groupthink. *Science, 328*(5981), 987–988. doi:10.1126/science.1190372.

Raghunathan, R., & Pham, M. T. (1999). All negative moods are not equal: Motivational influences of anxiety and sadness on decision making. *Organizational Behavior and Human Decision Processes, 79*(1), 56–77.

Reimann, M., & Bechara, A. (2010). The somatic marker framework as a neurological theory of decision-making: Review, conceptual comparisons, and future neuroeconomics research. *Journal of Economic Psychology, 31*(5), 767–776.

Reisenzein, R. (1983). The Schachter theory of emotion: Two decades later. *Psychological Bulletin, 94*(2), 239–264.

Renzi, E. De, Cavalleri, F., & Facchini, S. (1996). Imitation and utilisation behaviour. *Journal of Neurology, 61*(4), 396–400.

Sawyer, R. Keith. (2005). *Social Emergence: Societies as complex systems*. Cambridge: Cambridge University Press.

Schilbach, L., Timmermans, B., Reddy, V., Costall, A., Bente, G., Schlicht, T., & Vogeley, K. (2013). Toward a second-person neuroscience. *The Behavioral and Brain Sciences, 36*(4), 393–414. doi:10.1017/S0140525X12000660.

Schulte-Rüther, M., Markowitsch, H. J., Fink, G. R., & Piefke, M. (2007). Mirror neuron and theory of mind mechanisms involved in face-to-face interactions: A functional magnetic resonance imaging approach to empathy. *Journal of Cognitive Neuroscience, 19*(8), 1354–1372.

Singer, T., Seymour, B., & O'Doherty, J. (2004). Empathy for pain involves the affective but not sensory components of pain. *Science, 303*(February), 1157–1162.

Smith, A. (2006). Cognitive empathy and emotional empathy in human behavior and evolution. *Psychological Record, 56*, 3–21.

Smith, E. R., Seger, C. R., & Mackie, D. M. (2007). Can emotions be truly group level ? *Evidence Regarding Four Conceptual Criteria, 93*(3), 431–446.

Snelgrove, H., Gosling, N., & McAnulty, G. (2011). The dissenting opinion: Can simulation-based multi-professional training reduce 'groupthink'? *Postgraduate Medical Journal, 87*(1027), 323–324. Retrieved from Google Scholar.

Spengler, S., Von Cramon, D. Y., & Brass, M. (2010). Resisting motor mimicry: Control of imitation involves processes central to social cognition in patients with frontal and temporo-parietal lesions. *Social Neuroscience, 5*(4), 401–416.

Strack, R., Martin, L. L., & Stepper, S. (1988). Inhibiting and facilitating conditions of facialexpressions: A non-obtrusive test of the facial feedback hypothesis. *Journal of Personality and Social Psychology, 54*, 768–777.

Sunstein, C. R. (2006). *Infotopia: How many minds produce knowledge*. New York: Oxford University Press.

Tassy, S., Oullier, O., Duclos, Y., Coulon, O., Mancini, J., Deruelle, C., et al. (2012). Disrupting the right prefrontal cortex alters moral judgment. *Social Cognitive and Affective Neuroscience, 7*(3), 282–288.

Trimble, M. (2007). Body image and the parietal lobes. *CNS Spectrums, 12*(7), 540–544.

Umiltà, M. A., Kohler, E., Gallese, V., Fogassi, L., Fadiga, L., Keysers, C., et al. (2001). I know what you are doing: A neurophysiological study. *Neuron, 31*(1), 155–165.

Van Baaren, R., Janssen, L., Chartrand, T. L., & Dijksterhuis, A. (2009). Where is the love? The social aspects of mimicry. *Philosophical Transactions of the Royal Society of London. Series B, Biological Sciences, 364*(1528), 2381–2389. doi:10.1098/rstb.2009.0057.

Vaughan, K. B., & Lanzett, J. T. (1980). Vicarious instigation and conditioning facial expressive and autonomic responses to a model's expressive display of pain. *Journal of Personality and Social Psychology, 38*, 909–923.

Vaughan, K. B., & Lanzett, J. T. (1981). The effect of modification of expressive displays on vicarious emotional arousal. *Journal of Experimental Social Psychology, 17*, 16–30.

Wang, Y., Newport, R., & Hamilton, A. F. D. C. (2011). Eye contact enhances mimicry of intransitive hand movements. *Biology Letters, 7*(1), 7–10.

Waters, F. A. V., & Badcock, J. C. (2010). First-rank symptoms in schizophrenia: Reexamining mechanisms of self-recognition. *Schizophrenia Bulletin, 36*(3), 510–517.

Wegner, D. M. (1987). Transactive memory: A contemporary analysis of the group mind. In *Theories of group behavior* (pp. 185–208). Springer. Retrieved from Google Scholar.

Weiland, S., Hewig, J., Hecht, H., Mussel, P., & Miltner, W. H. R. (2012). Neural correlates of fair behavior in interpersonal bargaining. *Social Neuroscience, 7*(5), 537–551.

Wicker, B., Keysers, C., Plailly, J., & Royet, J. (2003). Both of us disgusted in my insula: The common neural basis of seeing and feeling disgust. *Neuron, 40*, 655–664.

Widen, S. C., & Russell, J. A. (2010). Descriptive and prescriptive definitions of emotion. *Emotion Review, 2*(4), 377–378.

Winecoff, A., Clithero, J. A., Carter, R. M., Bergman, S. R., Wang, L., & Huettel, S. A. (2013). Ventromedial prefrontal cortex encodes emotional value. *Journal of Neuroscience, 33*(27), 11032–11039.

Zaccaro, S. J., & Lowe, C. (1988). Cohesiveness and performance on an additive task: Evidence for multidimensionality. *Journal of Social Psychology, 128*, 547–558.

Zaccaro, S. J., & McCoy, M. C. (1988). The effects of task and interpersonal cohesiveness on performance of a disjunctive group task. *Journal of Applied Social Psychology, 18*, 837–851.

Zaki, J., & Ochsner, K. (2012). The neuroscience of empathy: Progress, pitfalls and promise. *Nature Neuroscience, 15*(5), 675–680.

Zaki, J., Weber, J., Bolger, Niall, & Ochsner, K. (2009). The neural bases of empathic accuracy. *Proceedings of the National Academy of Science, 106*(27), 11382–11387.

Chapter 2
With Feeling: How Emotions Shape Negotiation

Mara Olekalns and Daniel Druckman

Introduction

An increasingly popular topic in current research is how emotional expressions influence the course of negotiation and related interactions. Negotiation is a form of social exchange that pits the opposing motives of cooperating and competing against one another. Most negotiators seek to reach an agreement with the other party; they also strive for an agreement that serves their own goals. This dual concern is reflected in a process that consists of both bargaining and problem solving. A good deal of the research and practice literature concentrates on ways to perform these activities effectively. In earlier writing, emotions were viewed largely as factors that impede performance, preventing successful coordination from occurring. More recently, we have learned that emotions can both help and hinder progress. Expressions may convey useful information about preferences; they can also signal dislike or malevolent intentions. Whether emotions move a negotiation forward or backward—or improve/threaten a relationship—depends on a variety of process and context variables. We explore these variables in more depth in this chapter.

Authors' Note: This chapter was originally published in a somewhat different form in the *Negotiation Journal*, Volume 30, Number 6, October 2014. It is printed in this book with permission of the Journal and its publisher.

M. Olekalns (✉)
Melbourne Business School, University of Melbourne, Melbourne, Australia
e-mail: m.olekalns@mbs.edu

D. Druckman
George Mason University, Fairfax, VA 22030, USA
e-mail: ddruckma@gmu.edu

D. Druckman
Macquarie University, Sydney, Australia

B. Martinovsky (ed.), *Emotion in Group Decision and Negotiation*,
Advances in Group Decision and Negotiation 7,
DOI 10.1007/978-94-017-9963-8_2

The study of emotions has been neglected in a literature that emphasizes strategy and information processing. This emphasis is prominent in several dominant paradigms that have guided much of the research, including game and decision theory, behavioral approaches, cognitive framing/prospect theory, and the dual concern model. Concepts such as motives, trust, and identity that seem to have substantial emotional content have been described mostly in terms of strategy. Motives have been construed in terms of relative and absolute or joint gains (De Dreu et al. 2002; Hopmann 1995). Trust has been defined as calculus-, knowledge-, and identification-based (Irmer and Druckman 2009; Lewicki and Stevenson 1997). And, identity has been treated as constituent-based representative role obligations (Druckman 1994; Wall 1975; Bartunek et al. 1975). Because of this emphasis on cognition, progress in developing theories or frameworks for understanding the role of emotions in negotiation has been slow. However, a spate of recent studies bodes well for development of this topic.

This chapter is organized by the perspectives that have guided the research to date on emotions in negotiation. Each perspective highlights a particular aspect of negotiation influenced by or influencing emotional expressions, namely moves and exchanges (behavior), information processing (cognition), social interaction, and context. These perspectives capture several levels of analysis, including individual bargainers, dyads and groups, and the larger settings in which bargaining occurs. Taken together, the four perspectives cover much of what is known about emotions in and around the negotiation "table." They also identify gaps in knowledge discussed in a final section as questions raised for further research.

Behavioral Consequences of Emotions

Most researchers explore the effects of specific emotions—typically anger and happiness—on observed behavior during the negotiation process. The first wave of this research compared how expressions of anger by a negotiator influence the other party's willingness to make concessions. Using programmed computer messages to convey anger to a negotiator, Van Kleef and his coworkers (van Kleef et al 2004a) have consistently demonstrated that the strategic expression of anger elicits larger concessions from opponents. Consistent with the affect-as-information theories of emotion, the greater willingness to give concessions to angry opponents can be attributed to a negotiators' belief that angry negotiators have higher limits.

Subsequent research has focused on identifying the boundary conditions for this effect. This research shows that anger is most effective at eliciting concessions when there is pressure to close the deal. This pressure may be interpersonal, when negotiators have a high need for cognitive closure, or contextual, when negotiators are bargaining under time pressure (Van Kleef et al 2004b). These results suggest that anger may be most effective when negotiators are concerned about whether they will reach a deal, and diminish as the ease of reaching agreement increases. Consistent with this interpretation, Van Kleef et al. (2004a) show that angry communications induce fear in negotiators. The link between expressed and anger and fear implies that, when negotiators express anger, they increase the other party's concerns about whether settlement is possible. Further support for this interpretation is provided by the finding that, in ultimatum bargaining games, negotiators make higher offers but also obtain poorer outcomes when the consequences of having their offers rejected are low (Nelissen et al. 2011; Van Dijk et al. 2008). Importantly, this relationship is mediated by fear and perceived threat (Nelissen et al. 2011; Sinaceur et al. 2011).

The effectiveness of expressed anger is also affected by whether the anger is directed at the task or the other negotiators. Fisher and Ury (1981) exhort negotiators to focus on the problem, not the person. This maxim implies that emotions expressed in relation to the task will be more effective than emotions directed at the person. This reasoning holds in relation to anger. When negotiators express anger about the offer they have received, they elicit more concessions than when they direct their anger at the other negotiator because they infer that the other party has high limits (Lelieveld et at. 2011; Steinel et al. 2008). Interestingly, this effect is reversed when negotiators express either happiness or disappointment: Both of these emotions, when directed at the person (rather then the offer), elicit more concessions from the other party (Lelieveld et at. 2011; Steinel et al. 2008). Finally, Harinck and Van Kleef (2012) demonstrate that the benefits of anger are limited to conflicts about interests. When conflicts are about values, expressions of anger trigger retaliation and escalate conflict.

In a recent review, Van Kleef (2009) summarizes the conditions that influence the interpersonal effects of anger. Anger is beneficial in producing favorable outcomes when: (a) it is directed at the task rather than the person, (b) it is viewed by the other as being justified, (c) the relationship between bargainers is inter-dependent, (d) the expression has informational value, (e) the bargainers take a strategic approach that encourages using the expression as information that can aid coordination, and (f) the target of anger has few opportunities to deceive. As noted above, strategic information may come from the other's verbal and nonverbal emotional expressions. Based on this summary of findings, the authors address the question: When does it pay to be angry? The answer is: When the parties are interdependent, when they use anger expressions strategically, and when the anger is seen as being justified.

A second, negative emotion that has received research attention is disappointment. Disappointment, as a discrete emotion, appears to shape the other party's offers because it triggers guilt in the other party (Lelieveld et al. 2011; Nelissen et al. 2011). This finding provides further support for this interpretation that, in repeat PDGs and ultimatum games and in divorce negotiations, guilt encourages higher levels of cooperation (Ketelaar and Au 2003; Wietzker et al. 2012). Similarly, in ultimatum games, feelings of regret result in more prosocial behavior (Martinez et al. 2011). And, mirroring the effect when negotiators are the targets of disappointment, individuals who feel disappointed decrease their prosocial behaviors (Martinez et al. 2011). Taken together, the research we have discussed so far suggests that to fully understand the impact of emotions in negotiations, not only do we need to differentiate between emotions with a similar valence but we also need to consider whether negotiators are the targets of expressed emotion or are experiencing the emotion themselves.

So far, we have focused on the impact of emotional expressions on obtaining increased concessions from an opponent. This research informs us about the ways in which expressing anger and other options might affect value claiming, but tells us less about how emotional expressions affect value creation. Nonetheless, an opponent's emotions are likely to provide indirect information about the relative priorities that she has assigned to specific issues. Focusing on the relationship between value creating (integrative) behaviors and emotions, Pietroni et al (2008) show that when negotiators display happiness in relation to high-priority issues and anger in relation to low-priority issues, value-creating behaviors increase. However, when they display the reverse pattern (anger on high-priority issues, happiness on low-priority issues), integrative behaviors decrease.

This finding brings us to the role of positive emotions in negotiation. Negotiation researchers have, in recent years, paid considerably less attention to the consequences of positive emotions than to the consequences of negative emotions. Positive emotions, however, facilitate deal-making: Not only do they increase the likelihood that negotiators will reach a deal, but they also increase the likelihood that negotiators will be willing to deal with each other again in the future (Kopelman et al. 2006). Expressions of positive affect in employment negotiations result in greater willingness to implement the final agreement (Mislin et al. 2011). These findings suggest that positive emotions may help negotiators to adopt a future-focus, facilitating agreements and strengthening ongoing relationships. These findings provide a tantalizing link to temporal construal theory, which suggests that distant time horizons are more likely to trigger cooperation and creativity than proximal time horizons (Henderson et al. 2006; Trope and Liberman 2010). They raise the possibility that the different consequences of negative and positive emotions may be underpinned by a shift in negotiators' temporal horizons. This shift in temporal perspective is also recognized in studies of international negotiations. The distinction between backward- and forward-looking outcomes distinguishes between proximal pasts and distant futures. Forward-looking outcomes result from more cooperative (and creative) negotiation processes (Zartman and Kremenyuk 2005; Donohue and Druckman 2009). The question of concomitant emotions is raised to be studied in these contexts.

Linking emotion to decision frame, Carnevale (2008) tests the proposition that positive affect may shift negotiators' reference points and reverse the well-known framing effect. His research shows that happy negotiators are more cooperative. They make more concessions and more integrative offers to the other party. Importantly, he also demonstrates that the framing effect can be reversed under positive affect: Whereas affect-neutral negotiators were more resistant to making concessions under a loss frame, positive affect negotiators were more resistant to making concessions under a gain frame. Carnevale's findings raise several interesting questions for future research. The first is the link between affect and corresponding nonverbal behavior, the activation of neural systems and negotiators' behavior. Although this link between cooperative/competitive strategic choices and neural activity has been explored in the context of Prisoner's Dilemma Games, we are yet to understand how affective and neural systems shape strategic choices in the more ambiguous and uncertain context of negotiation. A start along these lines is made by the Druckman et al. (1986) study of the relationship between the P300 EEG waveform, nonverbal behavior, and surprise in a bargaining task. Carnevale also highlights the importance of emotion-as-information, the idea that negotiators use their own affective states to guide their behavior.

Cognitive Perspectives

This perspective focuses on the relationship between emotions and information processing (e.g., Clore et al. 2001). Information search during bargaining depends for its effectiveness on skilled problem solving and judgments of authenticity. The former is a vigorous cognitive activity that contributes to better, more integrative outcome (Kressel et al. 1994). The latter involves interpretation about the other's intentions, which have been shown to be influenced by emotional expressions (Baron 1990). Both skills, known as decoding (diagnosing the other's intentions) and encoding (conveying impressions), improve with practice (Thompson 1990).

The need to interpret and respond to the other negotiator's intentions suggests that the strategic bargainer may be a Bayesian. This can be illustrated with anger. First, she ascertains whether the anger (or other emotions) being conveyed has informational value. Then, she asks how often such outbursts have occurred in the past (*a priori* probabilities). The next step consists of updating. She may ask about whether the expression is justified, whether it is intended to communicate information about the other's limits, whether it is intended to convey information about the importance of the issue being discussed, or whether it indicates an impatience with the process or with herself, the target of the outburst. Each of these questions suggests a symptom that can be estimated in terms of probabilities. They are the contingent probabilities that contribute to a decision about reciprocating the anger (escalation) or mollifying the other (de-escalation): The former is a likely reaction to unjustified anger; the latter to justified anger. The bargainer's choice influences the chances that the process will move in the direction of an impasse or an agreement.

These judgments may be formed against a background of greater or lesser certainty: Tiedens and Linton (2001) differentiate emotions associated with certainty, such as happiness and anger, from those associated with uncertainty, such as surprise, hope, and fear. This distinction is based on whether, based on their experienced emotions, individuals are confident that they can (certain) or cannot (uncertain) predict what will happen next. A possible consequence is that predictions negotiators make about the other party are influenced not only by the valence of an emotion but also by the degree of certainty associated with that emotion. For example, happiness—a certain, positive emotion—will create strong optimistic expectations that the other party is skilled, that a settlement is likely, and that cooperation is an appropriate strategy (e.g., Forgas 1998). Conversely, anger—a certain, negative emotion—creates the expectation of a difficult, competitive negotiation, resulting in disinterest and withdrawal (Forgas 1998; Knapp and Miller 1985; Van Kleef et al. 2004a). This greater certainty is likely to result in greater confidence about what the other party will do next and decrease negotiators' responsiveness to the other's actual strategies. We know less about how uncertain emotions influence negotiation, but conclude that as the certainty associated with a specific negotiation decreases, negotiators are less confident about what the other party will do. This may result, on the one hand, in increased responsiveness and strategic flexibility but may, on the other hand, also increase vigilance and scrutiny of the other party's behaviors as negotiators strive to gain greater insight into their opponent's intentions.

Emotions are conveyed not only through speech, but also through nonverbal behaviors. Starting with Darwin's (1872) account of the processes of emotional expression in animals and humans, investigators have searched for the way in which different emotions are conveyed through speech and nonverbal behavior, particularly facial expressions. Woodworth's (1938) listing of primary emotions was the basis for studies designed to isolate expressions corresponding to each state (see Ekman and Friesen 1975). These emotions are as follows: happiness, surprise, fear, sadness, anger, disgust/contempt, and interest. A question asked in many of these studies is whether these are universal emotions or cultural-specific states (Ekman 1972). For negotiation researchers, an important question concerns the connection between emotions and intentions.

Research on nonverbal indicators of deception has explored this connection (Ekman and Friesen 1974; De Paulo et al. 1980). Honest and deceptive intentions have been shown to be associated with such emotional states as confidence, stress, and interest (Druckman et al. 1982). Each of these states has been found to be indicated by particular facial (and other bodily) expressions. For example, deceivers indicate confidence in defending positions through increased head shaking, rocking movements, and crossed hands; an attempt to evade an issue is accompanied by feelings of stress and indicated by frequent gazes away from the other person; an intention to be honest is accompanied by feelings of interest or involvement and indicated by frequent leg movements and increased speaking frequency. These correlational findings point to a connection between emotional states and particular intentions. They also highlight the possibilities for diagnosis (decoding) and impression management (encoding) in negotiation and related types of social exchange. Connections between the emotional expression of both negative and positive emotions and opportunities to deceive in negotiation are made in several recent studies (e.g., O'Connor and Canevale 1997; Olekalns and Smith 2009; Steinel and De Dreu 2004).

More broadly, neuroimaging research suggests that emotions and cognitions are not distinct. These processes do not differ in kind. Rather, they interact in producing decisions. Both are influenced by interactive brain regions involved in basic psychological operations (Lindquist et al. 2012). With regard to negotiation, this means that intentional tactics, which may include evading or deceiving, combine elements of thought and feeling in an integrative rather than a sequential, competing, or additive fashion.

Social Interaction Perspectives on Emotion

Emotional expression also serves important social functions and assists in the coordination of social action. For individuals, emotions facilitate survival; for groups, they facilitate social bonding and collaboration (Keltner et al. 2006; Shiota et al. 2004; Morris and Keltner 2000). Emotions influence interaction processes when negotiators regard their expression as social information. Van Kleef (2009) develops this idea in the form of a model referred to as the Emotions as Social Information (EASI) model. Drawing on research from a variety of areas, he demonstrates that expressions influence observers' behavior by triggering inferential processes and/or affective reactions in them. He regards inferences and affective reactions as different processes that vary in relative predictive strength depending on both the observer's information processing—for example, expressing sadness to solicit help or happiness to encourage volunteers to contribute to a cause—and such social–relational factors as the type of interpersonal relationship, prevailing norms, and the way the emotion is expressed (directed toward the person or the situation). Emotional expression is thus likely to play a role in the development of relationships between bargainers. Improved relationships have been shown to result from cooperative processes and mutually beneficial outcomes (e.g., Druckman 1998; Olekalns and Smith 2005). Importantly, the expression of positive emotion is identified as critical to forming and maintaining social bonds (Shiota et al. 2004).

This perspective suggests that emotions will influence not just a negotiator's behaviors and economic outcomes, but also social outcomes such as reputation and the ongoing relationship. One aspect of the social impact of emotions is the trust or mistrust that may develop between negotiators. The emotion–trust link, addressed by a small number of researchers, shows that the expression of positive emotions builds trust among negotiators, suggesting that it is critical to problem solving (Dunn and Schweitzer 2005). Refining our understanding of this relationship, Liu and Wang (2010) showed that whereas expressions of compassion are linked to trust, expressions of anger are linked to distrust. Srivastava et al. (2009) demonstrate a link between negative emotions, perceived unfairness, and the willingness to retaliate in experimental games. A further consideration is whether expressed emotions (specifically anger) are judged to be authentic or strategic: Strategically expressed anger reduces trust and elicits higher demands from opponents, whereas authentic emotion increases perceived toughness and elicits lower demands from opponents (Côté et al. 2013). An open question is whether emotional expression mediates the trust–outcome relationship or whether trust and emotions provide two distinct paths to shape negotiators' outcomes. The interlocking relationships between trust and emotions may increase in importance when, as we discuss in the next section, negotiations are among three or more parties.

Another approach, bridging the social interaction and cognitive perspectives, is provided by Goffman's (1969) analysis of strategic interactions. Referred to as an expression game, he focuses on interactive dynamics between the roles of subject (making an offer or demand) and observer (receiving an offer or demand). This idea is a departure from the way research on negotiation (and on emotions) has been done. These roles are separated in much of the research: The focus of analysis is usually on the person receiving information from another or on the person sending information to another as in buyer–seller concession making. Less attention is paid to the interaction process where observer–subject interactions consist of alternating moves, the one attempting to infer intent from the subject's expressions, while the other attempts to convey certain expressions. In this process, each person is in easy reach of both the observer and subject roles. Reversed roles are a feature of the interaction that occurs as a result of mutual attempts to influence the other; the participant's sense of being more the subject or more the observer depends on whether he or she is persuading or analyzing during a particular episode in the process (see also Argyle et al. 1968; Pruitt 1995). Interchangeable roles require that bargainers use both skills in the course of negotiation. And, both skills are essential for conveying and reading verbal and nonverbal emotional expressions in negotiation. Whether improved sensitivity to the meaning of expressions increases tactical proficiency in conveying intentions remains a research issue.

This approach assumes that the dyad or group is the unit of analysis. This assumption departs from a good deal of the laboratory research where half of the interaction is controlled by the experimenter: Messages are often sent from computers or confederates. Field research shows that, in the field, anger and other emotions may play out differently than in laboratory settings. For example, negotiators' outcomes are influenced not just by the valence of expressed emotions but also the linguistic patterns that evolve over time. In two studies of e-disputes, researchers showed that expressions of anger halved the likelihood of settlement and that the reciprocation of anger predicted a failure to resolve the dispute (Brett et al. 2007; Friedman et al 2004). Positive emotions, on the other hand, had no impact on the likelihood of reaching settlement in a buyer–seller dispute. However, Olekalns et al. (2010) showed that, in child-custody disputes, the expression of positive emotions by wives, as well as the extent to which husbands "caught" these emotions, shaped outcomes. Agreement was reached when husbands converged to wives' high levels of positive emotion, whereas impasses occurred when husbands converged to wives' low levels of positive emotion. Similarly, hostage negotiations are more likely to conclude successfully when negotiators and hostage-takers reciprocate positive affect (Taylor and Thomas 2008). Jointly, these findings suggest that positive and negative emotions may not mark two ends of an emotional continuum. They also suggest that the domain in which negotiations occur is linked to the relative efficacy of expressing positive or negative emotions.

Finally, negotiators may "catch" the emotion of the other party. Emotional contagion describes a phenomenon in which individuals experience others' emotion because of a general tendency to mimic and synchronize emotion (Barsade 2002; Hatfield et al. 1993). Early experiments by Carnevale and Isen (1986) and by Johnson (1971a, b) demonstrated impacts of socially induced affect on negotiation. The former showed that when positive affect was induced, few contentious tactics were used and joint benefits were improved. The latter studies showed that scripted communications of warmth increased the other's liking but did not result in improved outcomes compared to a "cold" (angry) script. The most effective strategy was alternating between negative (acting cold) and positive (acting warm) emotions: Negotiators compromised more and evinced a larger change in attitudes when faced with an opponent who alternated between showing anger and warmth than when faced with opponents who were consistently angry or warm throughout the interactions. This finding suggests that there may be an advantage to "fine-tuning" one's expressions. The direction of negative and positive expressions may also be important. Concession-making studies showed that creating expectations for toughness early and a willingness to compromise later in the process lead to better outcomes.

These effects may be due to increased trust. Consistent with findings that emotional contagion increases group cohesion and rapport (Sy et al. 2005), Swaab et al. (2011) showed that trust mediated the relationship between mimicking the other negotiator's language and outcomes: Linguistic mimicry during the early phases of the negotiation produced better outcomes for the mimicker. In an earlier study, Swaab and Swaab (2008) found that eye contact led to higher-quality agreements for females but not for males: The visual contact increased comfort for the female negotiators but increased discomfort for the males. Together, these studies suggest that behaviors that increase either perceptions of trust or feelings of comfort lead to better outcomes. The findings also provide a bridge between the cognitive and social interaction perspectives. Verbal and nonverbal behaviors have diagnostic value for the strategic negotiator. They are used to infer intentions that either facilitate or impede interactions with consequences for outcomes. Negotiators should thus be able to strategically induce emotions in others (potentially enhancing their outcomes, through the strategic expression of emotion. For a review of the more general literature on socially induced affect, see Druckman and Bjork 1994, Chap. 10.)

Contextual Influences on Emotion

Missing as well from many laboratory studies is the way that emotional expressions are shaped by the contexts in which they are displayed. A contextualized view of emotions would complement the process view preferred by many negotiation researchers. Consequently, a key contribution of Van Kleef's EASI Model is to provide a framework for research on the interpersonal effects of emotions, thus also providing a link between the cognitive and social interaction perspectives on emotion. By including such moderating variables as power, time pressure, and display rules into the model, Van Kleef also incorporates contextual variables into the framework. Support for the model comes from studies on conflict and negotiation (e.g., Van Kleef et al. 2006a, b). Further, the meta-analytic review conducted by Lindquist et al. (2012) shows that brain states evoked by emotional expressions are sensitive to context. Different brain states occur when the same emotion is elicited under different circumstances. This is illustrated by their example of fear and anger: The corresponding brain state depends upon labeling as fear or anger and the social setting as a physical or social context.

Power, frequently a very salient contextual variable in negotiations, provides an important lens through which to view expressions of anger. Social cognition research suggests that, because they process information systematically and are more attuned to the social consequences of their actions, low-power negotiators are likely to be more responsive to emotion displays than high-power negotiators. Consistent with these general findings, low-power negotiators concede more to others who express anger and also claim less value from angry opponents (Butt and Choi 2009; Van Kleef et al. 2006a, b; Van Kleef and Cote 2007; Sinaceur and Tiedens 2006). High-power negotiators are also influenced by anger; however, they respond both to their own and to the other party's emotional state. Responding to their own anger, high-power negotiators are energized: They report feeling more focused and assertive, claiming more value in the negotiation (Overbeck et al. 2010). In response to the other's anger, they increase their demands when they believe that anger is unjustified (Van Kleef and Cote 2007). Finally, powerful negotiators set the emotional tone for a negotiation: Their positive affect underpins the level of trust in the negotiation (Anderson and Thompson 2004).

Research on e-communication sheds further light on the expression of emotion in negotiations and disputes. When negotiations occur electronically, they are more likely to be successful if negotiators express positive emotions and agreeableness. Critically, although expressions of agreeableness at any time during an e-negotiation facilitate settlement, negative emotions affect success only when they are expressed in the second half of the negotiation. These findings in the domain of negotiation parallel research in the domain of dispute resolution. Two studies investigating eBay disputes show that the expression of negative emotions and anger delay and may prevent settlement (Brett et al. 2007; Friedman et al. 2004). This line of research highlights the importance of emotional tone as well as timing. When emotions are expressed, the extent to which others then converge to those emotions contributes to their impact on the outcome.

Because the expression of emotions is socially determined, we might also expect that the impact of emotional expression varies across culture. For example, the emphasis on harmony and preserving face in Asian cultures suggests that these cultures might be more reluctant to express negative emotions. Following this line of thought, Adam et al. (2010) show that expressions of anger elicit larger concessions for European American but smaller concessions from Asian and Asian American negotiators. Expressions of anger also affect what negotiators do next: Chinese negotiators are more likely than American negotiators to respond to anger by increasing their use of persuasive arguments (Liu 2009). Further insight into the impact of culture-based norms is provided by Kopelman and Rosette (2008), who explore the issue of culture-specific relationships between accepting offers and accompanying emotional expressions. They show that Asian negotiators are more likely to accept ultimatum offers that are made in the context of positive emotions than those made in the context of negative emotions; however, Israeli negotiators are indifferent to whether an offer is accompanied by expressions of positive or negative emotions.

The same reasoning about norms of appropriateness can be applied to gender: Like culture, gender might determine what is perceived as appropriate emotional expression and consequently affect the impact of those emotions. In general, women are expected to both experience and express a greater range of emotions than men. The two exceptions to this general expectation relate to expressions of anger and pride, both of which are seen as more typical of men than women (Plant et al. 2000). Consistent with this view, men who express anger are more likely to obtain positive organizational outcomes than women who express anger (Gibson et al. 2009). The idea that there are gender- and culture-based expectations about emotional expression is interesting, in light of work on expectancy violation and emotion in negotiation: Negotiators who switch strategies and thereby violate the expectations of the other negotiator influence that party's mood (Barry and Oliver 1996; Olekalns et al. 2005).

A broader context of interest, also associated with regulatory norms, is the organization. Directions for research on emotions in organizations is indicated by Fineman (1993: 217) and his contributors. He asks: "In what ways do decisions unfold over time as a function of the way people feel, and change their feelings—about themselves, their projects and significant others? How, for example does anxiety, suspicion, love, and hate take decision making through various paths towards particular outcomes?" These questions are also at the heart of research on negotiation. Stretching back to Walton and McKersie's (1965) intra-organizational model of labor negotiation, researchers have explored the way that negotiation occurs within and between organizations—particularly with regard to boundary roles (Adams 1976; Burke and Biggert 1997). The research has, however, been more concerned with strategies than with emotional expressions.

Context also changes when individuals move from dyadic to multi-party negotiations. As is the case in dyadic negotiations, expressions of anger and negative emotions decrease agreement. More importantly, negotiators who express anger are likely to be excluded from coalitions and hence lose their share of the outcome (Huffaker et al. 2011; Van Beest et al. 2008). However, if negotiators are forced or choose to form an alliance with an angry player, then, as is the case in dyadic negotiations, angry negotiators obtain large concessions. The flip side is that building perceived similarity, through linguistic convergence, increases agreement between coalition partners (Huffaker et al. 2011). When integrated with the positive emotion–trust link we described earlier, these findings suggest that positive emotions might strengthen alliances and enable negotiators to improve their outcomes (also, Olekalns et al. 2007). Our understanding of the role of emotion in multi-party negotiations is in its infancy. However, the possibility that emotional expression shapes coalition formation and agreement suggests that we need better understanding of the role that emotional expressions play in multi-party negotiations.

Finally, recent research has investigated the longer-term consequences of emotional expression. In their study, Van Kleef and De Dreu (2010) tested the long-term consequences of expressing anger in a negotiation. They contrasted a spillover model, which suggests that the target of anger would demand less in a subsequent negotiation, with a retaliation model, which suggests that a target would demand more in a subsequent negotiation. They found support for the spillover model: Negotiators demanded less when they had a second negotiation with the same angry negotiator because they perceived that negotiator to be tough. Taking the idea of timing in a slightly different direction, Filipowicz et al. (2011) compared the impact of consistently expressed emotions throughout a negotiation to the impact of emotional transitions. They found that, compared to negotiators who are consistent in their emotional expressions, negotiators who "become angry" obtain better outcomes and also conveyed a more positive impression than negotiators who "become happy." Similarly, Sinaceur et al. (2013) report that emotional inconsistency elicits greater concessions than emotional consistency.

New Directions for Research

To date, negotiation researchers have focused on a relatively narrow range of behaviors. Moreover, despite complex models of emotion in other domains, negotiators have neither connected with these literatures nor sampled systematically across different dimensions of emotion. Negotiation researchers continue to concentrate their work primarily on two emotions, happiness and anger. A few studies have examined impacts of surprise on bargaining moves (e.g., Druckman et al. 1986) and on the arousal of guilt when outcomes clearly favor oneself (Hegtvedt and Killian 1999). These and other emotional states have been studied in psychology more generally. One well-known model, the circumplex model of affect (Russell 1980), differentiates emotions based on their valence (positive or negative) as well as their arousal level (active vs. passive). We encourage negotiation researchers to more systematically assess how emotions around the affect circumplex affect negotiators' behaviors and outcomes.

More recent research also shows strong links between emotions and the activation different regions of the brain. The effects of mimicking have been shown to be associated with mirror neurons, which fire either when an individual acts or observes an action underlie the effects of mimicry that we described earlier (Van der Gaad et al. 2007; Wicker et al. 2003). Similarly, emotions from different quadrants of the affect circumplex trigger activity in different regions of the brain: Research shows that distinct brain regions activate depending on the valence and arousal of a specific emotion (Colibazzi et al. 2010; Posner et al. 2009). More recently, de Dreu and coworkers have linked oxytocin to in-group trust and cooperation in the face of intergroup conflict (De Dreu et al. 2010). These findings, because they show that different brain regions are activated by different emotions, underscore the importance of sampling emotions around the affect circumplex because they imply that similarly valence emotions may evoke distinctly different reactions. They further underscore the need to better understand the neurophysiological factors that drive our emotional experiences and our reactions to others.

Many of the studies we reviewed were conducted in laboratories. An advantage of the laboratory controls is that the direction of influence—from the computer/actor to the subject—is clear. Causal inferences can be made with confidence. A disadvantage is that interactive dynamics are ignored. The result is a loss in relevance to real-world negotiations. This trade off, favoring internal over external validity, is a feature of much of the research to date. A better balance between the two validities will materialize when researchers take on the challenge of field research. The interaction dynamics described by field researchers would complement the causal patterns inferred from the laboratory studies. Add to this the challenges of studying a phenomenon that is fleeting—as in changing moods during the course of an interaction—and vaguely defined—as when multiple meanings are inferred from expressions—and there is little wonder that the research to date has progressed slowly. Emotions are not easy to investigate. But there is little doubt that it is important to study them.

Of particular interest are research questions that cross the four perspectives. Examples include the following: (a) How are concessions (behavioral perspective) influenced by attributions of the other negotiator's intentions (cognitive perspective)? (b) How are interaction dynamics (social interaction perspective) shaped by the connection between decoding/interpretation and encoding/conveying expressions (cognitive perspective)? To what extent does Van Kleef's EASI model contribute to understanding this connection? (c) Which emotional expressions—and the corresponding link to negotiating behavior—are more or less influenced by such contextual variables as culture and gender? and (d) What role do emotional expressions play in the development of long-term relationships between negotiators? How is this connection—between emotions and social relationships—mediated by contextual variables?

Conclusions

The findings that we have discussed identify an interesting set of issues for continuing research within each perspective on emotions in negotiation. First, we can look forward to studies that examine other emotions such as surprise when expectations are disappointed, sadness when alternatives are unattractive and dependency increases, shame when face is lost, and interest or involvement when the stakes increase. Second, the interplay between emotions and cognitions present an interesting array of research challenges: for example, the way that bargainers use affective information to develop or change strategies. Third, process dynamics call for further investigation. In particular, interactive processes such as those described by the expression-game paradigm need to be better understood. A related issue is the coordination of emotional expressions: When does matching perpetuate impasses and when does it resolve them? Fourth, there is much yet to be learned about the contexts for emotional expression. Included in these contexts are the number of parties, organizational norms, and cultures. A question of interest is how these contexts shape the way emotions are expressed and read. The idea of cultural display rules may be relevant also for organizations and the institutional contexts within which negotiation occurs.

References

Adam, H., Shirako, A., & Maddux, W. (2010). Cultural variance in the interpersonal effects of anger in negotiations. *Psychological Science, 21*, 882–889.

Adams, J. S. (1976). The structure and dynamics of behavior in organizational boundary roles. In M. D. Dunnette (Ed.), *Handbook of industrial and organizational psychology*. Chicago: Rand McNally.

Anderson, C., & Thompson, L. (2004). Affect from the top down: How powerful individuals' positive affect shapes negotiations. *Organizational Behavior and Human Decision Processes, 95*, 125–139.

Argyle, M., Lalljee, M., & Cook, M. (1968). The effects of visibility on interaction in a dyad. *Human Relations, 21*, 3–17.

Baron, R. A. (1990). Environmentally-induced positive affect: Its impact on self-efficacy, task performance, negotiation, and conflict. *Journal of Applied Social Psychology, 20*, 368–384.

Barry, B., & Oliver, R. L. (1996). Affect in dyadic negotiation: A model and propositions. *Organizational Behavior and Human Decision Processes, 67*, 127–143.

Barsade, S. G. (2002). The ripple effect: Emotional contagion and its influence on group behavior. *Administrative Science Quarterly, 47*, 644–675.

Bartunek, J. M., Benton, A., & Keys, C. B. (1975). Third party intervention and the bargaining behavior of group representatives. *Journal of Conflict Resolution, 19*, 532–557.

Brett, J., Olekalns, M., Friedman, R., Goates, N., Anderson, C., & Lisco, C. (2007). Sticks and stones: Language and on-line dispute resolution. *Academy of Management Journal, 50*, 85–99.

Burke, W., & Biggert, N. (1997). Inter-organizational cooperation. In D. Druckman, J. Singer, & H. Van Cott (Eds.), *Enhancing organizational performance*. Washington DC: National Academy Press.

Butt, A. N., & Choi, J. N. (2009). Does power matter? Negotiator status as a moderator of the relationship between negotiator emotion and behavior. *International Journal of Conflict Management, 21*(2), 124–146.

Carnevale, P. J. (2008). Positive affect and decision frame in negotiation. *Group Decision and Negotiation, 17*(1), 51–63.

Carnevale, P., & Isen, A. M. (1986). The influence of positive affect and visual access on the discovery of integrative solutions in bilateral negotiation. *Organizational Behavior and Human Performance, 37*, 1–13.

Clore, G. L., Gasper, K., & Gavin, E. (2001). Affect as information. In J. P. Forgas (Ed.), *Handbook of affect and social cognition*. Mahwah, NJ: Lawrence Erlbaum Associates.

Colibazzi, T., et al . (2010). Neural systems subserving valence and arousal during the experience of induced emotions. *Emotion, 10*(3): 377–389.

Côté, S., Hideg, I., & van Kleef, G. A. (2013). The consequences of faking anger in negotiations. *Journal of Experimental Social Psychology, 49*, 453–463.

Daly, J. P. (1991). The effects of anger on negotiations over mergers and acquisitions. *Negotiation Journal, 7*, 31–39.

Darwin, C. (1872). *The Expression of the emotions in man and animals*. London: Murray.

De Dreu, C. K. W., et al. (2010). The neuropeptide oxytocin regulates parochial altruism in intergroup conflict among humans. *Science, 328*, 1408.

De Dreu, C. K. W., Weingart, L., & Kwon, S. (2002). Influence of social motives on integrative negotiation: A meta-analytic review and test of two theories. *Journal of Personality and Social Psychology, 78*, 889–905.

DePaulo, B. M., Zuckerman, M., & Rosenthal, R. (1980). Detecting deception: Modality effects. In L. Wheeler (Ed.), *Review of personality and social psychology* (Vol. 1). Beverly Hills, CA: Sage.

Donohue, W. A., & Druckman, D. (2009). Message framing surrounding the Oslo I accords. *Journal of Conflict Resolution, 53*(1), 119–145.

Druckman, D. (1998). Social exchange theory: Promises and prospects. *International Negotiation, 3*, 253–266.

Druckman, D. (1994). Determinants of compromising behavior in negotiation: A meta-analysis. *Journal of Conflict Resolution, 38*, 507–556.

Druckman, D., & Bjork, R. A. (1994). *Learning, remembering, and believing: Enhancing human performance*. Washington DC: National Academy Press.

Druckman, D., Karis, D., & Donchin, E. (1986). Information processing in bargaining: Reactions to an opponent's shift in concession strategy. In R. Tietz (Ed.), *Aspiration levels in bargaining and economic decision making*. Berlin: Springer.

Druckman, D., Rozelle, R., & Baxter, J. (1982). *Nonverbal communication: Survey, theory, and research*. Beverly Hills, CA: Sage.

Dunn, J. R., & Schweitzer, M. E. (2005). Feeling and believing: The influence of emotion on trust. *Journal of Personality and Social Psychology, 88*, 736–748.

Ekman, P. (1972). Universal and cultural differences in facial expressions of emotion. In J. K. Cole (Ed.), *Nebraska symposium on motivation*. Lincoln, Nebraska: University of Nebraska Press.

Ekman, P., & Friesen, W. V. (1975). *Unmasking the face: A guide to recognizing emotions from facial clues*. Englewood Cliffs, NJ: Prentice-Hall.

Ekman, P., & Friesen, W. V. (1974). Detecting deception from the body or face. *Journal of Personality and Social Psychology, 29*, 288–298.

Filipowicz, A. S., Barsade, S., & Melwani, S. (2011). Understanding emotional transitions: The interpersonal consequences of changing emotions in negotiations. *Journal of Personality and Social Psychology, 101*, 541–556.

Fisher, R., & Ury, W. L. (1981). *Getting to yes: Negotiating agreement without giving in*. London: Penguin.

Forgas, J. P. (1998). On feeling good and getting your way: Mood effects on negotiator cognition and bargaining strategies. *Journal of Personality and Social Psychology, 74*, 565–577.

Fineman, S. (Ed.). (1993). *Emotion in organizations*. London: Sage.

Friedman, R., Brett, J., Anderson, C., Olekalns, M., Goates, N., & Lisco, C. (2004). Emotions and rationality in mediation: Evidence from electronically-mediated disputes. *Journal of Applied Psychology, 89*, 369–376.

Gibson, D., Schweitzer, M., Callister, R., & Gray, B. (2009). The influence of anger expressions on outcomes in organizations. *Negotiation and Conflict Management Research, 2*, 236–262.

Goffman, E. (1969). *Strategic interaction*. Philadelphia: University of Pennsylvania Press.

Harinck, F., & Van Kleef, G. A. (2012). Be hard on the interests and soft on the values: Conflict issue moderates the effects of anger in negotiations. *British Journal of Social Psychology, 51*, 741–752.

Hatfield, E., Cacioppo, J. T., & Rapson, R. L. (1993). Emotional contagion. *Current Directions in Psychological Science, 2*, 96–99.

Hegtvedt, K. A., & Killian, C. (1999). Fairness and emotions: Reactions to the process and outcomes of negotiations. *Social Forces, 78*, 269–303.

Henderson, M. D., Trope, Y., & Carnevale, P. J. (2006). Negotiating from a near and distant time perspective. *Journal of Personality and Social Psychology, 4*, 712–729.

Hopmann, P. T. (1995). Two paradigms of negotiation: Bargaining and problem solving. *Annals of the American Academy of Political and Social Science, 542*, 24–47.

Huffaker, D. A., Swaab, R., & Diermeier, D. (2011). The language of coalition formation in online multiparty negotiations. *Journal of Language and Social Psychology, 30*, 66–81.

Irmer, C., & Druckman, D. (2009). Explaining negotiation outcomes: Process or context? *Negotiation and Conflict Management Research, 2*(3), 209–235.

Johnson, D. W. (1971a). The effects of warmth of interaction, accuracy of understanding, and the proposal of compromises on the listener's behavior. *Journal of Counseling Psychology, 18*, 207–216.

Johnson, D. W. (1971b). Effects of the order of expressing warmth and anger on the actor and listener. *Journal of Counseling Psychology, 18*, 571–578.

Ketelaar, T., & Au, W. T. (2003). The effects of feelings of guilt on the behavior of uncooperative individuals in repeated social bargaining games: An affect-as-information interpretation of the role of emotion in social interaction. *Cognition and Emotion, 17*, 429–453.

Keltner, D., Haidt, J. & Shiota, M. N. (2006). Social functionalism and the evolution of emotions. In M. Schaller, J. A. Simpson, & D. T. Kenrick, (Eds.), *Evolution and social psychology: Frontiers of social psychology*. Madison, CT: Psychosocial Press.

Knapp, M. L., & Miller, G. R. (1985). *Handbook of interpersonal communication*. Beverly Hills, CA: Sage.

Kopelman, S., & Rosette, A. (2008). Cultural variation in response to strategic emotions in negotiation. *Group Decision and Negotiation, 17*, 65–77.

Kopelman, S., Rosette, A., & Thompson, L. (2006). The three faces of eve: Strategic displays of positive, negative, and neutral emotions in negotiations. *Organizational Behavior and Human Decision Processes, 99*, 81–101.

Kressel, K., Frontera, E., Forlenza, S., Butler, F., & Fish, L. (1994). The settlement orientation vs. the problem-solving style in custody mediation. *Journal of Social Issues, 50*, 67–84.

Lelieveld, G., Van Dijk, E., Van Beest, I., Steinel, W., & Van Kleef, G. (2011). Disappointed in you, angry about your offer: Distinct negative emotions induce concessions via different mechanisms. *Journal of Experimental Social Psychology, 47*, 635–641.

Lindquist, K. A., et al. (2012). The brain basis of emotion: A meta-analytic review. *Behavioral and Brain Sciences, 35*, 121–202.

Liu, M., & Wang, C. (2010). Explaining the influence of anger and compassion on negotiators' interaction goals: An assessment of trust and distrust as two distinct mediators. *Communication Research, 37*, 443–472.

Liu, M. (2009). The intrapersonal and interpersonal effects of anger on negotiation strategies: A cross-cultural investigation. *Human Communication Research, 35*, 148–169.

Lewicki, R., & Stevenson, M. (1997). Trust development in negotiation: Proposed actions and a research agenda. Paper presented at the conference on Trust and Business: Barriers and Bridges. Chicago: DePaul University.

Martinez, L. M., et al. (2011). Behavioural consequences of regret and disappointment in social bargaining games. *Cognition and Emotion, 25*, 351–359.

Mislin, A., Campagna, R. L., & Bottom, W. P. (2011). After the deal: Talk, trust building and the implementation of negotiated agreements. *Organizational Behavior and Human Decision Processes, 115*, 55–68.

Morris, M. W., & Keltner, D. (2000). How emotions work: The social functions of emotional expression in negotiations. *Research in Organizational Behavior, 22*, 1–50.

Nelissen, R. A., Leliveld, M., van Dijk, E., & Zeelenberg, M. (2011). Fear and guilt in proposers: Using emotions to explain offers in ultimatum bargaining. *European Journal of Social Psychology, 41*, 78–85.

O'Connor, K., & Carnevale, P. (1997). A nasty but effective negotiation strategy: Misrepresentation of a common-value issue. *Personality and Social Psychology Bulletin, 23*, 504–519.

Olekalns, M., Lau, F., & Smith, P. (2007). Resolving the empty core: Trust as a determinant of outcomes in three-party negotiations. *Group Decision and Negotiation, 16*, 527–538.

Olekalns, M., Brett, J., & Donohue, W. (2010). Words are all I have: Linguistic cues as predictors of settlement in divorce mediation. *Negotiation and Conflict Management Research, 3*, 145–168.
Olekalns, M., & Smith, P. (2009). Mutually dependent: Power, trust, affect and the use of deception in negotiation, *Journal of Business Ethics, 85,* 347-365.
Olekalns, M., Roberts, C., Probst, T., Smith, O., & Carnevale, P. (2005). The impact of message frame on Negotiators' social judgments, moods and behavior.*International Journal of Conflict Management, 16*, 379–402.
Overbeck, J. R., Neale, M. A., & Govan, C. L. (2010). I feel, therefore you act: Intrapersonal and interpersonal effects of emotion on negotiation as a function of social power. *Organizational Behavior and Human Decision Processes, 112*, 126–139.
Pietroni, D., Van Kleef, G., De Dreu, C., & Pagliaro, S. (2008). Emotions as strategic information: Effects of other's emotional expressions on fixed-pie perception, demands, and integrative behavior in negotiation. *Journal of Experimental Social Psychology, 44*, 1444–1454.
Plant, E. A., Hyde, J. S., Keltner, D., & Devine, P. G. (2000). The gender stereotyping of emotions. *Psychology of Women Quarterly, 24*, 81–92.
Posner, J., et al. (2009). The neurophysiological bases of emotion: An fMRI study of the affective circumplex using emotion-denoting words. *Human Brain Mapping, 30*, 883–895.
Pruitt, D. G. (1995). Flexibility in conflict episodes. *Annals of the American Academy of Political and Social Science, 542*, 100–115.
Russell, J. A. (1980). A circumplex model of affect. *Journal of Personality and Social Psychology, 39*, 1161–1178.
Shiota, M. N., Keltner, D., & Hertenstein, M. J. (2004). Positive emotion and the regulation of interpersonal relationships. In P. Philippot & R. S. Feldman (Eds.), *The regulation of emotion*. Hillsdale NJ: Lawrence Erlbaum Associates.
Sinaceur, M., & Tiedens, L. (2006). Get mad and get more than even: When and why anger expression is effective in negotiations. *Journal of Experimental Social Psychology, 42*, 314–322.
Sinaceur, M., Adam, H., Van Kleef, G. A., & Galinsky, A. D. (2013). The advantages of being unpredictable: How emotional inconsistency extracts concessions in negotiation. *Journal of Experimental Social Psychology, 49*, 498–508.
Sinaceur, M., Van Kleef, G. A., Neale, M., Adam, H., & Haag, C. (2011). Hot or cold: Is communicating anger or threats more effective in negotiation? *Journal of Applied Psychology, 96*, 1018–1032.
Srivastava, J., Espinoza, F., & Fedorikhin, A. (2009). Coupling and decoupling of unfairness and anger in ultimatum bargaining. *Journal of Behavioral Decision Making, 22*, 475–489.
Steinel, W., Van Kleef, G. A., & Harinck, F. (2008). Are you talking to me?! Separating the people from the problem when expressing emotions in negotiation. *Journal of Experimental Social Psychology, 44*, 362–369.
Steinel, W., & De Dreu, C. K. W. (2004). Social motives and strategic misrepresentation in social decision making. *Journal of Personality and Social Psychology, 86*, 419–434.
Swaab, R. I., & Swaab, D. F. (2008). Sex differences in the effects of visual contact and eye contact in negotiations. *Journal of Experimental Social Psychology, 45*, 129–136.
Swaab, R. I., Maddux, W. W., & Sinaceur, M. (2011). Early words that work: When and how linguistic mimicry facilitates negotiation outcomes. *Journal of Experimental Social Psychology, 47*, 616–621.
Sy, T., Cote, S., & Saavedra, R. (2005). The contagious leader: impact of the leader's mood on the mood of group members, group affective tone, and group processes. *Journal of Applied Psychology, 90*, 295–305.
Taylor, P., & Thomas, S. (2008). Linguistic style matching and negotiation outcome. *Negotiation and Conflict Management Research, 1*, 263–281.
Thompson, L. (1990). An examination of naïve and experienced negotiators. *Journal of Personality and Social Psychology, 59*, 82–90.

Tiedens, L. Z., & Linton, S. (2001). Judgment under emotional certainty and uncertainty: The effects of specific emotions on information processing. *Journal of Personality and Social Psychology, 81*, 973–988.

Trope, Y., & Liberman, N. (2010). Construal-level theory of psychological distance. *Psychological Review, 117*, 440–463.

Van Beest, I., Van Kleef, G. A., & Van Dijk, E. (2008). Get angry, get out: The interpersonal effects of anger communication in multiparty negotiation. *Journal of Experimental Social Psychology, 44*, 993–1002.

Van Dijk, E., Van Kleef, G. A., Steinel, W., & Van Beest, I. (2008). A social functional approach to emotions in bargaining: When communicating anger pays and when it backfires. *Journal of Personality and Social Psychology, 94*, 600–614.

van der Gaad, C., Minderaa, R. B., & Keysers, C. (2007). Facial expressions: What the mirror neuron system can and cannot tell us. *Social Neuroscience, 2*, 179–222.

Van Kleef, G. (2009). How emotions regulate social life: The emotions as social information (EASI) model. *Current Directions in Psychological Science, 18*(3), 184–188.

Van Kleef, G., & Cote, S. (2007). Expressing anger in conflict: When it helps and when it hurts. *Journal of Applied Psychology, 92*, 1557–1569.

Van Kleef, G. A., & De Dreu, C. K. W. (2010). Longer-term consequences of anger expression in negotiation: Retaliation or spillover? *Journal of Experimental Social Psychology, 46*, 753–760.

Van Kleef, G. A., De Dreu, C. K. W., & Manstead, A. S. R. (2006a). Supplication and appeasement in conflict and negotiation: The interpersonal effects of disappointment, worry, guilt, and regret. *Journal of Personality and Social Psychology, 91*, 124–142.

Van Kleef, G. A., De Dreu, C. K. W., Pietroni, D., & Manstead, A. S. (2006b). Power and emotion in negotiation: Power moderates the interpersonal effects of anger and happiness on concession making. *European Journal of Social Psychology, 36*, 557–581.

Van Kleef, G. A., De Dreu, C. K. W., & Manstead, A. S. (2004a). The interpersonal effects of anger and happiness in negotiations. *Journal of Personality and Social Psychology, 86*, 57–76.

Van Kleef, G. A., et al. (2004b). The interpersonal effects of emotions in negotiations: A motivated information processing approach. *Journal of Personality and Social Psychology, 87*, 510–528.

Wall, J. A. (1975). Effects of constituent trust and representative bargaining orientation in intergroup bargaining. *Journal of Personality and Social Psychology, 31*, 1004–1112.

Walton, R. E., & McKersie, R. B. (1965). *A behavioral theory of labor negotiations: An analysis of a social interaction system*. New York: McGraw-Hill.

Wicker, B., Keysers, C., Plailly, J., Royet, J. P., Gallese, V., & Rizzolatti, G. (2003). Both of us disgusted in my insula: the common neural basis of seeing and feeling disgust. *Neuron, 40*, 655–664.

Wietzker, A., Buysse, A., Loeys, T., & Brondeel, R. (2012). Easing the conscience: Feeling guilty makes people cooperate in divorce negotiations. *Journal of Social and Personal Relationships, 29*, 324–336.

Woodworth, R. S. (1938). *Experimental psychology*. New York: Henry Holt.

Zartman, I. W., & Kremenyuk, V. (2005). *Peace versus justice: negotiating forward- and backward-looking outcomes*. Lanham MD: Rowman & Littlefield Publishers.

Chapter 3
The Cognitive–Affective Structure of Political Ideologies

Paul Thagard

Introduction

Many group conflicts are strongly influenced by ideologies. Political deliberation and discourse are shaped by ideologies such as liberalism, conservatism, communism, fascism, anarchism, environmentalism, and feminism. Each of these is a system of interconnected concepts, beliefs, goals, and attitudes. The aim of this chapter is to explain how such systems operate by drawing on current theories of cognition and emotion. Relevant questions include:

1. What is the mental structure of an ideology? That is, how are its concepts, beliefs, goals, and attitudes related to each other?
2. What role does affect (encompassing emotions, moods, and motivations) play in ideological thinking?
3. What are the mental mechanisms (cognitive and affective) that explain how individuals acquire, retain, and abandon ideologies?
4. What are the social mechanisms involving both cognitive and affective communication that explain how ideologies spread in *groups* of individuals?

This chapter attempts to answer these questions using novel accounts of the structure and development of conceptual systems.

Ideologies construed as emotionally laden systems of ideas and values are highly relevant to group decision and negotiation. When members of a group face a decision, they often have to deal with how ideologies held by various group members impede movement toward consensus. Negotiations among group members and between members of different groups can be hindered by misunderstandings and blockages resulting from the possession of conflicting ideologies.

P. Thagard (✉)
Philosophy Department, University of Waterloo, Waterloo, ON, Canada
e-mail: pthagard@uwaterloo.ca

B. Martinovsky (ed.), *Emotion in Group Decision and Negotiation*,
Advances in Group Decision and Negotiation 7,
DOI 10.1007/978-94-017-9963-8_3

Hence identifying ideologies and their effects on conflicts is an important part of negotiation.

At a minimum, negotiators need to recognize and understand the differences between their own ideologies and those of their opponents in order to overcome obstacles and move toward acceptable resolutions. Historical mistakes such as the appeasement of Hitler before the Second World War can result through lack of understanding of the character and intensity of competing ideologies. Although this chapter is primarily concerned with political ideologies, there are other kinds, for example religious ones, that have similar cognitive and affective properties. The term "affect" is used by psychologists to cover emotion, mood, and motivation. The cognitive–affective approach is consistent with conventional political work on ideology (e.g., Freeden 1996; Leader Maynard 2013), but provides much more detail about the underlying psychological processes. Like Haidt (2012), my approach views ideology as enmeshed with morality and emotion.

I will display the structure of ideologies using a new technique called *cognitive–affective mapping*. This technique can be used to portray the cognitive and emotional relations in both left-wing and right-wing ideologies. To show the full structure of more specific ideologies, however, we need to expand the technique to allow multimodal representations such as pictures and sounds in addition to verbal concepts. This chapter will present multimodal cognitive–affective maps of Nazi and anarchist ideologies. Cognitive maps, also known as concept maps or mind maps, have long been used to depict systems of mental representations (e.g., Axelrod 1976; Novak 1998; Sowa 1999), but are inadequate to show the emotional and nonverbal character of ideologies.

Cognitive–affective maps are useful for showing the structure of ideologies, but do not address the questions of how they are acquired, retained, and abandoned by individuals and groups. Fortunately, the maps are based on a theory of emotional coherence that can explain why people are attracted to various ideologies. A case can be made that emotional coherence is the main mental mechanism governing people's acquisition and retention of ideologies, producing such less-than-rational processes as motivated inference and fear-driven inference. Moreover, the psychological theory of emotional coherence meshes well with social mechanisms of cognitive and emotional transfer that can explain how ideologies spread through groups of individuals.

The Structure of Ideologies

The conceptual structure of ideologies can be conveniently displayed using the new method of *cognitive–affective maps* (Thagard 2010b, 2011, 2012a, b, 2015, in press; Findlay and Thagard 2014; Homer-Dixon et al. 2013, 2014). After a brief introduction to this technique, this section presents cognitive–affective maps (CAMs for short) of left-wing and right-wing ideologies.

A cognitive–affective map is a visual representation of the emotional values of a group of interconnected concepts. It employs the following conventions:

1. Ovals represent emotionally positive (pleasurable) elements.
2. Hexagons represent emotionally negative (painful) elements.
3. Rectangles represent elements that are neutral or carry both positive and negative aspects.
4. The thickness of the lines in the shape represents the relative strength of the positive or negative value associated with it.
5. Solid lines represent the relations between elements that are mutually supportive.
6. Dashed lines represent the relations between elements that are incompatible with each other.
7. The thickness of the lines in the connection represents the strength of the positive or negative relation.

When color is available, CAMs conventionally represent positive elements by green ovals, negative ones by red hexagons, and neutral ones by yellow rectangles. Figure 3.1 schematizes this kind of representation.

A CAM can be drawn by following these steps:

1. Identify the main concepts, beliefs, goals, and emotions of the person being modeled.
2. Identify these elements as emotionally positive or negative, and accordingly represent them by ovals or hexagons.
3. Identify relations between elements that are either complementary (solid lines) or conflicting (dashed lines).
4. Show the resulting map to other people to see whether it captures their understandings of the person and situation.

We can now apply this technique to ideologies.

Figure 3.2 shows a highly simplified account of a kind of right-wing ideology that is currently popular in many countries, for example in the Republican Party in the USA and in the Conservative parties of the UK and Canada. The most important

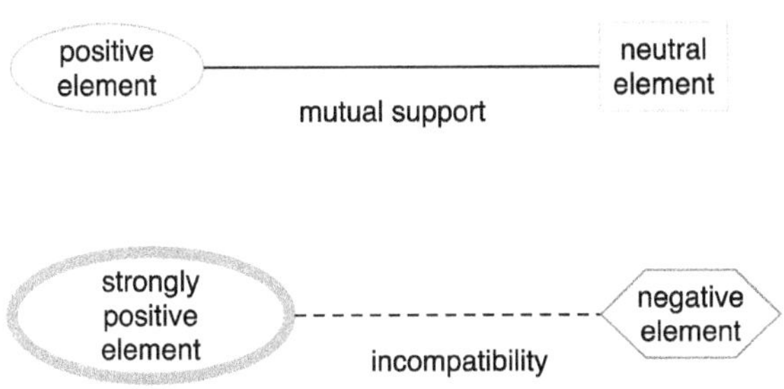

Fig. 3.1 Schema for a cognitive–affective map. Use of color is optional depending on the medium used

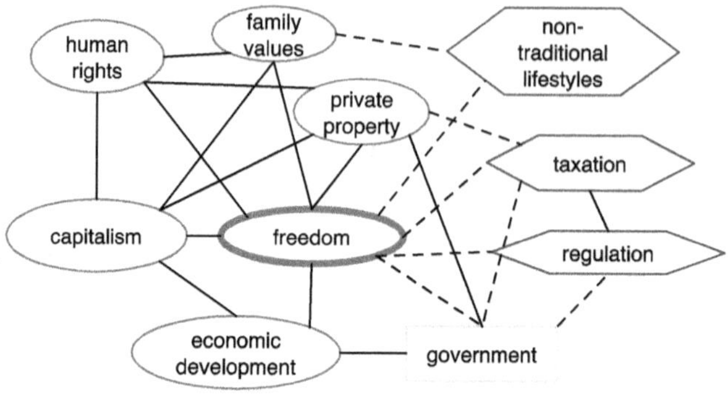

Fig. 3.2 Fragment of the conceptual structure of right-wing (conservative) ideology. *Ovals* represent emotionally positive concepts, *hexagons* represent emotionally negative concepts, and *rectangles* represent emotionally neutral or ambivalent concepts

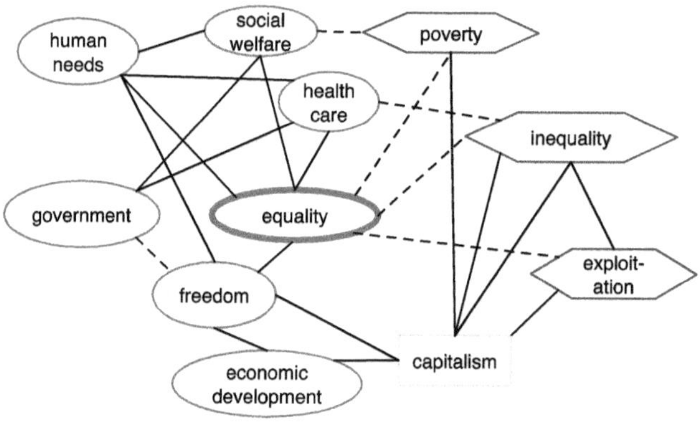

Fig. 3.3 Fragment of the conceptual structure of left-wing (progressive) ideology. Mapping conventions are the same as in Fig. 3.2

positive concept is *freedom*, which is accordingly shown with a thick oval. Freedom shows favorable associations (indicated by solid lines) with other positively valued concepts such as capitalism and private property. These positive values conflict with negative ones such as government regulation, taxation, and nontraditional lifestyles, whose emotional disfavor is shown by hexagons. I have portrayed the concept *government* using a neutral rectangle, indicating the ambivalence of conservatives: They dislike government for taxation and regulation, but appreciate it for its contribution to economic growth and military defense (not shown).

In contrast, Fig. 3.3 provides a highly simplified account of left-wing ideology that is espoused by progressive parties such as the Labor Party in the UK, the New Democratic Party in Canada, and many European social democratic parties. In the USA, related views occur among the more liberal members of the Democratic Party. In Fig. 3.3, the central and most positive concept is *equality*, with links to other emotionally valued concepts such as social welfare and health care. In contrast to the conservative picture in Fig. 3.2, *government* is viewed favorably, whereas *capitalism* is shown as neutral reflecting ambivalence about its positive contributions to economic growth and negative effects on equality.

The technique of cognitive–affective mapping is not just a drawing technique, but reflects a theory of emotional coherence that has been used to explain a wide range of phenomena including decision making, trust, and biased decision making (Thagard 2000, 2003, 2006). On this view, people's decisions and other judgments arise from a process of balancing different elements based on their emotional values, or *valences*. The theory of emotional coherence can be summarized in three principles:

1. Elements have positive or negative valences.
2. Elements can have positive or negative emotional connections to other elements.
3. The valence of an element is determined by the valences and acceptability of all the elements to which it is connected.

This theory is implemented in a computational model called "HOTCO" for "hot coherence," in which units (artificial neurons) have valences as well as activations. Positive emotional connections are implemented by mutual excitatory links between units, and negative emotional connections are implemented by mutual inhibitory links between units. The valence of a unit u_j is the sum of the results of multiplying, for all units u_i to which it is linked, the activation of u_i times the valence of u_i times the weight of the link between u_i and u_j.

The computational model HOTCO (hot coherence) shows precisely how this process can work in neural networks corresponding to cognitive–affective maps:

1. Every node in a CAM can be represented by a unit (artificial neuron) in a neural network.
2. Positive (oval) nodes in a CAM have a corresponding HOTCO unit with positive valence.
3. Negative (hexagon) nodes in a CAM have a corresponding HOTCO unit with negative valence.
4. Complementary connections (solid lines) in a CAM have corresponding excitatory links between the HOTCO units that represent the connected nodes in the CAM.
5. Conflicting connections (dashed lines) in a CAM have corresponding inhibitory links between the HOTCO units that represent the connected nodes in the CAM.

Once they are set up in this way, the HOTCO networks have a major advantage over the CAM diagrams: They come with a set of algorithms for spreading valences and activation among the units to make complex computations, including determinations of emotional coherence. Having concepts represented by single neurons is clearly not neurologically realistic, but HOTCO networks can be implemented in a much more neurologically realistic fashion using distributed representations of concepts in large populations of neurons (Thagard and Aubie 2008; Thagard 2010b; 2012a). A later section shows how emotional coherence can provide a mechanism to explain why people adopt ideologies.

There are other ways of visualizing emotions besides CAMs. For example, posts on the social network Twitter are displayed on a grid with the dimensions of pleasant versus unpleasant and active versus inactive (http://www.csc.ncsu.edu/faculty/healey/tweet_viz/).

Anarchism

The right and left ideologies shown in Figs. 3.2 and 3.3 are quite general, but cognitive–affective mapping can also be used to delineate more specific ideologies. Figure 3.4 presents a map of an ideology that has become remarkably popular among radical young people since the 1999 Seattle protests concerning globalization (Graeber 2009; Marshall 2010). The anarchist CAM depicts a core set of values including equality and solidarity that are used to support several kinds of practical activities, including highly democratic decision making by "spokescouncils" that operate by consensus rather than by voting or hierarchical direction. The anarchist values and practices conflict with negative values and institutions such as authority, capitalism, and especially the state, and the conflict is used to justify direct actions that confront governments.

The anarchist ideology shown in Fig. 3.4 had a large influence on the Occupy movement that produced major demonstrations in New York City and hundreds of other cities in 2011. Figure 3.5 shows the emotional values of the most important concepts behind the initial Occupy Wall Street action, which incorporated identification with ordinary people (the 99 %) as opposed to the wealthy elite (the 1 %). The analysis in Fig. 3.5 was largely derived from a book produced by participants, while the occupation was still in progress (Writers for the 99 % 2011).

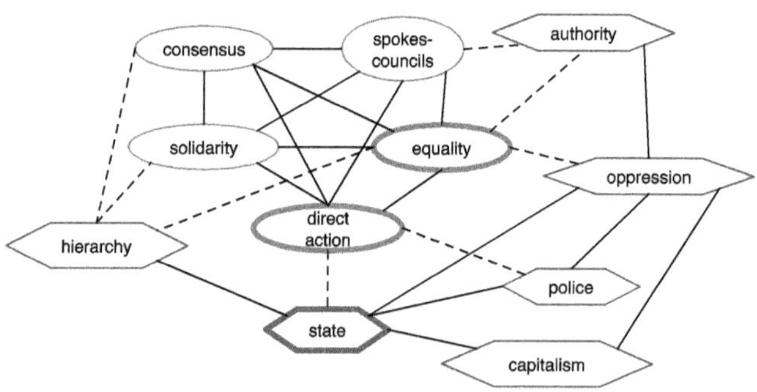

Fig. 3.4 Fragment of the conceptual structure of contemporary anarchism. Mapping conventions are the same as in Fig. 3.2

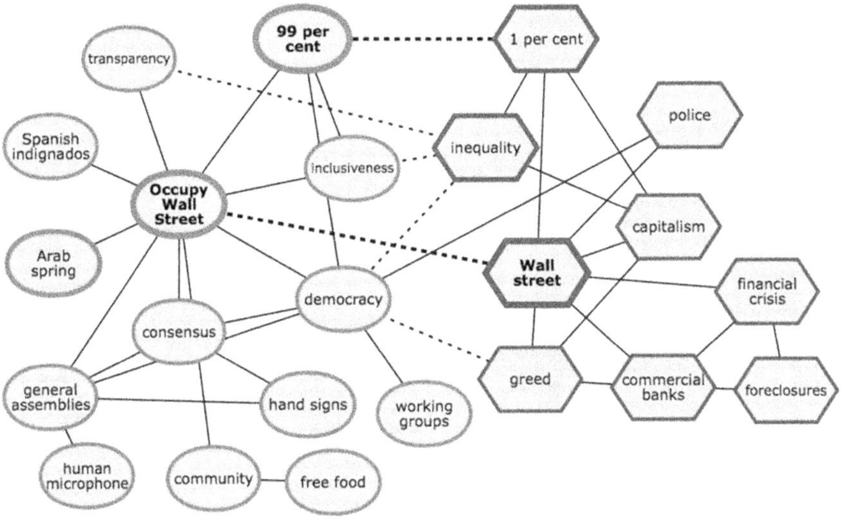

Fig. 3.5 Cognitive–affective map of the Occupy Wall Street movement of 2011. This uses the same conventions as earlier figures, but looks different because it is drawn using the free tool Empathica (http://cogsci.uwaterloo.ca/empathica.html)

Right-Wing Social Movements

CAMS can also be useful in describing and explaining the rise of right-wing social movements such as the Swedish Democrats, the Danish People's Party, the National Front in France, the neo-Nazi Golden Dawn in Greece, and the Tea Party Movement in the USA. Figures 3.6 and 3.7 display CAMs that show mental representations without and with the nationalist solution. The maps below apply to European movements, but not so well to the Tea Party which is more libertarian.

Fig. 3.6 Cognitive–affective map of fear and anger arising from right-wing concerns about immigration and crime

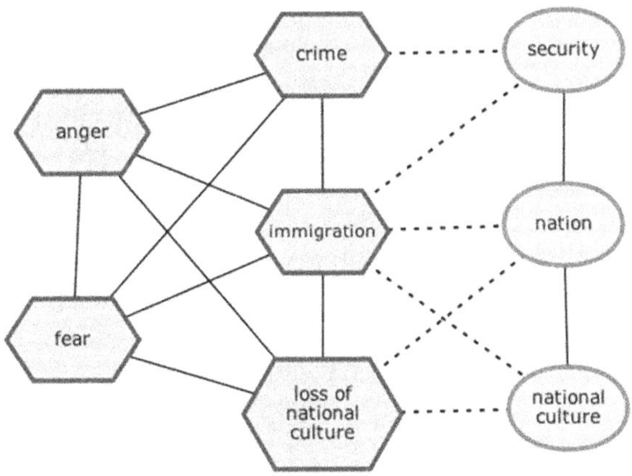

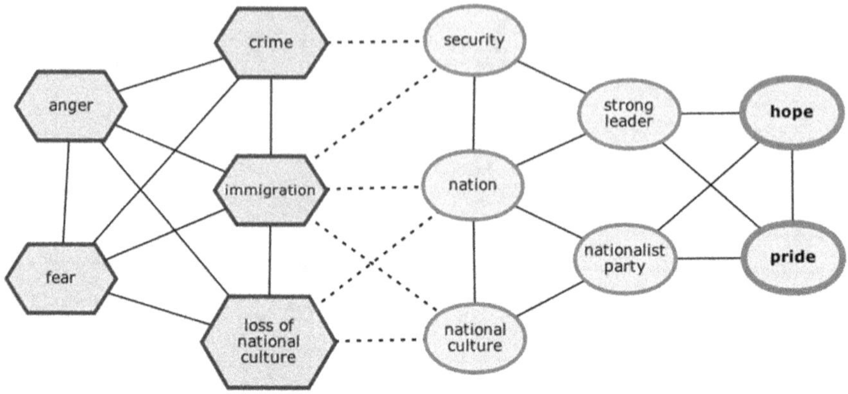

Fig. 3.7 Cognitive–affective map of hope and pride arising from the right-wing prospects of a nationalist party and leader

Figure 3.6 displays some of the concerns of citizens that make people worried about their current political situation, and Fig. 3.7 shows how a right-wing party can provide an emotionally appealing solution to the negative emotions shown in Fig. 3.6. These figures include the specific emotions of anger, fear, hope, and pride, which are beyond the scope of the HOTCO model which only deals with positive and negative valences. Later neural network models of emotion, however, can explain the generation of specific emotions (Thagard and Aubie 2008; Thagard and Schröder 2014).

Explaining Atrocities

In 1994, the Hutu majority in Rwanda slaughtered more than 500,000 members of the Tutsi minority. One of the factors contributing to this action was the explicit development of a Hutu ideology. The role that ideologies play in the causal explanation of atrocities is case specific, but in general ideologies lead to plans that lead to actions. Figure 3.8 is a sketch of the causes of the Rwanda massacre, based primarily on Melvern (2004). The cognitive–affective structure of the Hutu ideology is depicted in the CAM shown in Fig. 3.9.

Figure 3.9 could valuably be supplemented by representation of specific emotions, such as the pride associated with the oval concepts, and various negative emotions associated with the hexagon: fear, anger, contempt, and disgust. These emotions in turn can be linked to actions, such as killing Tutsis. Ideologies and plans are adopted because they fit with the beliefs and goals of the people exposed to them. The social mechanisms by which ideologies and plans spread through groups of individuals are described below.

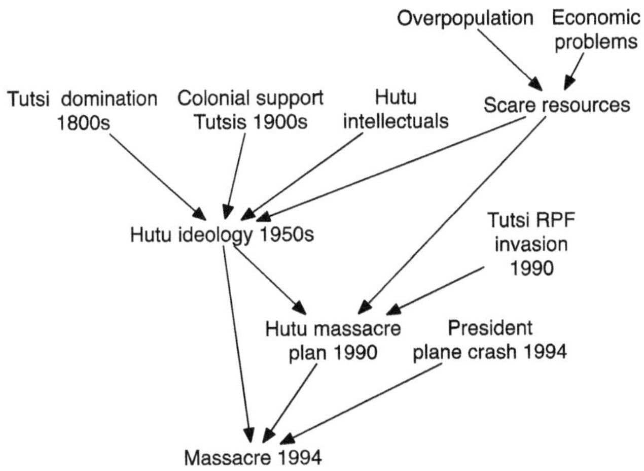

Fig. 3.8 Hutu ideology as one of the causes of the 1994 massacre. *Arrows* indicate causality

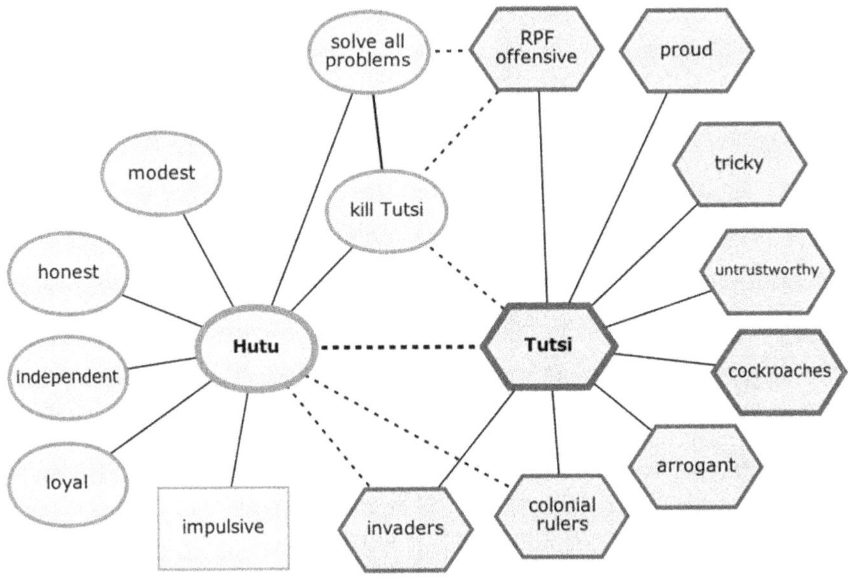

Fig. 3.9 CAM of Hutu ideology, based primarily on Melvern (2004)

Multimodal Cognitive–Affective Maps

All of the cognitive–affective maps shown so far, as well as those in previous papers, employ verbal concepts such as *equality* and *freedom*. This section extends the technique of cognitive–affective mapping to include nonverbal representations

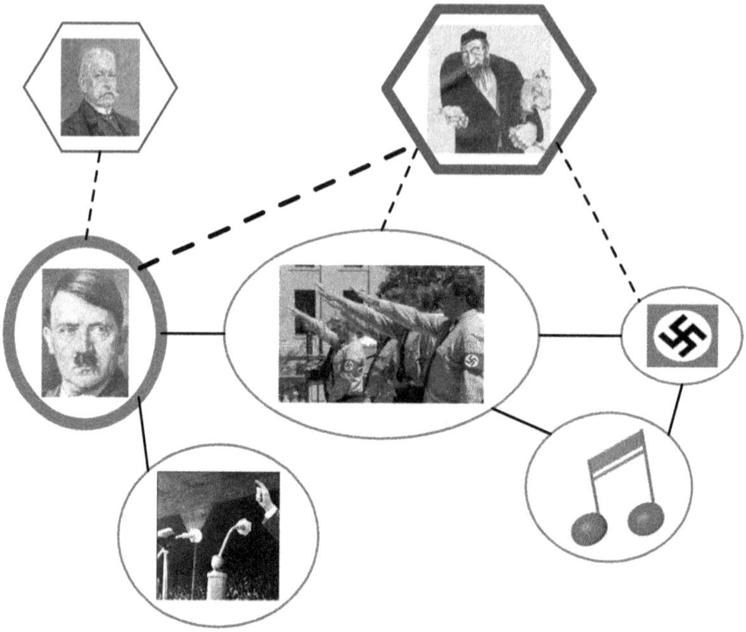

Fig. 3.10 Multimodal cognitive–affective map of Nazi ideology. The mapping conventions are the same as in Fig. 3.2, but the elements include visual images, gestures, and sounds

such as visual images, sounds, and gestures. Like verbal concepts, these representations have emotional associations that can be indicated using the same conventions (ovals, hexagons, links) as the CAMs already portrayed, but they add to the understanding of ideologies important but neglected cognitive and emotional aspects.

It would be easy to draw a CAM of Nazi ideology using verbal concepts such as *Deutschland, national socialism, Führer*, and so on. Figure 3.10, however, shows how such a map could be supplemented by powerful nonverbal representations that contribute to the emotional coherence of an ideology. The visual images in Fig. 3.10 include Hitler's portrait, which displays strength and determination in contrast to the old and weak Hindenberg who led Germany before Hitler came to power. Hitler is positively associated with the ancient swastika that was adopted by the Nazi party in 1920, and with the Heil Hitler (sieg heil) gesture, which is also a visual image that has an associated sound. The main image shown in Fig. 3.10 as incompatible with Nazi symbols depicts an ugly Jew as a gold-loving communist; this image comes from the cover of a 1937 Nazi pamphlet. Finally, the musical note is a placeholder for a collection of songs that were important to the Nazi movement, such as the Horst Wessel song, the German anthem proclaiming "Deutschland Uber Alles," military marches, and Hitler's beloved Wagnerian operas. It is notable that some of the main nonverbal elements of Nazi ideology—the swastika, the Heil Hitler gesture, and the Horst Wessel song—are still illegal in Germany.

The rather loose right and left ideologies shown in Figs. 3.2 and 3.3 are too vague and general to have nonverbal symbols associated with them, but all more specific ideologies such as variants of fascism and communism have nonverbal representations that are emotionally important. For example, communism has visual images such as the hammer and sickle and the portrait of Stalin that was ubiquitous in the Soviet Union under his rule. Communism has also had associated songs such as the Internationale and radical folk songs, and the associated gesture of the raised fist. Figure 3.11 shows some of the visual and auditory images associated with anarchism, including the black (anti-state) flag, the circle-A symbol, the physical activities of the Black Bloc (here shown at the Toronto G20 protests in 2010), and anti-state punk rock music. Contrasting images and values include the police.

Nationalisms are also ideologies, and they usually come with a set of nonverbal symbols. For example, pro-American views are associated with visual images such as the stars-and-stripes flag, songs such as The Star-Spangled Banner and God Bless America, gestures such as the hand-on-chest during the pledge of allegiance, and even foods such as apple pie. Religious ideologies can also be represented by cognitive–affective maps that are multimodal as well as verbal. For instance, the Roman Catholic Church has a wealth of visual and auditory symbols, including

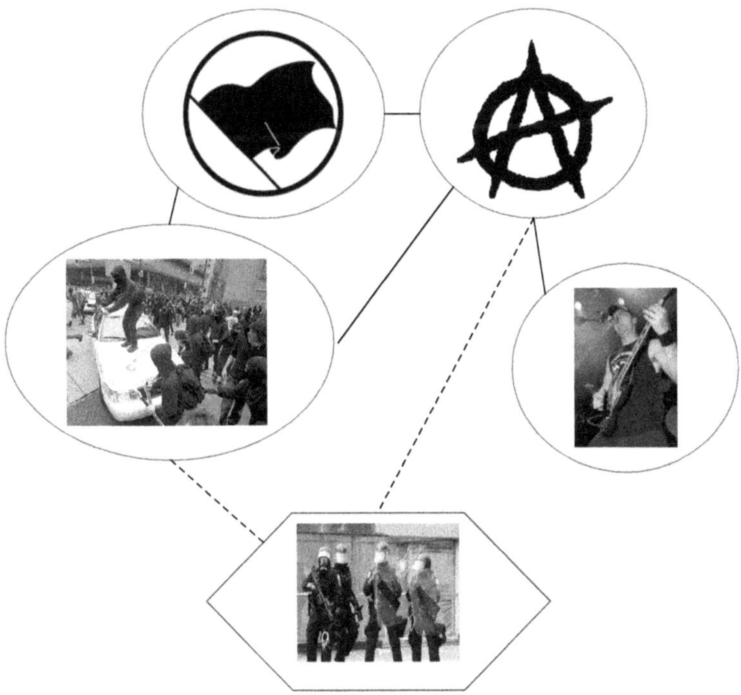

Fig. 3.11 Multimodal cognitive–affective map of parts of anarchist ideology. The mapping conventions are the same as in Fig. 3.2, but the elements include visual images, gestures, and sounds

cathedrals, crosses, the Pope's hat, prayers, and hymns. In sum, it seems that most ideologies have emotionally important nonverbal representations, and these can be captured in a natural, multimodal expansion of cognitive–affective maps.

The cognitive–affective maps presented so far have been useful for sketching important parts of ideologies, particularly concepts and emotional attitudes. They are not so effective at portraying other important parts, namely beliefs and goals. A full account of the psychological and social origins of ideologies will require a more general cognitive theory that we will now consider.

Mental Mechanisms

In 1920, Hitler's party had fewer than 100 members, but in 1933, the National Socialists received more than 17 million votes (43.9 %) in the German federal election (Evans 2005). How can we explain the rapid spread of Nazi ideology? Explanation should operate both at the individual level, accounting for why individuals such as the philosopher Heidegger became Nazis, and at the social level, accounting for the spread of ideas in groups of people. This section contends that the primary mental mechanism by which individuals come to adopt an ideology is emotional coherence.

According to the theory of emotional coherence, people make decisions and other inferences based on how well competing alternatives fit overall with their beliefs and goals, including the emotional values (valences) that they attach to these representations. Decision making is not a mathematically careful calculation of probabilities and utilities, but rather an emotional assessment of how well opposing actions might accomplish valued goals. For example, an undergraduate student deciding what to do after graduation might consider several options such as getting a job, going to graduate school, or traveling around the world. These options have different impacts on various goals typical of young adults, such as making money, preparing for an interesting career, and having fun. The priority of these goals for an individual is captured by their emotional valences, which spread to representations of the options which compete for the highest valence. This process can be precisely described using equations for information processing in neural networks, but mathematical details are omitted here. What matters for understanding ideology is that emotional coherence affects not only decisions but also beliefs, by virtue of the phenomenon of motivated inference.

Motivated inference, the tendency to reach conclusions unduly influenced by personal goals, is a well-researched phenomenon in social psychology (Kunda 1990, 1999; Bastardi et al. 2011; Redlawsk et al. 2010). For example, a coffee drinker will be inclined to be skeptical about claims that caffeine has negative health effects, but will tend to be gullible about claims that it has positive health effects. Motivated inference is more complex than mere wishful thinking, in that people do not simply believe whatever makes them happy. Rather, their goals leads them to be selective about how they acquire and evaluate evidence. Emotional coherence easily explains motivated inference: People naturally misinterpret the attractiveness of a conclusion arising from its fit with their goals as attractiveness arising from fit with evidence. For instance, the decision by the O.J. Simpson jury to acquit him of murder charges can be understood as a case of motivated inference arising from the mechanism of emotional coherence (Thagard 2003).

Emotional coherence can also explain other kinds of inferential distortions that are driven by negative rather than positive emotions. Motivated inference is desire-driven, in that people believe what they want to on the basis of their goals. Another kind of emotional distortion occurs when evaluation of evidence is affected by fears and anxieties. On the face of it, it seems ridiculous that people should adopt beliefs that both lack evidence and make them unhappy, but many instances of this kind of fear-driven inference occur in a wide range of domains, including personal relationships, health, politics, and economics (Thagard and Nussbaum 2014; Elster 2007, who writes of "countermotivated inference" and Mele 2001, who writes of "twisted self-deception").

Fear-driven inference arises from emotional coherence when attempts to rationalize worries away using motivated inference fail: One can swing from irrational exuberance to irrational despair if the negative feelings that arise from considering worrisome outcomes are misinterpreted as evidence supporting the likelihood of those outcomes. In such cases, one's beliefs cohere with fears for which there is little independent evidence. A famous example is Shakespeare's Othello, who becomes convinced on the basis of scant evidence that his wife Desdemona is unfaithful to him. But Othello gets caught in a vicious emotional circle in which his fear itself becomes mistaken as evidence that he has something to fear, so that his belief arises from an amplifying feedback loop rather than careful assessment of alternative hypotheses.

A third kind of emotional inference that has not received the attention it deserves is driven by intense anger or rage. Rage-driven inference occurs when people become so angry at what they perceive as wrongs done to them (or to others whom they care about) that they are impelled to take extreme actions that may not be well suited to accomplish their goals. Radical movements on both the left and right are often driven by anger arising from perceived wrongs, generating zeal to commit extreme acts such as terrorism, attempted revolution, and intense state repression. Rage-driven inference arises from emotional coherence through a chain of connections something like the following: Intense anger means that someone has done something very bad, and the anger is itself evidence that they deserve to be punished. It is misleading to characterize the mental process in such verbal terms, making its illogical character all too evident. In the minds of radicals, however, there may be no explicit awareness of the connection between anger and action, so the force of the determination to take extreme measures is concealed. That is not to say that rage-driven inference is always irrational, as sometimes both the anger and the extreme actions that result from it are fully justified, for example in the American civil rights movement of the 1950s and 1960s that included massive civil disobedience. Sometimes ideologies are fully justified by aspects of social and psychological reality.

Emotional Coherence and Ideology

The adoption of ideologies is emotionally coherent through the more specific mechanisms of motivated, fear-driven, and rage-driven inference. Consider, for example, the rapid rise during the 1920s and 1930s in support in Germany for Hitler and the Nazi Party. Obviously, there were different factors operating in the millions of Germans who became Hitler supporters, but for many people they included:

- Desire and hope that Hitler could lead Germany out of economic depression and international weakness.
- Fear that, without Hitler, Germany would succumb to communism, which had considerable popular support, and to Jewish influence.
- Anger that Germany had been defeated and humiliated in the Great War.

These emotional components, respectively, contributed to motivated, fear-driven, and rage-driven inference, all of which combined to make Nazism highly emotionally coherent for many people, including philosophers.

The multimodal cognitive–affective map of Nazism presented in Fig. 3.10 captures only part of the multifaceted inference processes that produce adoption of that ideology. Figure 3.12 provides a richer model of the appeal of Hitler and Nazism to many Germans, showing three of the main sources of emotional reasons to support him. People naturally wanted improvement to the dismal economic situation of Germany in the 1920s and early 1930s and made the motivated inference that Hitler's peculiar "national socialism" could provide a solution, as it in fact did when military expansion produced a dramatic drop in unemployment. Hitler also gained support by fanning the flames of anti-Semitism and anti-communism. Fear-driven inference served to make people even more afraid of Jews and communists than they already were. Not shown in Fig. 3.12 is an additional step of motivated inference in which people are led to believe that they can best manage their enhanced fears about Jews and communists by putting Hitler in charge. Similarly, the rage-based inference that something extreme must be done about Germany's military humiliation feeds into a motivated inference that Hitler is the solution. Many other kinds of potential support for Hitler and the Nazis are not shown in Fig. 3.12, for example German nationalism based on cultural traditions involving language, literature, and history. Also not shown in Fig. 3.12 are interconnections between the different kinds of inference: Fear of Jews and communists was also exploited by the Nazis through the motivated inference that Hitler would control them.

The Nazis, led by Joseph Goebbels, were masters of propaganda, exemplified by Leni Riefenstahl's 1933 film *The Triumph of the Will* and the appalling 1940 pseudo-documentary *The Eternal Jew,* both available on YouTube. Propaganda provokes a reaction in people building on motivated, fear-driven, and rage-driven inference. Most advertising exploits people's motivations, using multimodal emotional coherence to convince people that they can be sexier, richer, or healthier merely by purchasing the advertised product.

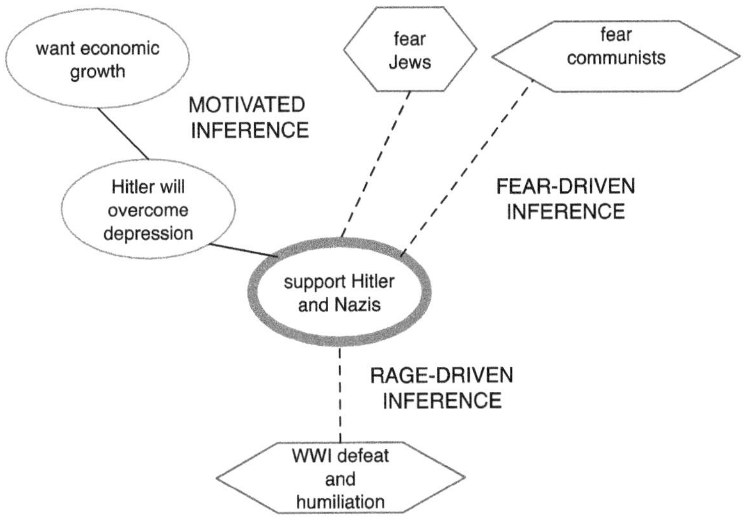

Fig. 3.12 The emotional coherence of the decision to support Hitler and the Nazis, deriving from motivated, fear-driven, and rage-driven inference

It would be easy to show that other ideologies, such as various kinds of nationalism, are also based on emotional coherence that generates motivated, fear-driven, and rage-driven inference. For example, American nationalism is sometimes motivated (the USA is the best country in the world), sometimes fear-driven (the threat of communists or, more recently, Arab terrorists), and sometimes rage-driven (the reaction to the 9/11 attacks). A recent ideological trend is the revival of anarchism since 1999 as part of the anti-globalization movement. A cognitive–affective analysis of this ideological development building on Figs. 3.4 and 3.5 would explain its appeal among young people in terms of several kinds of inference: motivations such as bringing about a more equitable world, fears such as oppressive governments and their police forces, and rage leading to direct action (Graeber 2009).

Religious ideologies often arise from a combination of motivated and fear-driven inference (Thagard and Nussbaum 2014). Religious leaders intensify people's fear of punishment and death, and then incite the motivated inference that salvation can come via religion. Rage-driven inference can also contribute to religion when people are angry at what they see as the moral transgressions of others, generating the motivation to believe in divine retribution.

The discussion so far may have given the impression that ideologies are always unjustifiable distortions that are best avoided. On the contrary, the idea of an "end of ideology" was itself ideological, and no one can operate at a sophisticated political level without an interconnected system of concepts, beliefs, goals, and attitudes. Although inevitably emotional coherence will play a role in the acquisition of an ideology, it is also possible to assemble evidence that can support comparative judgments about the value of differing ideologies. For example, Thagard (2010a) argues that psychological and biological evidence about the nature of human needs, along with political and historical evidence about the quality of life in the world's countries, supports the conclusion that the best kinds of government are ones that incorporate social democratic values like those shown in Fig. 3.3. Although ideologies often arise from motivated, fear-driven, and rage-driven inferences that ignore relevant evidence, it is possible to build and defend a set of concepts, beliefs, goals, and attitudes based on evidence about the nature of human minds and societies. Not all ideologies are evil.

The same emotional psychological mechanisms that lead people to acquire ideologies can be used to explain why they continue to hold ideologies, spurred by ongoing motivated, fear-driven, and rage-driven inferences. But what causes people to abandon or modify ideologies, for example when people became disillusioned with Nazism or communism or various kinds of nationalism? It would be an interesting exercise to model several ways in which people move away from ideologies, including:

- gradual disinterest that operates in the same way that some people slowly lapse from religious beliefs and practices;
- decisive events that lead people to abandon an ideology, for example when many people abandoned communism in 1956 as the result of the Soviet Union's invasion of Hungary and Krushchev's revelations about Stalin's atrocities; and
- replacement of one ideology by a competing one, for example when some American Trotskyists of the 1930s became neo-conservatives.

The mechanisms that cause abandonment of ideologies, such as those that lead to their adoption, are not merely psychological, but can also depend on social interactions.

Social Mechanisms

A full explanation of the rise of ideologies such as Nazism needs to pay attention, not only to psychological mechanisms such as emotional coherence, but also to social mechanisms by which emotional attitudes spread from one person to another. I will not attempt a comprehensive discussion here, but will merely list with appropriate references a group of methods of emotional communication. All of them contribute, I suspect, to the spread of various ideologies. Other chapters in this volume discuss related social mechanisms, including empathy by neural resonance (Moore and Iacaboni) and verbal negotiation (Olekalns and Daniel Druckman, Meerts and Vukovic, Martinovski).

1. Mirror neurons. There are neural populations in both monkeys and humans that are activated in similar ways by both actions and perceptions of actions (Rizzolatti and Craighero 2004). Similar mirroring occurs in the perception and experience of pain and may occur in the perception and experience of some

emotions (Iacoboni 2008). If I see you displaying an emotion, I can have some of the same neural activity that I would have if I were experiencing the same emotion myself, leading me to actually have that emotion. This process provides a neural mechanism by which emotions can spread from one person to another, leading to the acquisition of desires, fears, and angry reactions.

2. Emotional contagion by mimicry. A more indirect kind of emotional spread occurs via facial and bodily mimicry (Hatfield et al. 1994). People naturally mimic the facial expressions of those with whom they interact, inclining them to acquire similar emotional reactions because emotions are in part responses to bodily changes.
3. Attachment-based learning. Minsky (2006) described how emotional attitudes can be easily acquired from people such as parents to whom a person is emotionally attached. People commonly acquire ideologies from their parents and other close associates. Mirror neurons and emotional contagion by mimicry may account for part of this kind of transmission, but verbal communication also contributes.
4. Empathy. In empathic learning, people acquire an emotional response from others by imagining themselves in the others' situations and experiencing emotions similar to theirs. The underlying mechanisms for empathy include basic physiological responses such as mirror neurons and also higher-level cognitive operations such as analogy (Thagard 2010a). Empathy can be either a direct physiological response or a cognitive construction in which people view themselves as analogous to others and therefore transfer over their emotions.
5. Altruism and sympathy. Except for psychopaths, humans are generally capable of caring for other people and acting toward them altruistically, taking into account the needs of others rather than mere self-interest (Batson 1991; Hoffman 2000). A key part of altruism is sympathy, feeling sorry for the misfortunes of others. Through altruism and sympathy, people can acquire emotional responses directed toward the well-being of others.
6. Social cuing. Giner-Sorolla and Espinosa (2011) describe how, in the social context of a group, people's facial expressions can cue negative emotions in their targets. For example, expressions of anger cue guilt, and expressions of disgust cue shame. Thus, negative social emotions can be induced in others. This kind of social cuing is unlike the five social mechanisms so far discussed, all of which produce in the observer approximately the same emotion as in the person observed: Here, we get different emotions produced in the observer.
7. Power manipulations. Many social scientists have discussed the importance of power in interpersonal relations (e.g., Mann 1986). From the perspective of emotions, there seem to be two main ways in which one person gains power over others: by offering them something they desire or by offering to protect them from something that they fear. The first kind of power manipulation provokes motivated inference, while the second instigates a combination of fear-driven inference (making them even more afraid than they might be otherwise) and motivated inference (encouraging them to think that the manipulator can protect them). Either way, a person or group achieves power by enhancing peoples' desires, fears, and beliefs about how to manage those desires and fears.

8. Propaganda and other forms of advertising can be effective for such emotional management. For example, propaganda can be used to generate rage-driven inference when it displays the enemy as evil and disgusting and therefore deserving of extreme retribution. One subtle way to make propaganda work is to use text and images to prime associated ideas and behaviors, for example when odious stories images of reviled ethnic groups are used to prime a full negative stereotype. Priming results from mechanisms that operate at neural, psychological, and sociological levels (Schröder and Thagard 2013) in social media such as Facebook and Twitter can facilitate the spread of propaganda.

These eight social mechanisms all can contribute to the spread of emotions from one individual to another. They complement the psychological mechanism of emotional coherence and the kinds of inference generated by it, showing how emotional information can be transmitted from one person to another, leading to emotional change in groups of individuals. Thus, ideological change can be a social phenomenon as well as an individual one. Understanding of ideologies as cognitive–affective structures does not assume a kind of methodological individualism in which the behavior of groups is just the result of the behavior of individuals, because social processes are as important as what goes on inside the head of an individual.

The spread of ideologies in groups instantiates the *principle of social recursion* (Thagard 2012b): The actions of groups result from the actions of individuals who think of themselves as members of groups. Thinking of oneself as a German, Canadian, Nazi, communist, or social democrat has major effects on one's behaviors and inferences and can in turn lead to the sorts of social interactions that produce emotional communications that affect psychological processes. The principle of social recursion provides the start of a solution to the problem of the relation between individual agents and social structures such as institutions and states (Giddens 1984; Wendt 1999). This person–group (or agent–structure) problem cannot be solved by attempting to reduce the behavior of groups to the behavior of individuals or by treating groups as unanalyzed wholes. Rather, a solution to the person–group problem requires understanding the interactions between psychological mechanisms such as fear-driven inference and social mechanisms such as emotional contagion.

Conclusion

This chapter has tried to show how attention to cognitive–affective structures and mechanisms can help to explain the rise and influence of political ideologies. Ideologies can be informatively analyzed using cognitive–affective maps, including ones that employ multimodal, nonverbal representations. The acquisition and maintenance of ideologies by individuals can be explained by the mechanism of emotional coherence that gives rise to motivated, fear-driven, and rage-driven inferences. The spread of ideologies requires social mechanisms in addition to psychological ones, including at least mirror neurons, emotional contagion by mimicry, attachment-based learning, empathy, altruistic sympathy, social cuing, and power manipulations.

The explanations of ideological change provided here complement the two main psychological theories of ideology acceptance: system justification theory and terror management theory. According to the former, adoption of ideologies often stems from a psychological motive to defend and justify the status quo (Jost and Hunyady 2005; Jost et al. 2009). For example, political conservatism holds that traditional institutions should be preserved even if they produce social and economic inequality. The cognitive–emotional antecedents of system-justifying ideologies include: needs for order, structure, and closure; perception of a dangerous world, anxiety about death, and system instability. It is easy to see how all of these concerns can lead to the motivated inference that the current system should be maintained. This inference allows personal goals rather than evidence-based beliefs to determine what conclusions are reached concerning political reality.

According to another major psychological approach to ideology, terror management theory, humans are "motivated to quell the potential for terror inherent in the human awareness of mortality by investing in cultural belief systems (or worldviews) that imbue life with meaning, and the individuals who subscribe to them with significance (or self-esteem)" (http://www.tmt.missouri.edu/). On this view, thoughts of death can lead to "suppressing death-related thoughts or pushing the problem of death into the distant future by denying one's vulnerability", and also to "maintaining self-esteem and faith in one's cultural worldview … to control the potential for anxiety that results from knowing that death is inevitable" (Pyszczynski et al. 1999, p. 835). Terror management thus appears to rely on motivated inference, adjusting beliefs based on the goal to avoid the anxiety associated with death. Fear-driven inference may also contribute, if obsession with death leads to anxiety that erroneously becomes taken as evidence that it is something fearful (for reasons not to fear death, see Thagard 2010a).

Detailed simulations of experimental results would be required to make plausible the conjecture that system justification and terror management theories are special cases of emotional coherence. One problem with both those theories is that they seem better suited to explain conservative ideologies than radical ones such as Nazism, communism, and anarchism. Worldviews that advocate overthrowing the established order hardly contribute to system maintenance or quelling of terror. In contrast, emotional coherence leading to motivated, fear-driven, and rage-driven inference can account for various ideologies that reject conservatism in favor of radical change.

A limitation of this chapter's discussion of the role of emotion in political ideologies is that it has emphasized one central dimension of emotion: evaluation of positive and negative valence. Other relevant dimensions include activity (arousal) and potency (control over action). Thagard and Schröder (2014) provide a much broader neural theory of emotion that can explain the differences between particular emotions such as happiness, fear, and anger. The relevance of specific emotions to ideologies needs further investigation. As the discussion of the rise of Nazism indicated, fear is a major contributor to the impact of ideologies when it facilitates their plausibility and adoption. Ideologies also incite and exploit anger and hate when they identify an external group as responsible for alleged wrongs, for example when Nazis blamed Jews and Hutus blamed Tutsis for economic problems and national failures. Other negative emotions that interact with valences in ideologies include blame, contempt, resentment, envy, and regret. On the positive side, an ideology can be more attractive when it fosters feelings such as happiness, pride, and hope. A fuller account of the affective structure of political ideologies will need to show how social influences based on the dimensions of activity and potency can generate specific emotions that enhance the appeal of a system of ideas.

Acknowledgments This work is supported by the Natural Sciences and Engineering Research Council of Canada. I am grateful to an anonymous referee for comments and to Tobias Schröder and Thomas Homer-Dixon for helpful discussions.

References

Axelrod, R. (Ed.). (1976). *Structure of decision: the cognitive maps of political elites*. Princeton: Princeton University Press.

Bastardi, A., Uhlmann, E. L., & Ross, L. (2011). Wishful thinking: Belief, desire, and the motivated evaluation of scientific evidence. *Psychological Science, 22*, 731–732.

Batson, C. D. (1991). *The altruism question*. Hillsdale, NJ: Lawrence Erlbaum Associates.

Elster, J. (2007). *Explaining social behavior*. Cambridge: Cambridge University Press.

Evans, R. J. (2005). *The coming of the Third Reich*. London: Penguin.

Findlay, S. D., & Thagard, P. (2014). Emotional change in international negotiation: Analyzing the Camp David accords using cognitive-affective maps. *Group Decision and Negotiation, 23*, 1281–1300.

Freeden, M. (1996). *Ideologies and political theory*. Oxford: Clarendon Press.

Giddens, A. (1984). *The constitution of society*. Berkeley: University of California Press.

Giner-Sorolla, R., & Espinosa, P. (2011). Social cuing of guilt by anger and of shame by disgust. *Psychological Science, 22*, 49–53.

Graeber, D. (2009). *Direct action: an ethnography*. Oakland, CA: AK Press.

Haidt, J. (2012). *The righeous mind: Why good people are divided by politics and religion*. New York: Pantheon.

Hatfield, E., Cacioppo, J. T., & Rapson, R. L. (1994). *Emotional contagion*. Cambridge: Cambridge University Press.

Hoffman, M. L. (2000). *Empathy and moral development: Implications for caring and justice*. Cambridge: Cambridge University Press.

Homer-Dixon, T., Leader Maynard, J., Mildenberger, M., Milkoreit, M., Mock, S. J., Quilley, S., et al. (2013). A complex systems approach to the study of ideology: Cognitive-affective structures and the dynamics of belief systems. *Journal of Social and Political Psychology, 1*, 337–364. doi:10.5964/jspp.v1i1.36.

Homer-Dixon, T., Milkoreit, M., Mock, S. J., Schröder, T., & Thagard, P. (2014). The conceptual structure of social disputes: Cognitive-affective maps as a tool for conflict analysis and resolution. *SAGE Open, 4*. doi: 10.1177/2158244014526210.

Iacoboni, M. (2008). *Mirroring people: The new science of how we connect with others*. New York: Farrar, Straus and Giroux.

Jost, J. T., & Hunyady, O. (2005). Antecedents and consequences of system-justifying ideologies. *Current Directions in Psychological Science, 14*, 260–265.

Jost, J. T., Kay, A. C., & Thorisdottir, H. (2009). *Social and psychological bases of ideology and system justification*. New York: Oxford University Press.

Kunda, Z. (1990). The case for motivated reasoning. *Psychological Bulletin, 108*, 480–498.

Kunda, Z. (1999). *Social cognition: Making sense of people*. Cambridge, MA: MIT Press.

Leader Maynard, J. (2013). A map of the field of political ideologies. *Journal of Political Ideologies, 18*, 299–327. doi:10.1080/13569317.2013.831589.

Mann, M. (1986). *The sources of social power*. Cambridge: Cambridge University Press.

Marshall, P. (2010). *Demanding the impossible: A history of anarchism*. Oakland: PM Press.

Mele, A. R. (2001). *Self-deception unmasked*. Princeton: Princeton University Press.

Melvern, L. (2004). *Conspiracy to murder: The Rwandan genocide*. London: Verso.

Minsky, M. (2006). *The emotion machine: Commonsense thinking, artificial intelligence, and the future of the human mind*. New York: Simon & Schuster.

Novak, J. D. (1998). *Learning, creating, and using knowledge: Concept maps as facilitative tools in schools and corporations*. Mahwah, NJ: Lawrence Erlbaum Associates.

Pyszczynski, T., Greenberg, J., & Solomon, S. (1999). A dual-process model of defense against conscious and unconscious death-related thoughts: An extension of terror management theory. *Psychological Review, 106*, 835–845.

Redlawsk, D. P., Civettini, A. J. W., & Emmerson, K. M. (2010). The affective tipping point: Do motivated reasoners ever "get it"? *Political Psychology, 31*(4), 563–593.

Rizzolatti, G., & Craighero, L. (2004). The mirror-neuron system. *Annual Review of Neuroscience, 27*, 169–192.

Schröder, T., & Thagard, P. (2013). The affective meanings of automatic social behaviors: Three mechanisms that explain priming. *Psychological Review, 120*, 255–280.

Sowa, J. F. (1999). *Knowledge representation: Logical, philosophical, and computational foundations*. Pacific Grove: Brooks Cole.

Thagard, P. (2000). *Coherence in thought and action*. Cambridge, MA: MIT Press.

Thagard, P. (2003). Why wasn't O. J. convicted? Emotional coherence in legal inference. *Cognition and Emotion, 17*, 361–383.

Thagard, P. (2006). *Hot thought: Mechanisms and applications of emotional cognition*. Cambridge, MA: MIT Press.

Thagard, P. (2010a). *The brain and the meaning of life*. Princeton, NJ: Princeton University Press.

Thagard, P. (2010b). EMPATHICA: A computer support system with visual representations for cognitive-affective mapping. In K. McGregor (Ed.), *Proceedings of the workshop on visual reasoning and representation* (pp. 79–81). Menlo Park, CA: AAAI Press.

Thagard, P. (2011). The brain is wider than the sky: Analogy, emotion, and allegory. *Metaphor and Symbol, 26*(2), 131–142.

Thagard, P. (2012a). *The cognitive science of science: Explanation, discovery, and conceptual change*. Cambridge, MA: MIT Press.

Thagard, P. (2012b). Mapping minds across cultures. In R. Sun (Ed.), *Grounding social sciences in cognitive sciences* (pp. 35–62). Cambridge, MA: MIT Press.

Thagard, P. (2015). Value maps in applied ethics. *Teaching Ethics, 15*, 115–127.

Thagard, P. (in press). Emotional cognition in urban planning. In J. Portugali & E. Stolk (Eds.), *Complexity, cognition, urban planning and design*. Berlin: Springer.

Thagard, P., & Aubie, B. (2008). Emotional consciousness: A neural model of how cognitive appraisal and somatic perception interact to produce qualitative experience. *Consciousness and Cognition, 17*, 811–834.

Thagard, P., & Nussbaum, A. D. (2014). Fear-driven inference: Mechanisms of gut overreaction. In L. Magnani (Ed.), *Model-based reasoning in science and technology* (pp. 43–53). Berlin: Springer.

Thagard, P., & Schröder, T. (2014). Emotions as semantic pointers: Constructive neural mechanisms. In L. F. Barrett & J. A. Russell (Eds.), *The psychological construction of emotions* (pp. 144–167). New York: Guilford.

Wendt, A. (1999). *Social theory of international politics*. Cambridge: Cambridge University Press.

Writers for the 99 %. (2011). *Occupying wall street: The inside story of an action that changed America*. Chicago: Haymarket Books.

Chapter 4
Reputation and Egotiation: The Impact of Self-Image on the Negotiator

Paul Meerts and Siniša Vuković

Introduction

In the realm of international relations, negotiations represent a "process of combining conflicting positions into a joint decision" (Kissinger 1969). Since the negotiation process prescribes a dynamic through which parties seek a suitable alternative position to their initial conflicting viewpoints, not surprisingly, the negotiations are often (maybe naively) exchanged for a bargaining process which entails a concurrence of conflicting and cooperative elements. In international relations, alternatives to a negotiated agreement are attainable through unilateral actions—varying from straining diplomatic relations to an employment of a series of coercive means such as sanctions, threat of, and/or the use of forceful means. Parties decide to negotiate when they perceive that the negotiations will generate gains that are unavailable to them by unilateral action. As pointed out by Zartman, negotiations "involve some action of mutually overcoming a conflict between the parties, each of whom holds a veto over the joint outcome. It is giving something to get something" (Zartman 2001a, b, 137). Reflecting on these dynamics Iklè pointed out, "without common interests there is nothing to negotiate for, without conflict nothing to negotiate" (Iklè 1985, 2). Therefore, for Iklè, negotiation represents "a process in which explicit proposals are put forward" for the "realization of a common interest where conflicting interests are present" (Iklè 1985, 3–4). As such, the key feature of any negotiation process is not a mere achievement of an

P. Meerts (✉)
Processes of International Negotiation (PIN) Program, Netherlands
Institute of International Relations 'Clingendael', Hague, The Netherland
e-mail: pmeerts@clingendael.nl

S. Vuković
School of Advanced International Studies (SAIS), Johns Hopkins University,
Washington, DC, USA
e-mail: svukovi1@jhu.edu

B. Martinovsky (ed.), *Emotion in Group Decision and Negotiation*,
Advances in Group Decision and Negotiation 7,
DOI 10.1007/978-94-017-9963-8_4

agreement, but rather the promotion and protection of one's own interests—which may also be strengthened by a potential agreement. In fact, some parties may use negotiations for tactical reasons—such as "buying" time and/or improving one's international reputation—that would allow them to improve their current position in the conflict without any intention of reaching an actual agreement (Stedman 1997; Richmond 1998). Therefore, negotiations can be considered as concluded "when the parties find a solution that is preferable both to continued conflict and to continued negotiation" (Zartman 2002, 7).

Along with explanations that emphasize the importance of process and structure in negotiations, some studies have yielded significant insights from a sociopsychological perspective. A growing body of literature makes an attempt to explain the impact of cultural factors on international negotiations (Avruch 1998; Blaker et al. 2002; Wittes 2005; Cogan 1997, 2003; Smyser 2002; Solomon 1999; Solomon and Quinney 2010). According to these studies, negotiations are affected not only by parties' incompatible interests and goals, but also by cultural differences that are characteristic for each party involved in the negotiation process (Avruch 1998). For instance, in order to explain French negotiating behavior, Cogan (2003) argues that "mixing rationalism and nationalism, rhetoric and brio, self-importance and embattled vulnerability, French negotiators often seem more interested in asserting their country's "universal" mission than in reaching agreement." As Freeman points out, international negotiators often conduct their affairs "in a foreign language, and on persons and peoples whose moral and political outlook is always different from, and often at odds with, their own" (Freeman 1997, 92). Cohen claims that negotiators are supposed to understand "the chemistry that occurs when negotiators representing mutually discordant traditions come into contact," as it is not rare that in such circumstances "typical patterns of miscomprehension can be observed to recur" (Cohen 2001, 473).

Argument

While cultural traits are practical heuristic tools that assist the parties in understanding their counterparty's behavior, these often provide a limited degree of information as no individual is ever defined by a single cultural trait. Rather, each negotiator brings to the table numerous cultural aspects related to his/her social, professional, family, educational, and other similar backgrounds. Nevertheless, stereotyping is not a rare phenomenon in everyday communication. As such stereotyping is also present in the negotiation process and has a potential of affecting the outcome. Jönsson (2012) points out that social stereotypes represent an important type of categorization. According to him, categorization "is basic to human thought, perception and action. Without the ability to categorize things and people we would not function in our physical and social environment" (Jönsson 2012, 174). Moreover, "stereotyped perceptions of "the other" constitute a key element of national identity, along with mythical perceptions of one's own nation's past and unique features" (Jönsson 2012, 175). In the negotiation process, stereotyped perceptions might have a direct impact on the reputations that each party assigns to a respective counterpart. Reputation inevitably precedes any form of interaction between the parties, and it is based on either a previous interaction or the information provided by a credible third party. As Jönsson points out, "a counterpart's reputation evokes a stereotype of that counterpart" (idem).

Numerous conflicts worldwide have been subject to the negative effects of obstinate use of stereotyping and reputation. Relations between the USA and the Soviet Union during the Cold War and between Israel and the neighboring Arab states have been constantly influenced by the "reputational effect." Similarly, attempts to negotiate a peaceful solution to the violent conflicts that followed the dissolution of former Yugoslavia were often hampered by mutual creation of national stereotypes and consequent negative reputation that each party in conflict assigned to "the others." Jönsson argues that "by amplifying the conflictual elements of negotiations, national stereotypes may give rise to vicious circles of self-fulfilling prophecies" (idem). Similarly, Holsti argues:

> When the other party is viewed within the framework of an "inherent bad faith" model the image of the enemy is clearly self-perpetuating… at the interpersonal level such behavior is characterized as abnormal – paranoia. Different standards seem to apply at the international level; inherent bad faith models are not considered abnormal, and even their underlying assumptions often escape serious questioning (Holsti 1968, 17).

Evidently the anarchical system of international relations, where parties are focused on preserving their survival and maximizing their utility, allows for a more paranoid categorization of "the others."

Some recent studies have shifted their focus from parties' perceptions of one another to their judgments about each one's biases. Pronin et al. (2004) point out that people tend to assign self-serving bias to their counterpart, while being unaware of the similar processes on their own judgments and behavior. However, the importance of self-image and self-perception is still quite understudied when it comes to the process of (international) negotiation. Present research aims to provide some insights on this phenomenon. We depart from the assumption that the negotiation process is affected not only by negotiators' perceptions of their counterparts, but also of their own (mis)perception of themselves. In order to illustrate this dynamic, we propose the inclusion of the term "ego" in our analysis. However, we are not referring to the classical Freudian classification of Ego, Super Ego, and Id. Rather, we employ a more colloquial use of the term ego, which in international negotiations would represent self-esteem, pride, and/or status. Consequently, we propose a new term—egotiation. While negotiation could be observed as a process in which the parties strive to satisfy and enhance their material and nonmaterial needs, both for the negotiator and the organization (country) that he/she represents, egotiation refers to the process where the parties strive to the preserve and enhance the "face" of the negotiator—face being a combination of self-esteem, pride, and/or status.

In a nutshell, present research aims to explain a reverse mechanism from the one just described by Jönsson regarding reputation effect. We look at the perception of one's own role, reputation, and image and claim that it has a direct impact on the behavior of that actor during the negotiation process. Depending on the circumstances, the negotiator's character, personal preferences, and emotions can take precedence over the interests of the stakeholders and their representatives. In such a situation, we might talk about "egotiation" instead of "negotiation," meaning that the ego of the negotiator is an obstacle to effective representation of interests (Meerts 2010, 28–29). Here, we do not mean ego in the Freudian sense, but in the political sense: the self-image and the prestige of the negotiating politician or diplomat and, by extension, of his or her country. In certain situations, protecting self-image and prestige will be seen as more important than the object of negotiation. While Olekalns and Druckmann offer a discussion on how emotions affect negotiations, we focus our attention on a face-saving dynamic: We postulate that the protection of the leader's "face" and of the country represented will take priority over the needs and the interests of the state, or even of the negotiator (Faizullaev 2006). By analyzing the role of leading personalities, this chapter will first look at seven turning-point conferences in the twentieth century, after which it will briefly profile 14 leading negotiators who did not take part in these meetings. This cannot and will not provide us with a comprehensive study of "egotiation" in the last century, but it will provide us with some indications of the effects of personality on the processes of international negotiation in recent times (Faizullaev 2006).

Politicians are power brokers, people who want to gain power and to use it as a tool in controlling others, thereby harvesting profits for themselves and for their party. In order to do this, they need to have a positive self-image, while they strive to be respected by others, either through doing well or through fear (for the emotions related to the group level, see the chapter by Christov Moore and Iacobini). Legitimacy, in whatever form, will make the wielding of power more effective, and a leader with a strong reputation will have no insurmountable problems in governing his or her people. Reputation is therefore indispensable and will have to be defended against those who want to damage it. This in turn might lead to situations in which upholding reputation becomes more important than defending specific material interests. In that sense, reputation can be defined as immaterial interest which can have both positive and negative effects on striving for material profits. Behind the façade of reputation sits the ego of the politician, and we postulate further that the more powerful the leader, the bigger his or her ego, the bigger the impact of his ego-state on the negotiation process. While we do not focus on particular ideologies that these leaders endorse (this issue was discussed by Thagard in this volume), we treat reputation in negotiation as a phenomenon that does not only have an impact on the perception of actors' counterparts, and following the logic of "your reputation precedes you" impacts the negotiation process; we also propose that reputation has also an impact on the self-perception of the actor itself as he/she will aim to protect the mentioned reputation as it represents an asset for any future interaction.

We will focus on some of the most powerful negotiators of the twentieth century, trying to discover the egotiation effects related to their behavior, under the understanding that their ego is to some extent situational. As Goldman and Rojot pointed out, "our ego state can be influenced not only by what surrounds our bodies but what enters them as well" (Goldman and Rojot 2003, 139). Though we have defined "egotiation" as a phenomenon connected to personality, one should not overlook the dynastic and state dimension of the term. Dynasties and states have a reputation. They have some measure of prestige, and the defense of this prestige is important as it will help the dynasty or the state to assert its position in the world and thereby facilitates the defense of its material interests. In that sense, the dynasty or the state has an "ego" as well, including its positive or negative impact on the processes of international negotiation. The decision of President George Bush to help the Northern Coalition of Tajik and Uzbek to drive the Taliban out of Kabul can be seen as a rational action aimed at destroying the protectors of al-Qaeda. However, it can also be seen as a show of force: We do not let our reputation as the most powerful country in the world be damaged by some bunch of terrorists. Furthermore, it can be looked upon as old-fashioned revenge, and finally as an ego-decision by the president, feeling that his prestige and his "face" is at stake. In short, both the people and the president were outraged, so action had to be taken, even more so because action orientation is a dominant feature of American societal and political culture. This action might, and to us it did, lead to a situation of entrapment, not being in the interest of the USA, neither of the well-willing nonterrorist segments of the Afghan population. It resulted in "an international conflict for the sake of pointless goals—national prestige or the vainglory of a ruling elite" (Joll 1982). Maybe the reaction was not pointless, but the process and outcome were.

The seven conferences are characterized by the limited number of real decision makers. The wheeling and dealing is done by the most powerful, surrounded by other less important negotiators, as well as their advisers. One of the negotiations that is examined is de jure multilateral (Paris in 1919), but de facto trilateral. Another (Munich in 1938) is de jure a four-party negotiation, but de facto bilateral. We then have a true trilateral negotiation (Yalta in 1945) and four bilateral meetings (Vienna in 1961, Beijing and Moscow in 1972, and Geneva in 1985). The chapter will examine why self-image and prestige—the software of negotiation—took precedence over the hardware, and what the consequences of this were for the negotiation processes in which they played a decisive role.

The multilateral case is the Paris Peace Conference at the end of the First World War, which led to the Treaty of Versailles in 1919. Of all the negotiators, this chapter will focus on the main three—Georges Clemenceau of France, Lloyd George of Britain, and Woodrow Wilson of the United States—although it will not completely disregard the others. George Clemenceau was the President of the Paris Peace Conference, and all substantial negotiations took place between him and the other two political leaders. Although the Prime Minister of Italy, Vittorio Orlando, was an integral member of the core group of negotiators—the Council of Four—he never played an important role and even left the conference before it was over. The chapter will also ignore people like the Japanese Prime Minister Saionji Kinmochi, the Romanian Prime Minister Ion Bratianu, and the Chinese Prime Minister Lou Tseng-Tsiang, as they were outside the actual decision making. Although others were very influential as advisers, including John Maynard Keynes for example, they were not the real decision makers and are therefore also omitted from this discussion. It is interesting to observe, by the way, that most important multilateral conferences of the past two centuries were actually negotiations among a very limited set of actors. This was true for the Congress of Vienna in 1814–1815 and Paris in 1919, while today we have a UN Security Council of only five parties.

The bilateral and trilateral cases are Munich 1938 between Chamberlain, Daladier, Hitler, and Mussolini; Yalta 1945 between Churchill, Roosevelt, and Stalin; Vienna 1961 with Kennedy and Khrushchev; Beijing and Moscow 1972 with Nixon, Mao Zedong, and Brezhnev, respectively; and Reagan and Gorbachev in Geneva 1985. The impact of "secondary negotiators" like Kissinger and Zou Enlai will of course be taken into account, as their behavior has probably even more decisive and reaching an outcome, than that of the official decision makers. To conclude, we will also look at profiles of those Presidents of the USA, Secretary Generals of the Communist Party of the Soviet Union, Presidents of France, and Prime Ministers of the United Kingdom who were not connected to the seven case studies.

We realize the shortcomings of such a limited number of conferences, all of which more or less center on Europe, as well as such a select group of leaders from the traditional Great Powers of the world. However, it has nevertheless been extremely difficult to distill the characteristics of each personality from the available records and biographical details of the pivotal people. The emotional side of their behavior is thoroughly underexposed, let alone their actions, which could be labeled as being the consequence of the projection of their self-image and the defense of their prestige, which run counter to the material interests of their countries and even of themselves. While participants in negotiation seminars will easily recognize the concept of "egotiation," as they have experienced this problem in their own dealings with political leaders, it is extremely difficult to prove it from the existing literature. After all, it is not only about the character and the behavior of the negotiator, but very much about his or her actions during the negotiation process.

The First World War: Closure Through Conference Diplomacy

The Paris Peace Conference had to create a new order for Europe and thereby for the world (MacMillan 2001; Sharp 2008). Between January and June 1919, negotiators from all over the world, excluding those who had been defeated in the First World War, gathered in Paris to settle the war issues and to lay the foundations for a more stable system of international relations than the "Balance of Power" of the nineteenth century. Like at the Congress of Vienna in 1814–1815, there was no prepared agenda, nor a procedure upon which all of the interested parties agreed. Although the Paris negotiators were aware of the shortcomings of the Congress of Vienna because of the very disorderly way in which that conference had developed, they nevertheless made the same mistake of incomplete preparation. The Paris Peace Conference was not institutionalized, unlike the League of Nations that it produced, let alone the United Nations that we have today, or the African Union, European Union, Association of Southeast Asian Nations, Organization of American States, or the North Atlantic Treaty Organization. Whatever the differences between these international organizations, with the European Union being far more institutionalized than the African Union, they at least have a fixed set of rules and regulations, thereby protecting the negotiation processes inside their institutions against too much volatility.

The Paris Peace Conference had to do without this, with the consequence of great ups and downs. On January 13, 1919, the representatives of France, Britain, the USA, Italy, and Japan formed the "Council of Ten" (also referred to as the "Supreme Council") as it had two representatives from each of the states, namely the government leader as well as the minister of foreign affairs. In March 1919, the negotiations became more difficult and more intense, and the Supreme Council reduced itself to the "Council of Four," consisting of US President Woodrow Wilson, and Prime Minsters Clemenceau of France, Lloyd George of Britain, and Orlando of Italy. Prime Minister Orlando did not play an important role, however, and the real negotiations became truly trilateral. The Council met on a daily basis, using English and French as their languages of negotiation and French and English were also decided upon as the languages of the official documents. Not only were the ministers of foreign affairs of the four countries kept at bay, but also were the Japanese and their head of delegation, Marquis Saionji Kinmochi, a former Japanese Prime Minister. The rest of the negotiators of other concerned states had to wait until they were invited into the triangle to state their wishes and to try to negotiate them, although they were not allowed in as decision makers. Therefore, the personalities of the "big three" were the only ones with a decisive impact on the negotiation process (Sharp 2008).

The Outer Ring

The most concerned of the other countries, besides those represented in the "Supreme Council," were the countries of the Central Powers that had lost the war: Germany, Austria and Hungary, the Ottoman Empire, and Bulgaria. The most important of these, Germany, was seen as the real evil and therefore kept out of the discussion until the very end. The Germans were in no way involved in the negotiations and were given a document to sign during the concluding weeks of the conference, with hardly any possibility of changing it. The victors were a little more forthcoming to the other defeated members of the Central Alliance. One of the former allies of the victorious Entente, Bolshevik Russia, was also kept out and had anyway no inclination to join the negotiations with the "capitalist" countries of the West. Poland and Romania, however, profited from the West's fear of communist Russia, by having their claims rewarded in order to create a bulwark against the emerging USSR. The other successor states of the former Austrian–Hungarian Empire also fared well: Czechoslovakia and Yugoslavia (i.e., the Kingdom of the Serbs, Croats, and Slovenes). Belgium and Greece could take their spoils and so could the British Dominions, South Africa, Australia, and to some extent Canada. China, Ireland, the Arabs, and the Zionists were basically ignored, as were others, such as the Latin American countries and Siam (now Thailand) (MacMillan 2001, 5).

Several of the representatives of these countries in the outer circle, however, were reasonably influential, partly because of the need of the big three to have a second layer of involved states to help to stabilize the whole process. Big powers need middle powers to help control the smaller powers. The middle powers will then "borrow" power from the dominant nations, disciplining the host of small states in the international system. Of the six countries that were allied to the "Victorious Three," Poland was first, as it was after all the only major power in Europe that had been washed from the map more than a century before, but that now had to perform an important function in the postwar system as a buffer between Germany and Russia. Whatever the Allies wanted with Poland, Polish General Josef Pilsudski created his own reality by defeating the Red Army outside Warsaw in August 1920 and thereby creating a large Poland including substantial Ukrainian and other minorities. Romania sent Ion Bratianu to Paris, a chief spokesman for the ideal of a greater Romania. Bratianu managed this by blackmailing the Allies with the Soviet threat, as well as by creating new realities on the ground, as Poland did. He was backed up by the assertive Romanian Queen Marie, who travelled to Paris to court the Big Three. The Czechs, who now controlled the heartland of Austria–Hungary's industrial potential, could easily take the spoils as well: Hungary's Slovakia and Ruthenia. The Czech leaders, Eduard Benes and Thomas Masaryk, managed to build a democratic state in the heart of Europe—quite an exception. The charming and diplomatic Benes, representing the Czech Republic in Paris, was helped enormously by the delays in decision making, which gave his country the opportunity to annex regions with large Hungarian and Ukrainian minorities (MacMillan 2001, 240–242). Austria, which was completely dismembered, remained alive as an orphan that was cut off from the "German Fatherland" until the Second World War, when it tried to settle its identity, with two civil wars as a consequence.

Although at odds with each other, the Serbs—represented by Nikola Pašić—and the Croats—by Ante Trumbić—were overtaken by realities when Prince Alexander of Serbia proclaimed the Kingdom of Serbs, Croats, and Slovenes, including Bosnia, Montenegro, Macedonia, and Kosovo, and occupying the Banat in the process. Hungary became independent, sent the communist leader Béla Kun to Paris, but lost most of its territory in the wars against Romania in 1919, just after the end of the so-called Great War. Alexander Stamboliski, the Bulgarian Prime

Minister, did what he could in Paris, but Bulgaria was diminished to its core, be it less savagely than in Hungary. The Greeks, who sent Prime Minister Venizelos to Paris, managed to keep the territories that it had conquered during the war, expanding even to Eastern Trace and Smyrna, which were lost when Ataturk drove them out of Turkey a few years later. The Ottoman Empire, which collapsed like Austria–Hungary, successfully regained its lost territories in Anatolia, Kurdistan, and Trace after the Turkish war of independence. China, which was represented by Prime Minister Lou Tseng-Tsiang, refused to sign the Treaty of Versailles, as the former German territory of Shandong—occupied by the Japanese—was not returned to the Middle Kingdom. China was the only participating country that did not sign.

Belgium received minor compensations for its enormous losses in lives and goods, and the Dominions remained in the British Empire, but received a higher status and were allowed separate membership of the League of Nations. Some of the Dominions, such as South Africa and Australia, could expand their reach, being enlarged with former German colonies as "trust territories."

Germany, meanwhile, was a special case (MacMillan 2001, 492–493). It lost its colonies, its fleet, big chunks of its territory, and it had to pay huge reparations. Count Ulrich von Brockdorff-Rantzau led the German delegation at the signing ceremony at Versailles on April 29, 1919. The delegation was kept waiting for several days before it received the terms, and had only a few days to respond. The Diktat was born.

The Inner Ring

There were, of course, others inside the delegations of the Big Three who exerted influence on their leaders, although the overall impression remains that French Prime Minister Georges Clemenceau, British Prime Minister David Lloyd George, and President of the United States Woodrow Wilson were much more influenced by their own personality and the personality of their co-decision makers than by their foreign ministers, advisers, or minute takers, etc. Before turning to the personalities of the main decision makers, the seven most important players in the inner circle around the Supreme Council will have to be listed in alphabetical order (Duke International Security Conference 2005, 1–10): Alfred Balfour, member of the British delegation and foreign minister during the Great War, was seen as having a thoughtful demeanor that proved a balance to Lloyd George's boisterous, charismatic style. Count Macchi di Cellere, the Italian Ambassador in Washington DC, who worked closely with President Wilson, tolerated no disrespect, whether by action or by word, toward his country or its representatives. Edward House was the most important and loyal adviser to US President Wilson and worked well with Clemenceau and Balfour, but felt that Wilson could not effectively administer negotiations and agree to peace successfully. He strongly discouraged the President's decision to attend the conference and had hopes of leading the

American delegation in Paris himself. John Maynard Keynes was the leading economist of the British Treasury Department and saw Wilson as the only person with the moral authority to save Europe from another self-destructive war. Robert Lansing was former US Secretary of State to President Wilson and also wanted to be head of delegation, making President Wilson and Colonel House suspicious of his motives, which tainted their relations through the rest of the conference. French Foreign Minister Stephan Pichon's most important asset was his diplomatic skill, as he was skilled at finding points of agreement between negotiating parties and at gaining favorable compromises. Finally, Baron Sidney Sonnino, Minister of Foreign Affairs of Italy, had little belief in the concept of the League of Nations or any other Wilsonian ideals and had an extremely negative attitude toward the French.

Of the main decision makers, French Prime Minister Clemenceau, who presided over the conference, will be discussed first. A provincial French medical doctor and shrewd negotiator, he was nicknamed "the Tiger." It was said that "he comes from a family of wolves," which did not mean that he was estranged from his own feelings, as "when he heard that the Germans had agreed to an armistice [...] he put his head in his hands and wept" (MacMillan 2001, 38–39). Clemenceau's main drive was the interests of France and, above all, his hatred of the Germans, which had been kindled by the Franco–German War over 40 years earlier. This hatred obviously blinded him to solutions that might not later have sparked the resentment of the Germans, which was one of the main inducements of the Second World War. As Machiavelli once said, a statesman should always avoid creating resentment among his adversaries. This obsession with his eastern neighbor made Clemenceau open the Paris Conference on the day of the anniversary of the coronation of Wilhelm II in Versailles and to close it with the formal signing of the treaties in the Hall of Mirrors in Versailles, where the Prussian King had been crowned Emperor of Germany in 1871. His hatred also induced Clemenceau to occupy the Rhineland and the Saarland and to demand enormous reparations, which caused the economic downfall of the democratic Weimar Republic with its unstable coalition governments. He ignored voices in the French government against these measures, including from one of his young assistants in that government, Jean Monnet. The time was not yet ripe for cooperation, just for competition, or, better, domination and oppression.

Clemenceau was politically isolated, so he had to rely on himself and his closest friends. He did, however, have a good relationship with the French military and the French press. His frictions were with parliament. The newly elected Chamber of Deputies of the French National Assembly was hostile toward him, as he kept the parliamentarians out of the peace talks. His main struggle, however, was with France's President Raymond Poincaré. Clemenceau and Poincaré disliked each other intensely. According to the President, Prime Minister Clemenceau was a "Madman [...] vain man" (MacMillan 2001, 40), as he wrote in his diary. Clemenceau's relationship with his two direct co-negotiators was not too bad, but was not too good either. Wilson and Lloyd George had much more contact with each other than with Clemenceau. Lloyd George saw the French prime minister as being a “disagreeable and rather bad tempered old savage” (MacMillan 2001, 43). For his part, Clemenceau mistrusted Lloyd George, seeing him as unreliable, while he regarded Wilson as a naïve man whose ideas about self-determination would produce a powder keg in the new Europe. Although Clemenceau presided over the negotiation sessions with authority, he could turn savage, as he regularly did if the negotiations reached stalemate. He literally created hurting stalemates by shouting and storming out of the negotiation room. Whether this was pure tactic, or indeed a genuine emotional rage, is unknown, but it could have been both.

Lloyd George seemed to love devious methods. “He was a politician of formulae rather than principles, […] quick-witted and voluble—the septuagenarian Clemenceau lamented ‘si je pouvais pisser comme Lloyd George parle’—his adroitness in debate was sharpened by long practice and by unconcern for self-contradiction” (Pearton 1993, 73). One is tempted to link this to the opinions about British negotiation style: highly effective but quite unreliable, and perhaps therefore so successful in reaching the desired results in the British interests. While training British civil servants for their presidency of the European Union, trainers observed the British diplomatic way of pragmatically dealing with the process of international negotiation, while striving without much scruple for an outcome that is favorable to the UK (Hemery and Meerts 2006). The British prime minister seemed to fit into his English culture perfectly. The question then arises of to what extent his attitude was a personal or a cultural characteristic. As was observed with Clemenceau, the answer is probably both. Lloyd George was not quite aware of the European issues and shared this lack of awareness with the British main negotiator at the Congress of Vienna in 1814–1815, Lord Castlereagh. He was careless with appointments, could be quite ruthless in attempts to prevail over others, was of a domineering character, and had a problem in personal bonding. At the same time, however, he could be extraordinarily persuasive and charming—again, the true stereotype of the typical British diplomatist. During the negotiations, Lloyd George tried to balance Wilson and Clemenceau, and when asked whether he thought he had been successful, he answered that he thought he had done well, being seated between “Jesus Christ and Napoleon.”

According to “Napoleon” (that is, Clemenceau), Lloyd George was “devious and untrustworthy,” “shockingly ignorant,” while “all arguments were good to him [Lloyd George] when he wishes to win a case and, if necessary, he uses the next day arguments which he had rejected and refuted the previous day,” while to Wilson, Lloyd George simply “lacked principle” (MacMillan 2001, 41, 43 and 48):

> He was a politician of formulae rather than principles. He preferred oral to written agreements. He did not command universal trust, […] had an unconcern for self-contradiction. He made decisions on grounds of authority to act at once […] His greatest weakness, namely the lack of detailed background in foreign affairs […] led him blithely to discuss the problem of Silesia in the belief that he was settling the fate of a province in Asia Minor (Pearton 1993, 73).

(That vilayet was obviously Cilicia in southeastern Turkey, rather than Silesia, the region in Central Europe.) His short sightedness did not preclude his far sightedness, however: "after the [signing] ceremony, Lloyd George commented presciently that 'we shall have to do the whole thing over again in 25 years at three times the cost'" (Reynolds 2007, 30)—he was exactly right. Like President Nixon and Henry Kissinger in their dealings with the Soviets and the People's Republic of China, Lloyd George did not consult the Foreign Office, which—just like in the cases of Nixon and Kissinger—boomeranged, as serious oversights could not be corrected by the experts. In conclusion, "He was universally respected for his boundless energy and strong work ethic, but his bluntness and sharp tongue endeared him to few people. Nevertheless, he was very popular among the British people and politicians of both parties" (Duke International Security Conference 2005, 3).

Finally, we come to Woodrow Wilson, perhaps the most complicated of the three main negotiators (Nordholt 1992). He was seen as a hypochondriac professional academic and as having a hard time understanding the Realpolitik of the epoch. His most important contribution was the (in)famous 14 points, including the creation of a League of Nations of which the USA was not going to be a member. He was an idealist, who thought of himself as being morally right. According to Clemenceau, "talking to Wilson is something like talking to Jesus Christ. In public, Wilson was stiff and formal, but with his intimates he was charming and even playful. He was usually in perfect control of himself, but during the Peace Conference he frequently lost control of his temper" (MacMillan 2001, 15 and 26):

> He became mesmerized by the strength and neatness of the phrases that he devised. [...] He regarded himself as a prophet designated to bring light to a dark world. Yet, if we read again the tremendous sermons that he delivered during 1918, we shall find in them the seeds of the jungle of chaos that today impedes and almost obliterates the processes of rational negotiation. He failed to realize that the public is bored by foreign affairs until a crisis arises; and that then it is guided by feelings rather than by thoughts (Nicolson 1998, 85 and 87).

Wilson's aim was to avoid another world war, but his concept of world peace did not last and did not work. The idea of self-determination, which was not even clear to Wilson himself, did spark a series of minor conflicts during the interbellum period. Self-determination is not at all equivalent to independence, but to the masses and the politicians who manipulated them, it was interpreted as such. Perception determines reality, and so many conflicts were born. Why independence for some and not for all? Wilson's own interpretation of self-determination, being the right of peoples to decide on their own form of government, was not concrete enough to preclude any other vision that might be at odds with it. Wilson was far from being straight in the implementation of his vision:

> On reaching Paris, President Wilson quickly decided that by 'diplomacy' he had not meant 'negotiation', but only the results of that negotiation, namely treaties. He decided that the Phrases 'openly arrived at' and 'in the public view' were relative only and contained nothing that need deter him from conduction of prolonged secret negotiations with Lloyd George and Clemenceau [...] The general public, however, [...] continued to assume that by 'diplomacy' was meant both policy and negotiation. This is perhaps the most confusing of all fallacies that we owe to President Wilson (Nicolson 1998, 85–86).

Finally, we come to the fourth member of the "Supreme Council," the Italian Prime Minister Vittorio Emanuele Orlando. A professor of law, diplomat, and politician, Orlando had striven for Italy to leave the bloc of the Central Powers and join the Entente. In doing so, Italy suffered severe losses, but gained South Tyrol, Trieste, and some other minor territories. This was perceived as a great injustice and gave rise to problems with Yugoslavia about Istria. As Orlando did not get what he wanted, and as his government was weakened beyond measure by his failure to get what he wanted, he left the conference in April 1919. Orlando saw himself and Italy as a victim of the Big Three: "I am indeed a new Christ […] and must suffer my passion for the salvation of my country" (MacMillan 2001, 306). He allowed Italy's conservative Foreign Minister Sidney Sonnino to play an important role in Paris, and he resigned as prime minister before the signing of the Treaty. Orlando later supported Mussolini's rise to power and was connected to the Mafia during his entire political career.

The Second World War: Opening and Closure in Munich and Yalta

To categorize negotiations on the basis of the number of participants is useful, but also difficult. It is useful because the number of participants has a great impact on the flow of the negotiation process: the more actors, the more complexity, but also the more richness. The struggle with complexity is the main issue in multilateral bargaining. How can one manage the chaos? One needs good procedures, rules and regulations, effective chairs, a strong secretariat, and negotiators who are well aware of the organization's culture to set the boundaries and inner structure of the conference, etc. The management of complexity might be the main skill that negotiators of conference diplomacy have to possess; their advantage will be the choices that they have. Multilateral negotiation does generate many obstacles, but a lot of opportunities as well: multi-party, multi-issue, a multitude of problems as well as solutions, plus partial solutions for the power problem. It is, after all, easier to counterbalance the power of the powerful if many of them are present. Coalitions will ease the differences in strength and give the weaker parties a tool in playing the strong off against each other. The advantage of bilateral or trilateral bargaining is its transparency and speed. Multilateral negotiations tend to be slow, although there might be more assured outcomes. Bi- or trilateral negotiations could be speedy, but there might be more less-assured outcomes. It is also more difficult to deal with the power problem, but procedures are less of an issue and the directness allows for more personal influence. In bi- or trilateral negotiations, as well as in multilateral negotiation, much remains the same as well: the question of mandates and the relationship with the constituency.

This chapter postulates that the smaller the circle of negotiators, the greater the impact of power and personality. What, however, about prestige? What about "egotiation"? One could expect them to be more of a problem than in multilateral negotiations, because the negotiators are, after all, more directly connected in small forums. The counter-argument would be that the defense of prestige, and thereby the risk of "egotiation," is less if the negotiator is not exposed to many colleagues, let alone to public opinion. This is why secret and back-channel negotiations are often the preferred mode. It is also less because it is much easier for negotiators who operate in small groups to influence each other and thereby to put a limit to the tendency to "egotiate." The downside is groupthink. The risk of groupthink is much bigger than in multilateral negotiation processes. Although the number of parties does influence the people, power structure, flow of the process, and the product of their work, it remains difficult to link this fully with maximized-party and minimized-party negotiations. After all, talks between two, three, four, or five negotiators are essential for progress in multilateral meetings. While we have to characterize the Paris Peace Conference as multilateral, we also saw that in reality it was very much a trilateral process. However, this trilateral negotiation also had multilateral aspects, as advisers in the Inner Circle were quite involved and influential, actors in the Outer Circle did exert some influence, and the constituency back home—as well as public opinion—was part of the overall flow as well. In other words, bi- and trilateral negotiations have a multilateral dimension and multilateral talks are dependent on bi- and trilateral meetings within them. It seems, however, that the essence of the process of international negotiation can only be handled in groups of up to five actors, which we might label as the "core caucus" of the negotiation.

Munich 1938

The Munich negotiation process can perhaps be termed the mother of catastrophic negotiation processes. It was seen by Western leaders as a huge mistake: Britain and France selling out Czechoslovakia to Adolf Hitler and thereby opening the road for German hegemony of Eastern Europe up to the borders of the Soviet Union. This is true, although the question remains of what the alternatives would have been. Adolf Hitler himself was not as happy with the outcome of the Munich conference as one would presume:

> [...] er wollte [...] alles, was ihm vorschwebte, zu seinem Lebzeiten schaffen. Er hatte keine Zeit. Das Münchener Abkommen, in dem Freund und Feind mit Recht einen märchenhaften Triumph Hitlers sahen, empfand er selbst geradezu als Niederlage: Es war nicht nach seinem Willen gegangen, er hatte aus der Hand Englands und Frankreichs entgegennehmen müssen, was er lieber mit Gewalt genommen hätte, und er hatte Zeit verloren. So erzwang er 1939 den Krieg, der ihm 1938 entgangen war (Haffner 2011, 125–126).

Hitler felt restrained by the Munich agreement and was taken by surprise by the peace efforts of British Prime Minister Neville Chamberlain:

> By the summer of 1938, Hitler was convinced that the Czech problem had to be resolved by war: this had become for him a test of personality. At the same time, across the North Sea, a mirror-image situation was developing: for Chamberlain the search for peace had become almost an ego trip' (Reynolds 2007, 41).

Chamberlain's determination to be successful and to save Britain and the world from disaster had its root in his family history. His father, Joseph, was one of the heroes of liberal politics in the nineteenth century, although he never became prime minster. The son wanted to do better than the father and he was ready to take the necessary risks for that, in competition with his half brother Austin: "As the marginal man in this fiercely proud family, Neville would always be less than human if he did not sense a chance to outdo his father and his brother in the battle for reputation. [… He] was always measuring himself against his father and brother" (Reynolds 2007, 50). In order not to be hindered in his endeavor concerning Adolf Hitler, he ignored his Foreign Minister Anthony Eden, who resigned because he felt bypassed. Chamberlain's personal mission took off, and nobody could stop him but reality. He began to overestimate himself and told his sisters: "now I have only to raise a finger and the whole face of Europe is changed." Acknowledging the publication of H.A.L. Fisher's new History of Europe in March 1938, he replied: "At the present moment I am too busy trying to make the history of Europe to read about it" (Reynolds 2007, 49).

Without consulting the British Foreign Office, Chamberlain offered to visit Hitler in his residence "the Berghof" on the Obersalzberg above the town of Berchtesgaden, although the German Foreign Ministry had been fully engaged through its Foreign Minister Joachim von Ribbentrop from the very first moment. It was an unprecedented step, to go to the wolf's lair, and Chamberlain did not even take an interpreter with him. Dr Paul Schmidt, interpreter of the German Foreign Ministry, acted as interpreter. This, of course, could and did lead to miscommunications, as Chamberlain could not check on Schmidt's words. At first he did not even receive a transcript of the minutes made by Schmidt. The talks lasted for one day and were a mere exchange of opinions and arguments. They nevertheless raised expectations of a peaceful solution, as Hitler showed his readiness to discuss the contentious issues in something that looked like a dialog. As history showed later, however, this dialog was not for real, nor were the follow-up talks in Bad Godesberg. This second encounter was anyway much grimmer than the first. This time Chamberlain took his First Secretary Ivone Kirkpatrick, who spoke German fluently. Hitler did make some minor concessions, but in reality the British were eaten on the spot and Hitler got what he wanted on the question of the Sudeten Germans. The meeting did not give any reason for optimism and ended in an icy atmosphere (Reynolds 2007, 75–80).

As a next step, Chamberlain proposed a four-power meeting, with the Italians and the French also present. This was very much welcomed by Italy's Benito Mussolini (known as the Duce), who feared that a German invasion of Czechoslovakia would further upset the balance of power between the Hitler's Third Reich and Mussolini's fascist Italy. Hitler thus invited the Duce, Prime Minister of France, Édouard Daladier, and Chamberlain to come to Munich. This was the third time in a row on German territory, and the Czechs were not invited. At the end of the meeting, Chamberlain and Hitler held a bilateral meeting about the issue of Anglo-German relations in the future, whose resolution was reluctantly undersigned by Hitler. It stated that "We are resolved that the method of consultation shall be the method adopted to deal with any other questions that may concern our two countries, and we are determined to continue our efforts to remove possible sources of differences and thus to contribute to assure the peace of Europe" (Reynolds 2007, 95). The meetings were prepared amateurishly, and in that sense, there is not much of a difference from the Paris Conference discussed earlier in this chapter, or for that matter the Congress of Vienna in 1814–1815. There were no briefing papers, no position papers, no planning, no strategy, and no profiles of the main negotiators—nothing of the kind. In such a situation, the danger of so-called salami tactics being used by the other side is immanent. Without overall planning, it is difficult to trace the trade-offs, and one side might walk off with the biggest part of the cake because it got more in every distributive bargaining, precluding integrative win–win outcomes. "In short, Hitler was a much more effective negotiator than Chamberlain, but he never wanted to negotiate, whereas Chamberlain, a less skilled tactician, got what he really wanted—peace not war" (Reynolds 2007, 99). In other words, Chamberlain's need for a settlement was much greater than Hitler's, and by being the "demandeur," he had to concede much more than his opponent.

What about the personality and the position of Adolf Hitler? While Chamberlain had a short-term plan of preventing war, Hitler had a long-term strategy: dominating Europe in his lifetime (Reynolds 2007, 100). In order to do this, he had to swallow Austria and Czechoslovakia in a peaceful way in order to be able to attack Poland and thereby dominate the whole of Eastern Europe up to the Soviet border. The final goal was to conquer Russia, but in order to do so, he had to subdue France first in order to overcome the classic German dilemma of a war on two fronts. Britain, it was thought, would then be so isolated that it would have to accept German hegemony over Europe—actually, it would be more apt to say to accept Hitler as the hegemon. For Hitler, the German people were merely tools in his conquest and the fulfillment of his second aim: the destruction of the Jewish people on the European continent. After the German failure to take Moscow, Hitler's dream of a pan-European Third Reich dominated by the "Germanic race" withered away, leaving him with his second target: to sweep away the "Semitic race." He thought in terms of peoples, not of states. Actually, he destroyed the German state system, in order not to be bothered by laws and institutions. Everything should circle around "der Führer," and thus the state had to wither away, like in Marxism, but for reasons of autocracy, not of equality. He was a criminal, political Darwinist, with a complete lack of empathy—unable to make intimate friends among men and women—who did not allow for much of a compromise. His tool was war, not negotiation. Like Chamberlain, he grossly overestimated himself until the bitter end (Haffner 2011, 13).

Yalta 1945

While Munich stood at the beginning of the Second World War, Yalta marked the end. This exclusive trilateral negotiation by US President Franklin D. Roosevelt (FDR), Soviet Premier Joseph Stalin, and British Prime Minister Winston Churchill can be seen as the real closure negotiation of the Second World War. Although the Potsdam Conference in July and August 1945 was the last wartime summit, it did not change the foundations laid in Yalta in February 1945. The leaders' personalities played a prominent role:

> Of the three, Roosevelt probably had the greatest strengths and the least coherent conception of how to utilize them. Roosevelt was […] jaunty, self-possessed, confident, cheerful and capable of inspiring trust and affection. [However,] he held no well-defined or sophisticated world view […] Roosevelt saw himself as a realistic Wilsonian (Buhite 1986, 11–12).

Moreover,

> The President was a 'feely' politician, operating on a blend of intuition and experience, and his approach shaped his views of both Hitler and Stalin. FDR knew Germany well, or at least the Kaiser's Germany before the First World War. Speaking to [US] senators in January 1939, Roosevelt described the German leader as a 'wild man', 'walking up and down the room for hours on end', 'pounding the table and making speeches'. 'We should call him a "nut"'. The contest between Roosevelt and Hitler became very personal, whereas Churchill's animus was directed at German militarism and autocracy (Reynolds 2007, 108–109).

This brings us to Churchill:

> Churchill's world view rose from his concern that a single power, regardless of its ideology, might dominate the European continent. [He was] a man of great courage. […] especially his ability to use the language, stood unequalled among his countrymen […] What he possessed in learning and eloquence, he lacked in patience. He would be terribly impressed with his own performance, and then become bored, refuse to hear responses […] A better negotiator than Roosevelt, he was still surprisingly ill prepared. While voluble and emotional, at the same time he was insufficiently persistent. Churchill also suffered bouts of extreme depression, which tended to immobilize him. Many men of great prominence, whose aggressive behavior allows them to perform brilliantly toward opponents, turn their hostility inward once a foe is vanquished or an issue resolved. A man of massive ego […] 'Of course I am an egotist', he said to Clement Attlee. 'Where do you get if you aren't?' He had the egotist concept of leadership (Buhite 1986, 14–16).

As for Stalin, it has been observed that "Joseph V. Stalin [… était] un homme parvenu par les moyens les plus pervers au sommet de la puissance et n'y ayant pas trouvé ce qui'il en attendait, un homme totalement désabusé" (Laloy 1988, 15). Moreover,

> Stalin's style was that of recluse. The author of a psychological portrait of Stalin suggests that he was the quintessential paranoid personality. A vain, power-hungry man with a keen sense of his own inferiority, he harbored intense jealousies and a mean, vindictive spirit, […] mastering the art of manipulating people and laying them off against each other for his own benefit (Buhite 1986, 17).

In addition, "Although Stalin had a sharp mind and a prodigious memory, he had always had an inferiority complex about his lack of formal education; he was also deeply xenophobic" (Reynolds 2007, 115). "His greatest strength in Yalta lay in the Russian contribution to the war effort and the positioning of the Soviet forces" (Buhite 1986, 18). It was much more Roosevelt than Churchill who wanted to keep Stalin on board the alliance, also because Roosevelt still believed at Yalta that he needed the Russian war effort in the Pacific to underpin the American struggle against Japan: "Yalta est donc l'effort ultime de Roosevelt pour preserver l'entente avec l'URSS" (Laloy 1988, 9).

During the meeting, Stalin had the advantage of being on his home front, while Roosevelt in particular had to travel a long way and suffered increasingly from his weak health. Even Churchill arrived worn out by the long war years:

> Summitry requires quick wits and mental stamina. Arriving at Yalta, neither Churchill nor Roosevelt seemed to be at their best. Both he and Roosevelt listened intently to Stalin. Churchill watched the Soviet leader even when his words were being translated. [...] Conference diplomacy is about resolving differences through an interlocking set of compromises and trade-offs, in which no party gains everything but all get something and concede something. This is what happened at Yalta. Over the first two days, the Big Three brought most of the diplomatic issues to the table. From Wednesday, February 6, the deals began to be made (Reynolds 2007, 122–125).

The atmosphere seems to have been amicable, but the Soviet leader's position precluded many of the decisions that were taken. The facts on the ground were decisive, but this did not mean that emotions were absent:

> Of the two leaders [Roosevelt and Churchill], Churchill was more hard-line and often highly emotional. The only point when Roosevelt lost his cool was when Stalin protested about peace feelers made by the German army in Italy to US emissaries in Bern. [...] He was furious—face flushed, eyes flushing (Reynolds 2007, 150–151).

Roosevelt's answer to Stalin was, according to Churchill, "about the hottest thing I have ever seen so far in diplomatic intercourse" (Reynolds 2007, 151). It worked, because Stalin withdrew his complaint: "Stalin was indeed a skillful negotiator, letting the others do the talking and saving his succinct remarks for the right moment. Nevertheless, Churchill's more bombastic approach should not be underrated: it wore down the other two over France and German reparation" (Reynolds 2007, 159).

The Cold War: Attempts to Unfreeze in Vienna, Beijing, Moscow and Geneva

To negotiate during the Cold War was not an easy task. With the threat of nuclear destruction, both the USSR and the USA became increasingly aware of the necessity to start talking, to create a safety net in case of unintended escalation and the danger of unleashing their nuclear arsenals. While it was feasible during the First and Second World Wars to have a victorious party (not to belittle those wars' disastrous consequences), a Third World War would certainly end in catastrophe for all of the parties concerned: a lose–lose outcome. Negotiation, then, was the only way out. The first case in this section deals with a very difficult, but serious, attempt to bridge the gap between the two superpowers. It failed. The second and the third cases were already more successful and opened the road to the fourth case, which was indeed a success. Although a very precarious and bumpy process, it laid the foundations for the end of the Cold War half a decade later. With this, the chain of events that started with the Balkan Wars at the beginning of the twentieth Century came to an end with the inner-Yugoslav/Balkan War resulting from the implosion of the Federal Socialist Republic of Yugoslavia—one century from a Balkans to Balkans crisis, with negotiation processes trying to prevent, manage, and end the use of violence as an instrument in international relations in and around the European continent.

Vienna 1961

US President John F. Kennedy and Soviet Premier Nikita Khrushchev were the egos clashing at the summit meeting in Vienna in 1961. Khrushchev appeared to be the dominant figure in their encounters, being much more experienced than Kennedy. Actually, this took Kennedy by surprise and the Soviet leader exploited his situational advantage in a very skillful way by turning the negotiation into an ideological show of force. Khrushchev, from Ukrainian peasant ancestors and lacking serious formal education, appeared to be a ruthless negotiator, confirming the stereotypes about Russian bargaining styles (Meerts 2009, 4–8):

> Khrushchev retained a huge inferiority complex about his lack of education and culture and was always alert to condescension, real or imagined, at home and abroad. Stalin, too, had such a complex, but Khrushchev was not as good at concealing it. Nor, unlike his patron, could Khrushchev control his explosive temper: within seconds he could shift from good humor to foul-mouthed abuse. At their first meeting in Geneva in 1955, the Soviet leader seemed a frankly 'obscene figure' to the elegant, urban Macmillan [the UK Prime Minister], who wondered if 'this fat, vulgar man, with his pig eyes and his ceaseless flow of talk' could really be the head of a great country' (Reynolds 2007, 169).

Khrushchev's attitude was one of the reasons for his split with Mao Zedong (Reynolds 2007, 170), and it gave John F. Kennedy a very hard time.

Kennedy, a believer in negotiation as a tool in international relations, also saw the limits of this instrument. His famous saying that one should never negotiate out of fear, but nevertheless never fear to negotiate, is a case in point. Kennedy had a complicated family background. Like Chamberlain, he had to struggle with a dominant father figure, Joseph Kennedy, and an elder brother who was meant to be a politician but who died at too young an age, while his other brothers were groomed to play an important role in US politics as well. Given the Irish and Roman Catholic background of the family, there were also aspects of emancipation involved, perhaps not as much as in the case of Khrushchev—after all, Kennedy did attend Harvard Law School—but nevertheless. According to Thomas Mongar, ego structures are of two basic types, namely "satellizing" and deviant. "Satellizing" occurs when a child is intrinsically valued, but Mongar adds:

> Alternatively, if the child thinks he has been extrinsically valued, he will protect his omnipotent self-image (and) will attempt to increase his capacity to perform to meet the burden of vastly inflated aspirations. Kennedy's 'ego profile' is almost a perfect representation of the deviant structure. Deflation of aspiration was ruled out because of the

> neurotic pressures for achievement from the family. The only remaining alternative was a massive effort to inflate his performance capacities, which required a strategy of managing the symptoms of his neurosis and turning his weaknesses into competitive assets (Mongar 1969, 206–208).

Notwithstanding—or perhaps because of his chronic back problems—Kennedy managed to become US President.

In May 1961, Bobby Kennedy, John's younger brother, had a preparatory back-channel meeting with Georgi Bolshakov from the Soviet Embassy in Washington DC, a close friend of Khrushchev's son-in-law. Events then started to roll, partly managed through official diplomatic channels by US Ambassador to the USSR Llewellyn Thompson and his Soviet counterpart Ambassador Mikhail Menshikov and partly through the aforementioned back channel, trying to overcome the two main obstacles: Berlin and Vietnam:

> Each leader was going with his own list of priorities and with a confidence that, if he played it tough, the other man would come around. Each had fundamental blind spots about his adversary. The world has moved a long way since the days of Hitler and Chamberlain – communications had been transformed and information was much fuller – yet the psychological barriers to summitry were much the same (Reynolds 2007, 199).

The summit took place in Vienna from June 3 to 4, 1961. On the first day, Kennedy and Khrushchev met in the residence of the US Ambassador to Austria, surrounded by their staff. They exchanged ideological arguments about communism and capitalism, a debate in which the Soviet leader was much more versed that the President: "the [US] ambassador was shaken that Kennedy seemed to be taking one hit after another from the Soviet leader. In an effort at rational discussion, the president had ended up on the defensive in an ideological argument, even conceding that the Bay of Pigs had been a misjudgment" (Reynolds 2007, 203). On the second day, they met at the Soviet Embassy in Vienna. No progress was made and emotions rose, for example, with Khrushchev's comparison of the death toll of the USSR and the USA during the Second World War. A face-to-face bilateral meeting —with only interpreters present—did not bring any progress.

Beijing and Moscow 1972

Approximately ten years later, US President Richard Nixon was preparing for summitry with both Chinese leader Mao Zedong and Soviet Premier Leonid Brezhnev. The Americans had learned from Vienna, and they prepared much more thoroughly through back-channel preparatory talks, in which US Security Adviser Henry Kissinger played a decisive role, a role in which he himself was perfectly aware. In the run-up to the Moscow meeting, the Americans strengthened their position enormously by creating a "best alternative to a negotiated agreement," the alternative being talks with Beijing before the Moscow summit was due. It was vital that the back-channel talks with the Chinese would not be leaked to the Soviet Union. Kissinger therefore had to act without consulting the US State Department. He flew to Pakistan and from there, in secret and with only a few security men, to Beijing. As in the case of Chamberlain's flight to Berchtesgaden to meet with Hitler in 1938, Kissinger did not take an interpreter with him. Kissinger conferred with Chinese Prime Minister Zhou Enlai for seventeen hours. He was duly impressed by the cultivated Zhou.

> As we now know, Zhou was treated by Mao as his round-the-clock diplomatic factotum, forced at times to grovel even more basely than Gromyko did before Khrushchev. In 1972 Mao denied Zhou treatment for bladder cancer lest his premier outlive him, and even refused to pass full diagnosis' (Reynolds 2007, 240).

They decided that Nixon would fly to Beijing for a meeting with Mao before his summit in Moscow. The Kissinger mission upset the Russians so much that Nixon's hand in his negotiations with Brezhnev was substantially strengthened—one of the reasons why the Moscow meeting became a success.

Nixon was an unemotional and tough "Real Politiker." Nevertheless, like any other human being, he has an Achilles' heel: jealousy. As it was in US interests to make the trip to Beijing known to the Soviets, Kissinger talked to the media extensively, taking the credit for the meeting with Zhou Enlai. President Nixon was furious and decided that he would not allow Kissinger the same media attention in the case of Moscow: "Still chafing at Kissinger's self-promotion, Nixon stressed on numerous occasions during the flight that no one else must be in view when he and his wife descend from Air Force One. Just to make sure, a burly Secret Service agent blocked the aisle after they landed" (Reynolds 2007, 243). Nixon negotiated with Zhou Enlai and paid a courtesy visit to Mao Zedong. So-called ping-pong diplomacy was born. However, as the US State Department was only involved at the very last moment, while Secretary of State William Rogers was kept out of the talks with Zhou Enlai, Kissinger made two serious mistakes. He agreed to a wording in the final communiqué that was detrimental to Taiwan. He therefore had to renegotiate the communiqué, which could have been avoided if China experts had been involved in the drafting. Nixon was not amused.

Such a mistake was made again in the final joint statement after the Moscow meeting with Brezhnev, a few months after Beijing. Kissinger met Brezhnev in Moscow on April 21, 1972. Again, the US State Department had been left in the cold, but it was drawn in a little when Nixon finally flew to Moscow to talk to Brezhnev. The Soviets managed to slot the term "peaceful coexistence" into the final communiqué, an ideological term that Kissinger did not value, as it meant a continued struggle between communism and capitalism and a final victory of the first made possible by the avoidance of war. The Kremlinologists of the US State Department were not allowed to participate in the drafting and so could not correct the text.

US Secretary of State William Rogers felt that Kissinger was "deceitful, egotistical, arrogant, and insulting. Kissinger felt that Rogers was vain, uninformed, unable to keep a secret" (Reynolds 2007, 246).

Kissinger found Brezhnev to be:

> […] very forceful, extremely nervous, highly unsubtle, quite intelligent but not of the class of the other leaders we have met. Brezhnev, as much as Nixon, wanted to portray himself as a political virtuoso and take political credit for the eventual agreement. For his part, Nixon

> was struck by Brezhnev's physical presence and sheer 'animal magnetism'. [... As] Kissinger put it in his memoirs, 'Given Nixon's feelings about who should get the credit, I doubt that he would have agreed if we had proposed [to bring the arms control delegations to Moscow to work in conjunction with the summit]. We shall never know because I did not put forward the idea, not uninfluenced by vanity and the desire to control the final negotiation.' Time magazine had made [Kissinger] and Nixon joint Men of the Year for 1972, much to the president's fury. Even Kissinger begged the editors not to do it. If Watergate had not exploded, Kissinger might well have been a casualty of Nixon's jealousy in the second term (Reynolds 2007, 250, 268, 272 and 277).

Other personalities were involved, of course, such as President Nikolai Podgorny, Prime Minister Alexei Kosygin, and Foreign Minister Andrei Gromyko on the Soviet side, but they did not play a decisive role.

On May 22, 1972, Nixon landed in Moscow for his summit with Brezhnev. They met alone, with interpreters but without Kissinger. Members of both delegations were to be included later. The atmosphere changed from moment to moment, like a rollercoaster, but in the end the two leaders arrived at a common understanding on matters such as the Strategic Arms Limitation Talks (SALT) and basic principles governing relations between the two superpowers. Furthermore, they signed six bilateral agreements. Thus, "The Moscow meeting was not seen as a contest between victors and losers, but as an understanding from which both sides gained" (Reynolds 2007, 274).

Geneva 1985

In November 1985, Soviet Premier Mikhail Gorbachev and US President Ronald Reagan met in Geneva at a summit where they insulted each other, but also built a unique chemistry between them, as well as between their teams. This negotiation in Geneva foreshadowed the end of the Cold War. Ronald Reagan was a Cold War-monger, but he was averse to nuclear weapons and wanted them out of the international security arena. Mikhail Gorbachev needed an end to the arms race with the Americans, as he needed the money for restructuring the Soviet Union and putting an end to its stagnating economy. Moreover, he feared a new arms race because of Reagan's Strategic Defense Initiative (SDI), the so-called Star Wars Program. Just because Reagan did not believe in mutual assured destruction (MAD), he wanted to build a missile defense system, and this threatened the credibility of the Soviet potential to retaliate in the case of a US nuclear attack (Reynolds 2007, 346). Both sides therefore had good reasons to negotiate and they did so in Geneva, starting on November 19, 1985 in Fleur d'Eau, where the Americans hosted the first session. The next day they met on the grounds of the Soviet mission. The two leaders had long face-to-face bilateral fireside talks, keeping their delegations at arm length. Although they had grave problems on content, their personal relationship evolved in such a way that they became tenacious about solving the problems between the two superpowers, if not right away, then at least in the future. They cooperated in forcing their delegations to make headway. For example,

> [Reagan] concluded that earlier leaders had not accomplished very much. So he suggested, with Gorbachev nodding in agreement, that the two of them should simply say 'To hell with the past – we'll do it our way and get something done.' When an angry [US Secretary of State George] Schultz interrupted coffee to complain that [Soviet Deputy Foreign Minister Georgy] Kornienko [...] was blocking agreement on parts of the joint statement, Gorbachev said smilingly to Reagan: 'Let's put our foot down.' Each took his delegation aside. In fact the Soviet Leader leaned harder on his staff to sort things out (Reynolds 2007, 381).

They both saw summitry as a process, not as a one-time event.

Gorbachev came from humble origins, but contrary to Stalin and Khrushchev, he had enjoyed an advanced education. He had, however, experienced traumatic events in his childhood. His grandfather suffered under the Stalinist purges, although he was a good and loyal communist. His father and elder brother were sent to the Front to fight the Nazis, and his brother never returned. Although Gorbachev was a true believer in Marxism–Leninism, he was pragmatic by nature (Gruyter 1993). It was this attitude that brought him close to Reagan, who was a pragmatic politician as well, notwithstanding his seemingly ideological conservative utterances. Reagan, with an optimistic view of life, was a team player. He thereby avoided the "egotiation" mechanisms that bedevilled egotist loners such as Nixon and Kissinger. The personalities of the leaders set a series of summits in motion, melting away the Cold War. It is important to note that the extraordinary understanding between Reagan and Gorbachev was quite exceptional

> [... However,] most leaders find it difficult to disentangle their country's national interests from their personal political goals. Yet it is essential to intuit these needs and goals, and it is even more vital to understand the other leader as a political animal, rather than merely a newfound 'friend.' The ultimate question, more political than diplomatic, is whether the leader feels that in the last resort he can afford to walk away empty-handed from the summit. Summitry is predicated on the idea that better personal relations can yield diplomatic benefits. This makes most leaders reluctant to have an open row at the summit [... Nevertheless,] lower-level negotiations between specialists are [...] essential; they also allow the leader room to repudiate what has been tentatively agreed (Reynolds 2007, 429–431).

Discussion and Conclusion: Lessons for Theory and Practice

Looking back at the case studies, despite previously accepted limitations, a number of conclusions can be drawn regarding the impact of powerful prestigious personalities on the process and the product of international negotiation processes. Conventional understanding of potential negotiation failure emphasized the importance of preservation and promotion of specific interests through negotiation, which are generally prioritized over the achievement of a shared solution. In fact negotiations are rarely conducted for the sole purpose of achieving a solution.

Rather, the process is often constructed for the protection of particular negotiators' interests. Therefore, it is no surprise that negotiations often do not generate a commonly accepted solution as parties might use negotiations as a smokescreen and/or a tactical maneuver to regroup and garner outside sympathies and support. Looked from this rationalist angle, deadlocks in negotiations tend to be seen as a direct result of a calculated cost-benefit analysis by negotiators. However, as the case studies show, deadlocks are more than just a calculated choice. Individuals that act as negotiators bring to the table not only their mandate and set of priorities—they also bring their personal emotional profiles. As such, potential deadlocks can be liked also to their irrational side: the volatile nature of their emotional profile. While the mandate each negotiator has emphasizes a set of goals and priorities that need to be preserved, promoted, and potentially achieved through negotiations, depending on the circumstances negotiator's emotional profile—character, personal preferences, and emotions—can take precedence over the interests of the entity they represent. This process, which we termed "*egotiation*," inevitably has an impact on the negotiation process.

Parties opt to negotiate as a "way out" of their perceived deadlock. Consequently, the process serves as a "face-saving" method since the parties, aware that they are entrapped in the current conflict and are unable to escalate or de-escalate the situation to their favor, through negotiations aim to obtain more than what they can achieve by perpetuating the conflict (Zartman 2001a; Meerts 2005). The present case studies focused on the choices made by politicians and diplomats. The case studies support our initial proposition that under certain circumstances these actors will be more concerned with protecting the reputation (both personal and that of the entity/country they represent) than with finding a solution to the conflict they are currently in. The trade-off in this sense is that the face-saving aspect of negotiation is primarily related to the reputation which "precedes" the party, than with the potential image that party might obtain with the achievement of a specific solution. In other words, to borrow the terminology proposed by Zartman and Kremenyuk, the "face saving" becomes more "backward looking" than "forward looking" (Zartman and Kremenyuk 2005).

The second crucial element of our analysis represented the power aspect of negotiators. We defined power as a perceptive phenomenon: ability to induce a change in behavior on the part of one's counterpart/interlocutor, a change which otherwise would not be possible. In the realm of negotiation politicians are perceived as power brokers, individuals that strive to gain power and use it as a multi-functional tool: limiting and/or controlling others' behavior, and generating profits for themselves and the entity they represent. Among many forms of leverage in negotiation, reputation certainly represents one of the most important ones based on nonmaterial resources. Reputation can be observed as a two-way process: attributed characteristics from outside actors based on one's record of previous behavior and self-interpretation of these characteristic by the actor to whom they were attributed. In essence, reputational power allows an actor to bypass situations in which their involvement is either questioned or marginalized by their counterparts/interlocutors because "the reputation precedes the actor" in way that it allows to its counterparts to predefine the role and potential impact of the actor even before the negotiation process has even started. With this premise, we postulated that in a dynamic process such as negotiations, negotiators' reputation is an asset that needs to be preserved and defended even more than specific material interests. As case studies show, interpretation of one's reputation is directly related to the "ego" of a politician or diplomat. More importantly, the case studies provide sufficient support for our claim that the more powerful the leader the bigger his or her ego, the bigger the impact of his/her ego-state on the negotiation process. Countless deadlocks which occurred in all of the case studies were a direct result of a calculation made by negotiators which saw that their first task was to protect their and their country's reputation and only once that was not jeopardized a solution could be sought after.

In such circumstances ego-driven individuals, concerned primarily with reputation, might have both a constructive and destructive impact on the negotiation. On the one hand, if "egos" are the common stakeholders of a given issue, they will be proud of their success and their ego may thus steer the process away from disaster. If leaders realize that victory is not possible or that in fact defeat is looming on the horizon, they might opt for joint victory through cooperation. Finally, their ego might actually be comforted by a positive outcome. As the case studies show, despite their strong "ego" structures politicians might be induced to assume a great deal of responsibility where others back down. After all, somebody has to do the job. Their role appears to be indispensable in crisis situations. In that sense, the ego question might have more positive than negative effects on negotiation processes. It all depends on the leaders' motivation for wanting to be the leader. On the one hand, ego distorts an objective view of the negotiators' interests, "hardens" the negotiations, and contributes to the loss of flexibility—flexibility that is needed to enter the give-and-take bargaining phase in negotiations.

Looking more closely at our case studies, a number of avenues for future research seem to open. First of all, while we managed to find support in our claim that there is a tendency of prioritizing reputation over specific goals that are at the discussed at the negotiation table, future research needs to illuminate what circumstances trigger such behavior. For instance, how much impact time-constrained crisis situations have on the process of prioritizing reputation over material gains. At the same time, as each future research could shed more light on whether a combination of specific emotional profiles actually yields particular outcomes. For instance, whose ideas and interests will get most transposed into the final outcome? Will this depend on the perceived power of the entity a negotiator represents (i.e., country) or his/her particular emotional profile. Or is it a combination of the two? While practitioners find that emotional profiles of their interlocutors play an important role in their negotiation processes, it is still difficult to understand if there is a suitable strategy, potentially "one size fits all" to deal with each particular emotional profile. Quantitative studies in this regard would be of greater help and could pave the road for better understanding of how to approach and prepare for the negotiations given the likelihood that one's counterparts might be primarily focused in protecting and promoting their reputations instead of reaching a solution. Clues of how to avoid potential deadlocks stemming from such behavior thus represent an asset that should not be overlooked.

Acknowledgments The authors would like to thank Vlad Badea for his help in providing part of the literature that made this chapter possible.

References

Avruch, K. (1998). *Culture and conflict resolution*. Washington DC: US Institute of Peace Press.

Blaker, M., Giarra, P., & Vogel, E. (2002). *Case studies in Japanese negotiating behavior*. Washington DC: US Institute of Peace Press.

Buhite, R. D. (1986). *Decisions at Yalta, an appraisal of summit diplomacy*. Wilmington, Delaware: Scholarly Resources Inc.

Cogan, C. G. (2003). *French negotiating behavior: Dealing with the 'grand nation'*. Washington DC: US Institute of Peace Press.

Cohen, R. (1997). *Negotiating across cultures: International communication in an interdependent world*. Washington DC: US Institute of Peace Press.

Cohen, R. (2001). Negotiating across cultures. In C. A. Crocker, F. O. Hampson, & P. Aall (Eds.), *Turbulent peace: The challenges of managing international conflict* (pp. 469–482). Washington DC: United States Institute of Peace Press.

Duke International Security Conference. (2005). *Paris peace conference 1919, minister biographies* (pp. 1–10). Durham, US: Duke University.

Faizullaev, A. (2006). Diplomacy and self. *Diplomacy and Statecraft, 17*(3), 497–522.

Freeman, C. (1997). *Arts of power: Statecraft and diplomacy*. Washington DC: US Institute of Peace Press.

Goldman, A. L., & Rojot, J. (2003). *Negotiation: Theory and practice*. Netherlands: Kluwer Law International.

Gruyter de R. (1993) *Once upon a time, a historical and psychological analysis of gorbachev's reign*. Doctoral Thesis, University of Amsterdam.

Haffner, S. (2011). *Anmerkungen zu Hitler*. Frankfurt am Main: Fischer Taschenbuch Verlag.

Hemery, J., & Meerts, P. W. (2006). Training for practice, a practical approach. *The Hague Journal of Diplomacy*, 1(2), 197–208.

Holsti, O.R. (1968). Cognitive dynamics and images of enemy. In J. C. Farrell & A. P. Smith (Eds.), *Image and Reality in World Politics*. New York, NY: Columbia University Press.

Iklè, F. C. (1985). *How Nations negotiate*. Millwood: Kraus.

Joll, J. (1982). The ideal and the real, changing concepts of the international system, 1815-1982. *International Affairs, 58*(2), 210–224.

Jönsson, C. (2012). Psychological causes of incomplete negotiations. In G. O. Faure (Ed.), *Unfinished business: Why international negotiations fail* (pp. 167–184). Athens, GA: University of Georgia Press.

Kissinger, H. (1969). The Vietnam negotiations. *Foreign Affairs, 47*, 211–234.

Laloy J. (1988). *Yalta, Hier, aujourd'hui, demain*. editions Robert Laffort, Paris.

MacMillan, M. (2001). *Peacemakers, the Paris conference of 1919 and its attempt to end war*. London: John Murray.

Meerts, P. (2005). Entrapment in international negotiations. In I. W. Zartman & G. O. Faure (Eds.), *Escalation and negotiation in international conflicts* (pp. 103–130). Cambridge, UK: Cambridge University Press.

Meerts, P. (2009). Negotiating with the Russian bear: Lessons for the EU?. EU Diplomacy Papers, Vol. 8. College of Europe, Bruges.

Meerts, P. (2010). Egotiation: Ego as a factor in international negotiation processes. In *Pinpoints network newsletter* (Vol. 35, pp. 28–29). Laxenburg: IIASA.

Mongar, T. M. (1969). Personality and decision making: John F. Kennedy in four crisis decisions. *Canadian Journal of Political Science, 2*(2), 200–225.

Nicolson, H. (1998). *The evolution of diplomatic method, diplomatic studies programme*. University of Leicester, (being the Chichele Lectures in Oxford, 1953).

Nordholt, J. W. S. (1992). *Woodrow Wilson, Een leven voor de wereldvrede: Een biografie*. Amsterdam: Meulenhoff.

Pearton, M. (1993). The Paris peace conference. In AP. van Goudoever (ed.), *Great Peace Conferences in History, 1648–1990, Utrechtse Historische Cahiers*, (Vol. 14, # 2). University of Utrecht.

Pronin, E., Gilovich, T. D., & Ross, L. (2004). Objectivity in the eye of the beholder: Divergent perceptions of bias in self versus others. *Psychological Review, 111*(3), 781–799.

Reynolds, D. (2007). *Summits, six meetings that shaped the twentieth century*. New York: Basic Books.

Richmond, O. (1998). Devious objectives and the disputants' view of international mediation: A theoretical framework. *Journal of Peace Research, 35*(6), 707–722.

Sharp, A. (2008). *The versailles settlement, peacemaking after the first world war, 1919–1929*. London: Palgrave Macmillan.

Smyser, W. R. (2002). *How Germans negotiate: Logical goals, practical solutions*. Washington DC: US Institute of Peace Press.

Solomon, R. H. (1999). *Chinese negotiating behavior: Pursuing interests through 'old friends'*. Washington DC: US Institute of Peace Press.

Solomon, R. H., & Quinney, N. (2010). *American negotiating behavior: Wheeler-dealers, legal eagles, bullies, and preachers*. Washington DC: US Institute of Peace Press.

Stedman, S. J. (1997). Spoiler problems in peace processes. *International Security, 22*(2), 5–53.

Wittes, T. C. (2005). *How Israelis and Palestinians negotiate: A cross-cultural analysis of the Oslo peace process*. Washington DC: US Institute of Peace Press.

Zartman, I. W. (2001a). Negotiating identity: From metaphor to process. *International Negotiation, 6*(2), 137–140.

Zartman, I. W. (2001b). Timing of peace initiatives: Hurting stalemates and ripe moments. *Ethnopolitics, 1*(1), 8–18.

Zartman, I. W. (2002). What I want to know about negotiation. *International Negotiation, 7*(1), 5–15.

Zartman, I. W., & Kremenyuk, V. (2005). *Peace versus justice: Negotiating forward and backward looking outcomes*. Oxford UK: Rowman and Littlefield Publishers.

Chapter 5
Emotions in e-Negotiations

Michele Griessmair, Patrick Hippmann and Johannes Gettinger

Introduction

Electronically mediated communication (EMC) has become a central part of organizational life (Hedlund et al. 1998; Baltes et al. 2002; Hinds and Kiesler 2002), and also negotiations are increasingly conducted via electronic media instead of traditional face-to-face (f2f) discussions (Loewenstein et al. 2005; Thompson 2005; Holtom and Kenworthy-U'Ren 2006). Whereas first approaches to support negotiations are rooted in decision-related aspects for individual negotiators, the particular characteristics of negotiations called for the development of negotiation-specific tailored support (Kersten and Lai 2007). Therefore, negotiation support systems (NSS) are seen as a branch of decision support systems (DSS) (Arnott and Pervan 2005, 2008) and "constitute a special class of Group Decision Support Systems (GDSS) designed for noncooperative, mixed-motive task situations" (Anson and Jelassi 1990, p. 186). Further innovations in the fields of information and communication technologies and the increasing need to support negotiations between locally separated people resulted in the development of electronic negotiation systems (eNS). An eNS is commonly defined as "software that employs internet technologies and it is deployed on the web for the purpose of facilitating, organizing, supporting and/or automating activities undertaken by the negotiators

M. Griessmair · P. Hippmann
Department of Business Administration, University of Vienna,
Vienna Oskar-Morgenstern-Platz 1, 1090 Vienna, Austria
e-mail: Michele.Griessmair@univie.ac.at

P. Hippmann
e-mail: Patrick.Hippmann@univie.ac.at

J. Gettinger (✉)
Department of Organisational Communication, University of Hohenheim,
70593 Stuttgart, Germany
e-mail: Johannes.Gettinger@wi1.uni-hohenheim.de

B. Martinovsky (ed.), *Emotion in Group Decision and Negotiation*,
Advances in Group Decision and Negotiation 7,
DOI 10.1007/978-94-017-9963-8_5

and/or a third party" (Kersten and Lai 2007, p. 556). Although a number of systems for e-negotiations with focus on different functionalities have been developed (e.g., Rangaswamy and Shell 1997; Kersten and Noronha 1999; Schoop et al. 2003), at a minimum level they all consist of an individual DSS and an electronic communication channel (Lim and Benbasat 1992). Empirical evidence shows that both of these components have an impact on a variety of issues that are crucial in negotiations such as conflict escalation (Friedman and Currall 2003), trust (Rockmann and Northcraft 2008), fairness (Tangirala and Alge 2006), collaborative behavior (Foroughi et al. 1995; Delaney et al. 1997), decision-making accuracy (Hedlund et al. 1998), negotiation outcomes (Lim and Benbasat 1992; Delaney et al. 1997), or postnegotiation satisfaction (Foroughi et al. 1995; Gettinger et al. 2012a).

Initially, eNS were designed to direct negotiators toward more rational decision making and task orientation, as well as to help negotiators to avoid emotional behavior that was considered to be dysfunctional (DeSanctis and Gallupe 1987; Anson and Jelassi 1990; Rangaswamy and Shell 1997; Delaney et al. 1997; Foroughi 1998; Jonassen and Kwon 2001). However, recent theory and research show that emotions play a vital role in negotiations (Morris and Keltner 2000; Van Kleef et al. 2010b) and that eNS should also consider the effects emotions have in negotiations (Derks et al. 2008; Broekens et al. 2010). We argue that both components often implemented in an eNS, the communication and the decision component, influence the amount of communicational cues—the richness of a medium —that can be transmitted, as well as cognition and information processing. These two dimensions can be directly linked to two major streams of research on emotions in negotiation: the affect-cognition perspective and the social functional perspective of emotions (Morris and Keltner 2000) (see Fig. 5.1) (see Chap. 2 in this volume).

The first stream of research, represented by the social functional perspective of emotions, emphasizes the inter-personal effects of emotional expressions. Its focus is on the impact that conveyed emotions have on the receiver's decisions and behavior

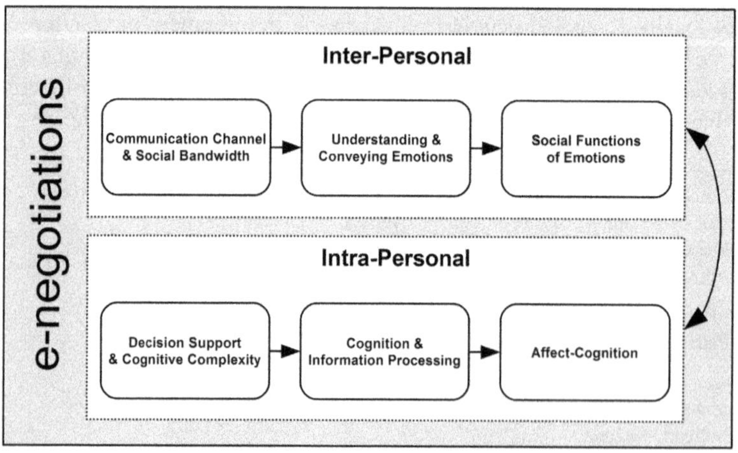

Fig. 5.1 Intra- and inter-personal effects of emotions in e-negotiations

(Keltner and Kring 1998; Morris and Keltner 2000; Van Kleef et al. 2010b). However, in order to fulfill their social functions, emotions must be conveyed and understood correctly. The bandwidth of a communication channel—the possibilities and limitations of expressing emotional and social content—has a direct impact on the degree to which emotions can be encoded and decoded in e-negotiations. For instance, in f2f negotiations a counteroffer can be accompanied by facial expressions, which are argued to be the major carriers of emotional information (Ekman 1993; Knutson 1996). These can indicate anger, happiness, or regret and clearly signal the social intentions of the reaction to the previous offer. When negotiating via an electronic communication channel that does not provide visual access (e.g., e-mail), alternative ways for communicating emotions must be found. If these are not as efficient as or more ambiguous than facial expressions, emotional expressions forfeit their vital functions in coordinating the negotiation interaction.

The second relevant stream, the affect-cognition perspective, addresses the intra-personal effects of emotions—how the emotions experienced by individuals are interrelated to their cognition and information processing (Bower 1981; Isen 1985; Damasio 1994; Loewenstein et al. 2001). The communication and the decision component influence negotiators' information processing capabilities and as a consequence mediate the interplay between affect and cognition. In particular, both components commonly implemented in eNS affect the cognitive complexity of a negotiation. For instance, subtle social information is more difficult to encode and decode in an EMC environment making the interaction process more cognitively demanding for the negotiators. However, eNS also provide functionalities reducing the cognitive load and allow the negotiator to expend more cognitive effort to decode and understand emotions.

In the subsequent sections, we address the linkages of the model proposed in Fig. 5.1. First, we provide an overview on the characteristics of electronic negotiations and how the two commonly implemented support components, text-based communication and analytic decision support, influence the encoding and decoding of emotional content. Subsequently, we describe intra- and inter-personal effects of emotions in negotiations and the extent to which they also hold true in e-negotiations. Finally, we elaborate on how the interplay between affect-cognition and social functions of emotions shapes the process and outcome of negotiations as well as how this relationship is potentially mediated by eNS.

Negotiating in an Electronic Environment: Communication and Decision Making

Whereas initial research in the area of electronically supported negotiations primarily focused on economic outcome dimensions of negotiations (Kersten and Lai 2007; Vetschera et al. 2013), the need to additionally consider socio-emotional factors has already been highlighted in the early stages of eNS research (Anson and

Jelassi 1990; Bui 1994; Foroughi 1998). Furthermore, e-negotiations should not be considered as simple translations of f2f negotiations into an electronic environment. Rather, the use of electronic means to support the decision making and the communication process shapes the negotiators' interaction and in consequence the negotiation process and outcome (Ströbel and Weinhardt 2003; Schoop 2010). In the following, we address the two components of eNS, the communication channel and decision support, and how they affect the way negotiators communicate and make decisions during the negotiation interaction.

Communication Channel and (Social) Bandwidth

Communication in negotiations follows the objectives of satisfying the needs and interests of the parties as well as to create a mutual understanding about the negotiation-relevant terms as a requirement for the execution of the reached agreement (Schoop et al. 2010). Communication quality is shaped by the levels of coherence and comprehension of transmitted information including factual information, ideas, and emotions (communication clarity), behavioral aspects of coordination and reciprocity (communication responsiveness), and mutually positively experienced interaction in terms of ease and pleasantness (communication comfort) (Liu et al. 2010).

In f2f negotiations, the creation of a shared sense of understanding about the communication between negotiators and their shared sense of participation in the conversation, referred to as grounding (Clark and Brennan 1991), is based on six characteristics: (i) co-presence within the same surroundings, (ii) visibility of the other negotiator, (iii) audibility of the other negotiator, (iv) co-temporality of expressed communication utterances, (v) simultaneity of sent and received messages, and (vi) sequentiality of turn-taking. In contrast, EMC is characterized by one-directional and intermittent communication—and thus is described as being of lower bandwidth than f2f communication. Most importantly for the present context, due to the lack of visibility and audibility of some communication media employed in e-negotiations, the major carriers of emotional cues available in f2f negotiations are missing. Hence, it is argued that the lower social bandwidth of EMC channels used in e-negotiations limits the extent of, or alters the way socio-emotional information can be transmitted and understood by the counterpart (e.g., Walther 1992, 1996). This, in turn, has a direct effect on the degree to which emotions can fulfill their social functions in e-negotiations.

The communication channel, however, does influence not only how (social) information is transmitted but also information processing by adding the communication features of (i) reviewability and (ii) revisability not available in f2f communication (Friedman and Currall 2003). Reviewability refers to the negotiators' ability to go through the entire communication record at any time, whereas revisability allows negotiators to work over messages several times before sending them to the counterpart. Moreover, an important characteristic of EMC is whether it is conducted synchronously (e.g., chat) or asynchronously (e.g., e-mail). Synchronous EMC is more comparable to f2f communication as both parties are present at the same time at the virtual bargaining table (Pesendorfer and Koeszegi 2006). Therefore, synchronous EMC is characterized not only by reviewability and revisability, but also by three characteristics present in f2f negotiations, namely co-presence, co-temporality, and simultaneity (Pesendorfer and Koeszegi 2006). In contrast, asynchronous communication does not include the aspects of real time and timely delays between exchanged messages are common. The slower turn-taking tempo in asynchronous communication "allows negotiators as much time between messages as they need to calculate the values of various outcomes and to consider the best counteroffers, and complete transcript of the communication allows for more careful information acquisition" (Moore et al. 1999, p. 39f). Consequently, intricate arguments are only effective in an asynchronous communication setting because the receiver has the possibility to reflect on and digest the arguments. Similarly, deceptive tactics are easier to use in asynchronous communication as it allows to carefully plan the deceptive message (Rockmann and Northcraft 2008). Research on time pressure, which may also be a consequence of the faster or slower turn-taking tempo, has further shown that when not under time pressure negotiators are slower at making concessions and make higher demands, increase integrative tactics, rely less on stereotypes, and are more likely to revise unfounded fixed-pie perceptions (Carnevale et al. 1993; Druckman 1994; De Dreu and Carnevale 2003). Thus, the communication channel does influence not only socio-emotional aspects but also information processing and thereby the interplay between affect and cognition in e-negotiations.

Cues Filtered in or Cues Filtered Out?

One of the primary questions relating to emotions in e-negotiations is whether they can be effectively transmitted at all given that the meaning of messages is determined to a considerable extent by nonverbal and para-verbal cues (DePaulo and Friedman 1998). Early theories addressing socio-emotional issues in EMC such as the lack of social context cues theory (Sproull and Kiesler 1986), social presence theory (Short et al. 1976), and the media richness theory (Daft and Lengel 1984, 1986; Daft et al. 1987) all postulated that the lower social bandwidth of EMC—the restricted number of different cues that can be used for communication—results in a "cues filtered-out" interaction.

Due to their textual nature and the lack of physical presence, most forms of EMC are devoid of these additional cues that serve important functions in encoding and decoding emotional communication. Furthermore, because of the potential lack of visibility and physical proximity, cues about and provided by the social context and the social presence are filtered out (Short et al. 1976; Sproull and Kiesler 1986). This results in reduced awareness of the other, a diminished appreciation of the inter-personal aspects of the interaction, and an increased social distance. Accordingly, early research reported that compared to f2f communication, EMC is less friendly, more depersonalized and hostile, as well as more task-oriented (Kiesler et al. 1984; Siegel et al. 1986; Sproull and Kiesler 1986; McGuire et al. 1987; Rice and Love 1987). Accordingly, e-negotiations should allow only for a limited exchange of socio-emotional and relational information, limit the possibilities to convey and recognize emotions, and alter the emotional climate of the negotiation.

The above-mentioned theories all assume that conveying emotional and relational information in an interaction is bound to the ability of a channel to transmit specific cues. This was soon called into question by a number of scholars positing that the characteristics of the communication channel are but one factor affecting the degree to which emotions can be conveyed and recognized (Lee 1994; Walther et al. 1994; Walther 1995; Zack and McKenney 1995; Carlson and Zmud 1999). Thus, although having a lower bandwidth, e-negotiations might be as suitable as f2f negotiations for establishing inter-personal relationships and exchanging socio-emotional messages. One crucial factor proposed by Walther's (1992) social information processing (SIP) perspective is time. Different communication channels do not differ with regard to the "amount of social information" but the "rate of social information" that can be exchanged (Walther 1996, p. 10). Accordingly, interacting in a computer-mediated environment does not inhibit but merely decelerate the transmission of socio-emotional information as it "forces both task-related and social information into a single verbal/linguistic channel" (Walther 1994, p. 476). Thus, e-negotiations do not necessarily hinder the exchange of emotions and their respective relational and informational functions but rather require more "real time" and/or additional media-specific communication strategies to convey them. Individuals also adapt to and expand a specific channel in order to filter cues back in (Walther 1996; Carlson and Zmud 1999). Hence, the bandwidth of a medium is determined not only by the medium itself, as posited by media richness theory, but also by the user (Carlson and Zmud 1999)—the more experienced negotiators are with EMC, the more effective they are in encoding and decoding messages and enriching the communication channel to convey socio-emotional content. Thus, although the medium may impose certain constraints on the interaction process, it is the way people make use of the electronic bargaining table that primarily shapes the negotiation interaction (cf. Boudourides 2001).

Conveying Emotional Cues in e-Negotiations

Despite the constraints imposed by a low-bandwidth medium, emotions can be communicated in an electronic environment. The most obvious way of expressing emotions in text-based EMC is indeed the direct and deliberate use of affective language and words such as the expression "this offer makes me really angry" (Van Kleef et al. 2004a, p. 513). Yet, there are also more subtle ways of conveying emotional information in EMC that are specific to the channel and function as substitute to facial expressions and vocal intonation in f2f interactions (see Chap. 6 in this volume).

First, e-negotiators can expand the communication channel to convey emotions by using emotext (Jaffe et al. 1999). Emotext can include intentional misspelling (e.g., "This offer is sooooo bad."), lexical surrogates (e.g., "hmmmm" to convey hesitation and thoughtfulness), strategic capitalization (e.g., "This offer is NOT FAIR AT ALL."), grammatical markers (e.g., "!??" in the sentence "Do you consider this offer as fair!??"), or emoticons (e.g., :)) (Jaffe et al. 1999). Other possibilities to transmit nonverbal emotional cues are the length, frequency, and timing of the messages (Walther and Tidwell 1995; Liu et al. 2001). The time of sending and receiving a message, the so-called chronemics, can convey information about dominance or submissiveness, as well as the degree of intimacy or liking (Walther and Tidwell 1995). For instance, a slow reply indicates more dominance than a fast reply, especially when task-oriented and sent at night-time. Also, a slow reply to a task-oriented message may convey a low degree of affection. Furthermore, both higher frequency and longer duration of message exchanges result in stronger impression formations regarding the counterpart (Liu et al. 2001). With respect to length and frequency of messages, Barry and Fulmer (2004) also speak of willful "underutilization" of a channel's possibilities. For instance, short messages and long response times when negotiating via e-mail signal negative affect. Furthermore, emotionally positive negotiations are characterized by a higher number of exchanged words than emotionally negative interactions (Hancock et al. 2007).

Whereas emotext and willful underutilization are not direct but primarily deliberate expressions of emotions in e-negotiations, negotiators "[...] often imply more information in a proposition than their words suggest or than the surface forms of their utterances denote" (Gibbons et al. 1992, p. 159f). Thus, even if a statement is not explicitly emotional or does not contain electronic paralanguage, it nevertheless conveys an emotional layer based on its content and the way the content is formulated. Furthermore, e-negotiators' language use does not only allow inferences about their abilities and intentions but also discloses information about their emotions (Sokolova and Szpakowicz 2006). This further implies that the lower the bandwidth of a communication channel, the more important becomes the role of language features in deriving emotional meaning from a message. For instance, the statements "Your offer is simply unacceptable!" and "Unfortunately, we cannot accept this offer." both inform the counterpart that the sender of the offer is unable or unwilling to accept the offer. However, despite having an identical factual content and no directly expressed emotions, the two messages differ in terms of valance and arousal. Whereas the former contains a certain degree of anger and frustration, the latter rather conveys regret or sadness (Griessmair and Koeszegi 2009). Accordingly, messages do not only consist of the factual content that informs the counterpart about what a negotiator wants, but contain multiple communicative layers (Watzlawick et al. 1967; Schulz von Thun 1981). The different layers neither require distinct messages nor have to be expressed explicitly, but are conveyed simultaneously within the same message. For instance, the type of offers negotiators make and how they are formulated convey not only the factual information about the offer (e.g., price) but at the same time how the sender relates to the receiver (e.g., feelings of dominance, feelings of submission). A more detailed investigation of this phenomenon is provided by linguistic approaches and works based on attribution theory (Weiner 1985). For instance, Schroth et al. (2005) showed that negotiators attribute emotional content to specific negotiation utterances. In particular, statements including negative attributions ("you are being unfair"), telling the counterparts what to do or what they can't do ("you need to give me a better deal than this one," or "no, that's impossible"), appealing to higher sources or blaming ("from a legal standpoint," or "my division is more important than yours"), as well as labeling the own behavior as superior ("I'm being reasonable") communicate and trigger negative emotions. Furthermore, linguistic features of written language such as polarization, immediacy, intensity, lexical diversity, and powerful or powerless style convey information of a negotiator's feelings to the counterpart (Gibbons et al. 1992; Sokolova and Szpakowicz 2006). For instance, language immediacy signals the degree to which negotiators wish to move closer to the counterpart and shows positive or negative directions of the negotiators' emotions. Emotions conveyed via language immediacy are not expressed explicitly but conveyed via subtle linguistic indicators such as whether a personal pronoun or a content noun is employed or the use of "there" and "he and I" rather than "here" and "we" (Gibbons et al. 1992; Sokolova and Szpakowicz 2006).

More subtle and implicit ways of communicating emotions in e-negotiations, however, also result in more ambiguity. For instance, individuals diverge greatly regarding their emotional perceptions or interpretations of e-mails (Byron and Baldridge 2005). Individuals also tend to be overly optimistic regarding their abilities to judge and interpret the emotional tone of e-mails (Kruger et al. 2005). Furthermore, respondents interpreting the emotional tone of e-mail mock-ups enriched with an emoticon were not directly influenced via the emoticons. Emoticons rather complemented message interpretations and intensified emotionally negative message interpretations (Walther and D'Addario 2001). Similarly, e-mail communication is supposed to suffer from neutrality and negativity effects (Byron 2008). Accordingly, whereas emotionally positive messages tend to be perceived as more neutral than intended by the composer, emotionally negative messages tend to be perceived as more intensely negative than intended.

Decision Support and Cognitive Complexity

The second component of eNS primarily considers negotiators' decision making processes and impacts the interplay between affect and cognition during the interaction process. The most common approach to supply decision support is the provision of analytic decision support and the visualization of decision-relevant information. An analytic approach uses formal representations and models to help negotiators achieve their goals on an individual and/or a negotiation group level (Sebenius 1992; Raiffa et al. 2002). From an economic perspective, Pareto efficiency of agreements is one core outcome criterion (Tripp and Sondak 1992; Raiffa et al. 2002). However, research argues that human decision makers have problems exploiting the full potential of conflict situations (Neale and Bazerman 1992; Sebenius 1992; Raiffa et al. 2002). As complexity increases, human negotiators face problems comprehending and evaluating all possible solutions (Anson and Jelassi 1990; Foroughi 1998). As the relationship between the level of information processing and the environmental complexity has the shape of an inverted "U" (Schroeder et al. 1967), negotiators face the problem of information overload in particularly complex conflict situations. Therefore, systems providing decision support to their users are seen as an extension of human mental abilities (Kersten and Lai 2007). While the functionalities of systems providing analytic decision support are still expanding, some eNS nowadays provide analytic decision support throughout the entire negotiation process (Kersten and Lai 2010). These systems elicit the individual negotiators' preferences and provide feedback about the exchanged offers in form of scorings (e.g., utility values) indicating to what extent the offers reflect the negotiators' individual preferences. Furthermore, several systems additionally offer a graphical presentation of the exchanged offers based on the focal user's preferences. A graphical presentation of the negotiation history gives an overview of the progress of the negotiation in terms of exchanged offers and reflects the dynamics of the supported negotiation (Weber et al. 2006). Such a problem presentation can serve as external information storage so that not all relevant information has to be kept into human memory (Zhang 1997). Furthermore, graphical decision aids aim to enable negotiators to "read-off" information such as whether the exchanged offers show a trend toward convergence or divergence. This process is called "computational offloading" and refers to the reduced cognitive effort to make informationally equivalent decisions (Scaife and Rogers 1996).

Empirical studies investigating synchronous negotiations show that a decision component alone without communication support is sufficient to improve objective outcome dimensions such as joint outcomes and the fairness of the final agreement (Delaney et al. 1997; Lim and Yang 2007). Similarly, the use of an eNS, consisting of a communication and an analytic decision support component, leads to higher joint (integrative) outcomes (Foroughi et al. 1995; Rangaswamy and Shell 1997), and more balanced (fairer) outcomes (Foroughi et al. 1995) in comparison with f2f negotiations. However, the use of an analytic decision component does not only shape objective dimensions, but also influences the negotiators' perceptions. Delaney et al. (1997) report that the combined use of decision and communication support compared to a DSS only results in a higher postnegotiation satisfaction in high and low conflict treatments. Furthermore, negotiators using communication and decision support express a higher postnegotiation satisfaction in low and high conflicting treatments (Foroughi et al. 1995). While negotiators perceive the same level of collaborative climate independently of their negotiation mode and the conflict level, negotiators in the f2f setting report to have experienced a higher negative climate in low conflict negotiations (Foroughi et al. 1995). Similar results have been found in asynchronous negotiations. Adding decision support additionally to the communication components leads to proportionally fewer exchanges of preference information, more infrequent usage of hard tactics, and more positive affective behavior (Koeszegi et al. 2006). Furthermore, negotiators also make proportionally more (integrative) package offers as well as concessions and reach more agreements. Similarly, the additional use of a decision component leads negotiators to express significantly more thoughts in negotiations (Schoop et al. 2014). However, the use of an analytic decision component decreases the post-settlement satisfaction of negotiators with relational aspects such as relationship building and mutual concern (Schoop et al. 2014). Vetschera et al. (2006) also found that the perceived usefulness of an analytic component in asynchronously conducted e-negotiations is positively related to the negotiators' overall subjective assessment of the used eNS.

Regarding visual analytical support based on utility values of exchanged offers in graphical form, Weber et al. (2006) compared asynchronous e-negotiations with and without a graphical presentation of utility values based on the exchanged offers. They report that negotiators require on average 334 words less in their text messages to reach an agreement. The use of such an additional graphical tool seems to help negotiators to clarify and support their arguments so that they require less direct communication. Similarly, another study investigating the effect of presenting the utility values in either tabular or graphical format to users found that negotiators provided with a graphical representation of the negotiation history engage in more integrative negotiation behavior and express a higher postnegotiation satisfaction (Gettinger et al. 2012b). Therefore, graphical decision aids based on analytic considerations can reduce the level of information ambiguity and the reproduced task complexity (Gettinger and Koeszegi 2014).

Overall, negotiating in an electronically mediated environment poses some challenges for negotiators in conveying and understanding emotions. However, e-negotiations also have some distinctive advantages over f2f negotiations resulting from reviewability, revisability, and the potential slower turn-taking tempo of the interaction. Furthermore, providing an adequate decision support component can reduce the cognitive complexity for the negotiators. Although these components were primarily designed to aid negotiators in dealing with rational-economic issues, research has shown that they also impact other crucial factors in negotiations such as communication patterns as well as socio-psychological and emotional dimensions.

Intra- and Inter-Personal Effects of Emotions in e-Negotiations

As discussed in the previous section, EMC alters the way emotions are used and transmitted, and negotiating (a)synchronously or (not) employing a DSS impacts negotiators' cognitive processes and, in consequence, their emotional experience. In the following sections, we provide an overview on the social functional and the affect-cognition perspective of emotions in negotiations and discuss whether the respective propositions of and findings derived from these perspectives also hold true in an e-negotiation setting. Put differently, we address the influence of emotions on the negotiator who is experiencing them (i.e., intra-personal effects), and the effect of expressed emotions on the counterpart (i.e., inter-personal effects) in e-negotiations. Finally, we outline how the two perspectives work together in shaping the negotiation process and how negotiating in an electronic environment might alter their interplay and, as a result, negotiation dynamics and outcomes.

Emotions and Social Functions: Inter-Personal Effects

The inter-personal approach investigates emotions as a social rather than individual phenomenon (Parkinson 1996; Keltner and Kring 1998; Morris and Keltner 2000; Fischer and Van Kleef 2010; Van Kleef et al. 2010b) (see Chap. 2 in this volume). This so-called social functional approach primarily addresses the relational functions of emotions and the effects that expressed emotions have on the interaction partner. Accordingly, emotions are conceptualized as "other-directed, intentional (although not always consciously controlled) communicative acts that organize social interactions" by communicating "social intentions, desired courses of actions, and role-related expectations and behaviors" (Morris and Keltner 2000, p. 13). In the context of negotiations, at least three emotional functions can influence the course of the interaction (Keltner and Kring 1998; Morris and Keltner 2000; Barry et al. 2004; Van Kleef and Côté 2007): (i) emotions are a central source of information, (ii) can serve as incentives or deterrents, and (iii) are likely to evoke reciprocal or complementary emotions in the counterpart.

Informational and Incentive Functions of Emotions in Negotiations

Negotiations are typically characterized by uncertainty about the counterpart and that negotiators must rely on a number of cues to decide which strategy to employ and which step to take next (Van Kleef et al. 2010b). The emotions displayed by negotiators provide valuable insights about their attitudes and intentions, their orientation toward, and how they perceive the status of a relationship as well as their willingness to agree and whether they conform with the counterpart's behavior (Daly 1991; Knutson 1996). Factual information such as offers and counteroffers is put into context by the accompanying emotional expressions that aid the receiver in making sense of the received information. Thus, emotions have an important informational, feedback, or signaling function (Keltner and Kring 1998; Morris and Keltner 2000; Barry et al. 2004; Pietroni et al. 2008). For instance, the display of anger may signal the importance of an issue, that negotiators' limits have been reached, or that they blame the counterpart for frustrating their goals (Van Kleef et al. 2004a; Schroth et al. 2005). Happiness, on the other hand, might indicate that the counterpart is satisfied with the progress of the negotiation but also that his or her limits are not yet reached and that a negotiator may be willing to, for example, make more concessions (Van Kleef et al. 2004a, b). Analogous to the informational function, in their incentive function emotions can serve as positive or negative reinforcers for other individuals' social behavior (Cacioppo and Gardner 1999; Fischer and Roseman 2007). Negotiators expressing positive emotions such as happiness or gratitude reward their counterparts for the performed behavior, increasing the likelihood that they will continue exhibiting congruous actions. Negative emotions, on the other hand, serve as punishment for a counterpart's undesired behavior, encouraging an adjustment of the performed course of action. In their function as incentives or deterrents, emotions help to regulate the negotiation interaction.

Emotional Contagion and Reciprocity in Negotiations

Extensive evidence in negotiation research shows that negotiators tend to respond-in-kind to their counterparts and investigate action–reaction sequences and their consequences in negotiations (Olekalns and Weingart 2003; Weingart and Olekalns 2004; Adair and Brett 2005). A similar phenomenon referred to as emotional contagion or emotional reciprocity is also observed with regard to affect (Hatfield et al. 1993; Friedman et al. 2004) (see Chap. 1 in this volume). Emotional contagion designates a process of automatic transfer of affect between interacting individuals (Hatfield et al. 1993, 1994). In other words, when emotional contagion occurs individuals start to feel the emotions expressed by the counterpart resulting in an affective synchronization (Barsade 2002). Emotional reciprocity is limited to the reciprocation of emotional expressions and does not necessarily include that the emotions are also evoked in the counterpart. Indeed, co-occurrence of these two phenomena is more likely; however, "contagion is not necessary to generate emotional reciprocity" (Friedman et al. 2004, p. 374) and vice versa. Furthermore, emotional contagion is more likely to occur in interactions which are characterized by high social and task interdependence (Hatfield et al. 1994; Bartel and Saavedra 2000). As in negotiations the parties are mutually dependent in achieving their goals and have to continuously adapt and adjust their behavior to each other, negotiations can be expected to be characterized by frequent emotional convergence. Finally, affective transfer is generally more likely with high-arousal and negatively valenced emotions (Bartel and Saavedra 2000; Rozin and Royzman 2001; Barsade 2002). Accordingly, it is likely to be the case in negotiations that spirals of negative affect are more easily triggered and maintained than positive dynamics.

The Social Functions of Emotions in e-Negotiations

By fulfilling the three aforementioned social functions, "emotions provide structure to social interactions, guiding, evoking, and motivating the actions of individuals in interactions in ways that enable individuals to meet their respective goals"

(Keltner and Kring 1998, p. 3). A number of studies investigated the functions and effects of expressed emotions in an EMC setting in which the negotiating parties had no visual access and communicated with each other only via text. These studies primarily focused on anger and happiness and showed, for example, that negotiators tended to concede more when the counterpart exhibited anger rather than happiness (Van Kleef et al. 2004a, b). The emotions expressed by their counterparts are used as information to infer their limits and adjust the own offers accordingly (Van Kleef et al. 2004b). This relation is, however, mediated by information, appropriateness, and power. Studies conducted via EMC show that negotiators are more influenced by the counterparts' emotional expressions when the informational value of emotions increases and they are motivated and able to consider them, for instance, when the offer is equivocal and they are not under time pressure (Van Kleef et al. 2004a, b; Van Kleef and Côté 2007). Negotiators also tend to retaliate rather than concede when the expression of anger is considered inappropriate (Van Kleef and Côté 2007). The counterparts' reaction to expressions of anger and its effect on value claiming and reaching an agreement is further dependent on whether the counterparts are vulnerable and the quality of their alternatives (Friedman et al. 2004; Sinaceur and Tiedens 2006; Van Kleef and Côté 2007). Research on the information function of emotions shows that providing affective rather than solely numeric statements increases the impact of a negotiator's toughness, respectability, and appearance of the counterpart's demands and concessions (Pietroni et al. 2007). Furthermore, emotional expressions influence the counterpart's perception of the other's priorities, which in turn results in an adaptation of the pursued negotiation strategy (Pietroni et al. 2008). Specifically, whereas expressing happiness about the counterpart's high priority issue and anger about the low-priority issue reduces fixed-pie perceptions and increases integrative strategies, the opposite emotional pattern amplifies the bias and reduces integrative behavior. The primer informs the counterpart about the possibility that her own high priority issue may be the other's low-priority issue. This information allows for making more differentiated demands and concessions in order to increase the negotiation pie. Conversely, expressing anger about the counterpart's high priority issue conveys the information that both parties value the same issue the most, resulting in zero-sum bargaining.

Only a few studies have directly assessed emotional contagion or reciprocity in e-negotiations. However, existing research indicates that this phenomenon also occurs in electronically mediated negotiation contexts. Indirect evidence stems from linguistic analyses showing that negotiators tend to reciprocate language and linguistic styles (Taylor and Thomas 2008). Furthermore, individuals are able to detect their partners' emotions, and negative emotional states tend to spill over from one interaction partner to the other when communicating synchronously via EMC (Hancock et al. 2008). Consequently, emotional contagion does not only take place when nonverbal cues such as facial expressions are possible but also occur in a cue-impoverished environment. Thus, also in e-negotiations, negotiators have the tendency to mimic the counterpart's text-based emotional expressions. Further research in this area shows that in asynchronous group negotiations via e-mail only one individual's emotional expressions are sufficient to increase positive or negative emotions of the other team members (Cheshin et al. 2011). As previously pointed out, strong and negatively valenced emotions such as anger are more likely to be contagious or reciprocated and, in consequence, may trigger a downward spiral of negative affect more easily. Similarly, in online auctions a single negative comment plays a more important role than many positive comments (Nielek et al. 2010). Furthermore, also in online auctions there is evidence for the reciprocation of negative affect and the emergence of a downward spiral as dominant pattern. Similarly, Friedman et al. (2004) showed that expressions of anger in online mediations trigger an angry response by the counterpart which, in turn, lowers the likelihood of resolving the conflict. Congruous with literature on response-in-kind behavior in negotiations (Olekalns and Weingart 2003; Weingart and Olekalns 2004; Adair and Brett 2005), emotional action–reaction sequences are not limited to reciprocation, a reinforcement of the ongoing emotional patterns, but also include complementary and structural sequences. In negotiations the expression of embarrassment, regret, or guilt after having violated a social norm may evoke the complementary emotion of forgiveness in the counterpart (Keltner et al. 1997; Van Kleef et al. 2010). Similarly, negotiators may also mismatch each other's affective expression by, for instance, countering anger with happiness. Displaying such complementary or structural emotions can aid negotiators to restore their relationship (Keltner et al. 1997; Van Kleef et al. 2010) and are vital for breaking negative cycles of reciprocity in negotiations (Brett et al. 1998). However, anti-complementary emotional pairs such as countering regret with anger may trigger a negative emotional dynamic and are detrimental for the maintenance of the relationship (Butt et al. 2005).

Overall, these studies provide evidence that major carriers of emotions such as facial expressions or intonation are not required to evoke similar emotions in the counterpart. Therefore, emotional contagion and reciprocity including their potential positive and negative consequences are phenomena that have also to be taken into consideration when negotiating online, even in asynchronous, text-based settings. Furthermore, the studies provide strong support that also in e-negotiations emotions coordinate the social interaction by providing information to the counterpart and act as an incentive or deterrent. However, these studies have primarily considered the deliberate and explicit use of emotional language and words. Other, more subtle ways of conveying emotions that are specific to a communication channel, as described in Sect. "Conveying Emotional Cues in e-Negotiations", are less researched. Only a limited number of studies have specifically addressed how emotions are implicitly conveyed in e-negotiations and how they shape the negotiation process and outcome. Research by Sokalova and colleagues (Sokolova et al. 2004; Sokolova and Szpakowicz 2006, 2007) showed that language patterns such as immediacy are valuable indicators for discriminating successful and unsuccessful e-negotiations. For instance, they found that "you" corresponds to politeness in e-negotiations in which an agreement was reached and to aggressiveness in failed e-negotiations. They also showed that "I can accept" appears three times more often in successful than in unsuccessful negotiations, whereas "you accept my" is used twice as often in unsuccessful than in successful negotiations. Similarly, Griessmair and Koeszegi (2009) investigated the emotional connotation of messages exchanged in e-negotiations as well as different formulations of logrolling statements. Although trade-offs and logrolling are the primary means for increasing joint outcome and a hallmark of integrative bargaining, the authors show that their effectiveness depends on the wording. For instance, whereas "If we both could agree on [issue Y], we would be able to accept [issue X]" is formulated as potential acceptance with a request, "We cannot accept [issue X] unless we get [issue Y] in turn" employs conditional language combined with a rejection to express the same factual content. A commanding tone or conditional language such as "you accept my" or "unless we get" is associated with attacking face (Brett et al. 2007) (see Chap. 4 in this volume) and a negative emotional undertone (Schroth et al. 2005). Finally, the aforementioned study by Cheshin et al. (2011), investigating emotional contagion in e-negotiations, also addressed the relation between factual content and conveyed emotions. Whereas communicating flexibility was found to be associated with happiness, expressing resoluteness, not giving in, and acting tough were found to be perceived as displays of anger. Furthermore, when the behavior and the emotion communicated via text were incongruent (e.g., the words are pleasant but the behavior is uncompromising), negative emotions were found to be elicited in the other team members.

Emotions and Cognitive Processes: Intra-Personal Effects

Whereas the previous section addresses the effects of expressed emotions on the counterpart, the current section is concerned with the effects of emotions on the individual who actually experiences them. Research in the tradition of this so-called affect-cognition approach shows that emotions are inextricably linked with cognitive information processing. Hence, emotions "color" cognitive processes and influence an individual's experiences, perceptions, and subsequent behaviors (Morris and Keltner 2000) (see Chaps. 1 and 2 in this volume). This assumption is discussed subsequently by addressing the questions of how emotions are tied to a negotiator's memory and judgments, how emotions provide intra-individual information functions, and whether cognitive processes and information processing are dependent on the type of perceived and experienced emotions. A number of theories provide an explanation of how emotions and cognitive processes are interrelated. Martinovski and Mao (2009), for example, discuss several theoretical contributions that influenced advancements of research in this field such as appraisal theory (e.g., Smith and Ellsworth 1985; Lazarus and Smith 1988; Scherer 1999) or Theory of Mind (Martinovski and Marsella 2005; Martinovski 2010) (see Chap. 6 in this volume). The present discussion puts a stronger focus on other theoretical concepts that are more closely tied to the affect-cognition perspective, in particular Bower's Semantic-Network Theory (Bower 1981), the Mood as Information Model (Schwarz and Clore 1983), and the Affect Infusion Model (Forgas 1995).

The interconnection of emotions and memory is addressed by Bower's Semantic-Network Theory (Bower 1981). The theory proposes that the judgment of the current situation occurs within a network of semantic and emotional memories. Thus, current information, experiences, or events are also judged on the basis of their emotional similarity to past situations. Hence, related memories (of related situations) that were stored in memory under similar emotional conditions are argued to have a strong impact on the interpretation of the current situation. Similarly, the somatic marker hypothesis postulates that the assessment of decision-making tasks, and hence the process of decision making itself, is influenced by past events that took place under comparable emotional conditions (Damasio 1994). For example, repeated negotiations with the same counterpart may induce positive emotions if past negotiation encounters with her were satisfactory or pleasant. In addition, emotionally rich information tends to be remembered and recalled more easily than more fact-based information. Hence, if negotiators express strong anger or happiness regarding an issue under negotiation, the opponent may be more attentive to this issue and attach more value to it. This also means that it will be recalled more easily in the remainder of the negotiation process. Thus, emotions tend to have an important impact on information recall, learning, and situational interpretations (Forgas and George 2001).

Moreover, according to the mood-as-information model, a negotiator's judgments are contingent on mood as intra-individual information (Schwarz and Clore 1983; Schwarz 1990, 2000). In particular, it states that negotiators use emotions that they experience or perceive to evaluate the current situation (Schwarz and Clore 1983; Schwarz 1990). Whereas positive emotions favor a positive situational interpretation, the opposite holds true for negative emotions (Keltner and Haidt 1999). For example, if negotiators are happy or pleased, they tend to perceive their environment as more positive and judge the information or offer that they receive from their counterpart in a more favorable way. In addition, also anticipated future emotional experiences or perceptions are believed to be judged and used in terms of their informational value when evaluating current situations and making decisions (Schwarz 2000). For example, when a potential agreement seems out of reach for the negotiators, they transfer their future unhappiness or anger to the current situation and judge it in a more negative light. An expected concession as reaction to a negotiator's own concession, on the other hand, may result in a more positive judgment of the current situation as a result of the anticipated happiness. The affect infusion model (AIM; Forgas 1995) incorporates the theories outlined above and additionally addresses when emotions are a more or less important source for decision making: The more motivated negotiators are to invest cognitive resources in a willful search for, interpretation of, and use of information, the more they may be induced to become deliberatively attentive to emotional perceptions, experiences, or information. Similarly, the EASI model (Van Kleef et al. 2010b) posits that the way individuals cognitively process emotions and subsequently act depends on their epistemic motivation, i.e., their willingness "to develop and maintain a rich and accurate understanding of the world" (Van Kleef et al. 2004b, p. 511).

Several studies confirm the relationship between affect and cognition as well as its effect on subsequent negotiation behavior. Positive emotions can, for example, increase negotiators' confidence and optimism, as well as impact their performance evaluation of the negotiation process and outcome (Kramer et al. 1993). Furthermore, negotiators in an emotionally positive condition may set higher negotiation goals (Baron 1990) and may have higher negotiation expectations (Yifeng et al. 2008). In contrast, intra-individual anger induces more dominating behaviors (Butt et al. 2005). Negative emotions may, however, also bias a negotiator in a positive way. Experienced negative emotions can increase negotiators' awareness about their own violations of social norms and can motivate negotiators to change their course of thinking and their subsequent behaviors (Forgas 1998). Moreover, negotiators with low epistemic motivation tend to relate the counterpart's expression of anger to the person rather than the task. This is not the case for negotiators with high epistemic motivation because they assess the displayed emotions more carefully and consider their deeper implications (Van Kleef et al. 2010a). Similarly, in the context of EMC, positive emotions result in more integrative bargaining (Carnevale 2008), and anger leads to more distributive positioning and competition. A direct test of affect infusion and epistemic motivation is provided by a study showing that negotiators were only affected by their counterparts' expressed emotions when they were able and motivated to consider them —when they had a low (vs. high) need for cognitive closure, were under low (vs. high) time pressure, and had low (vs. high) power (Van Kleef et al. 2004b).

The Interplay of Affect and Cognition in e-Negotiations

Cognitive resources play a central role for the experience, perception, and communication of emotions (Blascovich 1992). The global cognitive capacity that individuals possess is used to assess or judge internal as well as external stimuli (Feldman 1995). Thus, the less attention individuals (need to) pay to external stimuli (e.g., to search for information, or to formulate trade-offs), the more they can devote to internal stimuli (e.g., to judge offers, behaviors, and emotions, or to think about and use emotions more willfully). Consequently, if eNS provide a less cognitively demanding environment, the supported negotiators may redeploy more cognitive resources to intra-individual processes and activities. In line with channel expansion theory (Carlson and Zmud 1999), eNS may thus also be regarded as tools that enable negotiators to expand or enrich the limited set of communication cues that are available to them in lower-bandwidth communication environments. When viewed in the light of emotion regulation literature (e.g., Richards and Gross 2000; Ochsner et al. 2002; Côté 2005; Wadlinger and Isaacowitz 2011), eNS may then mitigate more uninhibited and extreme emotions, or enable negotiators to (better) focus their attention on specific aspects of the negotiation problem or process. Importantly, while literature on emotion regulation argues that the deployment of cognitive resources to certain activities, and hence the regulation of emotions, can be learned, a provision of decision support would mean that the regulation of emotions can also be supported by an eNS. Consequently, the use of an eNS and a decision support component reducing the cognitive load for the negotiator may increase the negotiators' ability to regulate (e.g., suppress or amplify) emotions more willfully. Providing negotiators with decision support may thus increase their "epistemic ability", i.e., their ability to increase their epistemic motivation, which then influences the way negotiators (can) cognitively deal with and use emotions. In the following we elaborate on the mediating effects of eNS on emotions by distinguishing between two potentially different (and opposing) cognitive settings: situations of higher cognitive complexity and situations of lower cognitive complexity.

e-Negotiations and Emotions in Settings of High Cognitive Complexity

Whenever e-negotiations are conducted via synchronous rather than asynchronous communication, and/or are not supported by a decision support component, negotiators need to invest more cognitive resources to deal with external stimuli. As a consequence, negotiators either increase their cognitive effort or focus their cognitive resources on certain activities while ignoring others and make use of mental shortcuts and heuristics. Empirical findings based on the media naturalness hypothesis (Kock 2005) showed that cognitive effort and communication ambiguity were higher in quasi-synchronous EMC than in f2f communication (Kock 2007). The EMC condition also led to a reduction in the fluency of communication and an increase in message encoding effort (Kock 2007). Investigations of flaming in instant-messaging negotiations (Johnson et al. 2008, 2009) show that negotiators who engage in flaming were less likely to reach an agreement and concluded that the intra-individual management (or regulation) of anger is important for the mitigation of flaming and its negative consequences. Johnson and Cooper (2009) further found that communication via instant-messaging was less emotionally positive than communication via telephone.

These results suggest that negotiators may be less cognitively able to control emotional processes or behaviors in environments of higher cognitive complexity and are also more influenced by their emotional experience (McKenna and Bargh 2000). As a result, negotiators may engage in more normatively inadequate, explicit, intense, or extreme (emotional) behaviors (Kiesler and Sproull 1992; Thompson and Nadler 2002; Friedman et al. 2004) than they would in situations of lower cognitive complexity. Moreover, Walther (1996) explicates that EMC environments can foster "hyperpersonal communication" (p. 17): When negotiators have a limited amount of social information at their disposal, they tend to consider these information in their judgments more than actually warranted and make "overattributions". Accordingly, if negotiators focus their attention and cognitive resources on specific issues, they may regard and interpret these issues as more important than others. Negotiators also rely more strongly on these issues when making inferences about the situation and the counterpart as well as when taking subsequent actions. For example, if a negotiator's counterpart uses a dominating language style, and the focal negotiator's attention is drawn to this piece of information, then she might overattribute this input and judge the opponent as angry or aggressive, even if the opponent's offers are fair and generous.

e-Negotiations and Emotions in Settings of Low Cognitive Complexity

Whenever e-negotiations are conducted via asynchronous rather than synchronous communication and/or are supported by a DSS, negotiators need to invest less cognitive resources to deal with external stimuli. As a consequence, eNS may help to reduce a negotiator's cognitive effort, or, put differently, an eNS may help to increase negotiators' ownership of their cognitive resources (Silver 1988; Singh and Ginzberg 1996; Foroughi 1998; Weber et al. 2006; Kersten and Lai 2007). Research comparing asynchronous e-mail and synchronous f2f negotiations (Morris et al. 2002) finds rapport building via emotional disclosures is more difficult to achieve with e-mail communication. If e-mail negotiators, however, talk to each other over the phone prior to the start of the negotiation, the negotiators managed to build more or a better rapport. A comparison of instant-messaging and e-mail negotiations shows that, due to the higher interaction speed and reduced information processing time, negotiators use more dominating communications when interacting via instant-messages (Loewenstein et al. 2005). Similarly, Pesendorfer and Koeszegi (2006) show that negotiators interacting via a synchronous communication channel engage in more affective, disinhibited, and competitive behaviors, than negotiators who interacted with each other asynchronously. Their results suggest that, because negotiators interacting in an asynchronous manner have more time to act and react, they also have time to cool down and reflect. Since cooling down and reflecting are related to the possibility of partitioning cognitive resources over a longer time period, these results also indicate that, when negotiating asynchronously, negotiators are better able to regulate their emotions. In other words, supplying e-negotiators with more time to (re)act can increase their epistemic ability.

Only limited empirical evidence is available on the impact of decision support on affect-cognition in e-negotiations. Koeszegi et al. (2006), for example, provide such evidence for text-based asynchronous e-negotiations. While negotiators, independent of their use of analytic decision support, express a similar relative frequency of negative emotions, negotiators express more positive emotions in task-related as well as private communication. Similarly, the use of an analytic decision support component in asynchronous negotiations is found to increase the absolute amount of expressed thought units in negotiations (Schoop et al. 2014). However, in contrast to the prior study, negotiators provided with decision support show more negative emotions than negotiators not provided with decision support. While the results of these two studies may seem at odds with each other, it is worth pointing out that in the latter study negotiators were provided with a more sophisticated communication support technology giving negotiators more control and understanding about their communication. As a consequence, negotiators may have been less cognitively taxed and thus better able to use negative emotions more willfully in line with their signaling functions.

The Interplay Between Social Functions and Affect-Cognition in e-Negotiations

Although we discussed intra- and inter-personal effects of emotions separately, affect-cognition and social functions of emotions are inextricably interwoven and have to be considered in conjunction to fully grasp the impact of emotions in e-negotiations. As depicted in Fig. 5.2, the behavior of negotiator A and the emotions she conveys when setting the behavior causes a cognitive evaluation by negotiator B. The cognitive evaluation does not only trigger an emotional experience but is also influenced by the current emotional state of the negotiator. This, in turn, will determine the behavior with corresponding emotional expressions that negotiator B shows in response to negotiator A's first move. Negotiator B's behavioral–emotional reaction serves as input for negotiator A's cognitive-emotional evaluation triggering her reaction. This cognitive-emotional fugue (Lewis et al. 1984) performed during the ongoing interaction shapes the dynamic of the negotiation and its outcome.

Fairness in negotiations can be used to exemplify Fig. 5.2 and the complex interrelations between affect and cognition and the social functions of emotions. Fairness evaluations have long been thought as purely cognitive process; however, a number of authors argue that fairness can be thought of as an affective event and that cognitive fairness evaluations are only performed after fairness-related

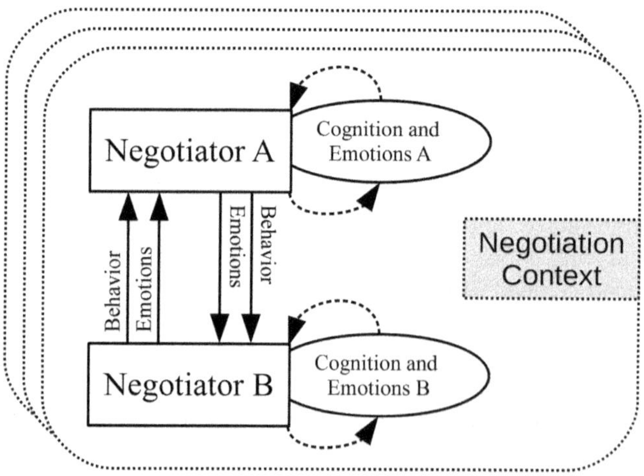

Fig. 5.2 Interplay of social functions and affect-cognition

emotions have been experienced (Solomon 1989; Weiss and Cropanzano 1996; Weiss et al. 1999). Furthermore, following appraisal theories of emotions (Frijda 1986; Lazarus 1991), the emergence of emotions in negotiations is primarily related to the progress individuals make toward achieving their goals (Kumar 1997; Fischer and Van Kleef 2010; Van Kleef et al. 2010b). If negotiator A, for example, makes an unfair offer while conveying positive emotions, this behavioral–emotional information constitutes the input for negotiator B's cognitive-emotional evaluation. The unfair offer and the resulting goal frustration are likely to trigger feelings of anger in negotiator B (Hegtvedt and Killian 1999; Weiss et al. 1999; Barclay et al. 2005). Also, the incongruence between communicated emotion and actual behavior by combining an unfair offer with the display of positive emotions might further exacerbate negotiator B's experienced negative emotions (Cheshin et al. 2011). Furthermore, if negotiator B is already in a negative emotional state as a result from previous interaction steps, she is likely to scrutinize the offer in more depth and evaluate it even more negatively (Staw and Barsade 1993). This cognitive-emotional evaluation determines negotiator B's subsequent behavior and emotional expression. Thus, negotiator B is likely to respond in kind to the unfair offer and display anger. The anger displayed by negotiator B has an important informational function for negotiator A and signals that the previous behavior was unacceptable and that a change of the course of action is required in order to reach an agreement (Morris and Keltner 2000). If negotiator A chooses to respond to negotiator B's expression of anger with guilt and a fairer offer, she signals that she is willing to make up for the transgression (Van Kleef et al. 2010b). Displaying guilt as complementary emotion to the previous expression of anger introduces a structural sequence (Adair and Brett 2005; Van Kleef et al. 2010b) which can aid the negotiators to re-introduce a constructive negotiation dynamic and restore their relationship (Keltner et al. 1997; Van Kleef et al. 2010b). Conversely, if negotiator A would have responded in kind by reacting to anger with anger, a conflict spiral of negative emotional dynamics, resulting in an impasse, might have been triggered (Brett et al. 1998).

The example shows how affect-cognition and social functions work together in shaping the negotiation process and outcome. However, the described effects are further mediated by the negotiation context. The EASI model (Van Kleef et al. 2010b) also provides a comprehensive rational for the different effects emotions have in social interactions. Accordingly, the specific social functional effects of positive and negative emotions depend on whether the negotiation setting is competitive or cooperative. In a competitive context, the display of anger in the aforementioned example is more likely to induce the counterpart to react with more cooperative behavior and make concessions as it signals that limits are reached and the willingness to retaliate or terminate the negotiation. Conversely, in a cooperative setting the same emotional display is more likely to reduce cooperative behavior as it conveys adverse signals and elicits similar emotions in the counterpart. Negotiating via EMC or employing a DSS is yet another context factor influencing the cognitive-emotional fugue as well as how and to what extent emotions have beneficial or detrimental social functions in negotiation interactions (see Fig. 5.3).

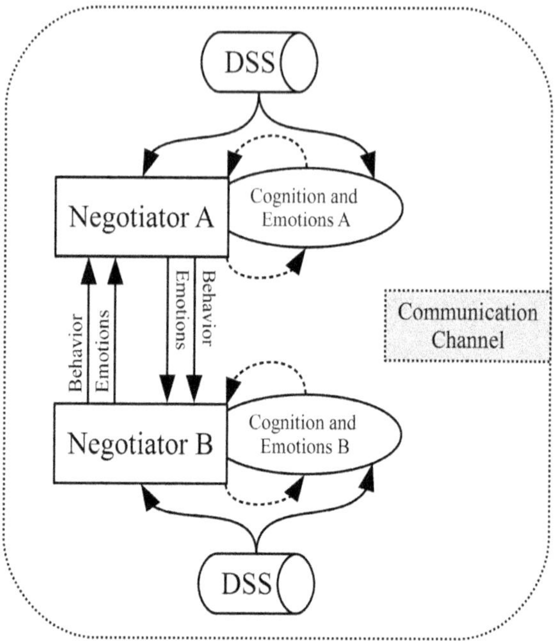

Fig. 5.3 Role of DSS and the communication channel

Research addressing the impacts of e-negotiation contexts on the inter-personal social functions of emotions as well as on intra-personal affect and cognition, as depicted in Fig. 5.3, is rather limited from a joint perspective. Thus, to illustrate the potential influence the communication and decision support components of an eNS can have on emotions in e-negotiations, we subsequently extend the example given above. For instance, negotiator B in the previous example might have e-mailed "Your previous offer makes me angry!" as response to negotiator A's unfair offer. By doing so she communicates a direct emotional signal that a change of action is required. However, she might also have replied with "Your offer is simply unacceptable!!!" employing the grammatical marker "!!!" and a specific language choice to implicitly convey feelings of anger via such emotext or "electronic paralanguage." Yet, the lower the bandwidth of a communication channel in terms of lacking primary carriers of emotions such as facial expressions, the more important become alternative and more subtle ways of conveying emotions. The efficiency and clarity with which negotiators can convey and understand emotions transmitted via an electronic channel determines whether and to what degree emotions can fulfill their vital functions in coordinating the interaction in e-negotiations. For instance, negotiator B intended to signal her anger with "Your offer is simply unacceptable!!!"; however, negotiator A might not have been able to decode the emotional language correctly because the negotiators have yet not been able to establish a common emotional code in the electronic environment. Negotiator B has introduced ambiguity by expressing her emotions with electronic paralanguage and negotiator A was not capable of deriving the emotional meaning of the messages.

As a result, the conveyed emotion did not fulfill its informational function and negotiator A might not have responded with a fairer offer and regret in order to restore the relationship and re-introduce a constructive negotiation dynamic. Thus, with respect to the second message, the eNS may make a difference regarding its interpretation. If we, for example, assume that the negotiators interact via a synchronous text-based communication channel and have no DSS available, the eNS is rather cognitively demanding, which means that negotiators may (implicitly) partition their cognitive resources to certain activities. As a consequence, the second exemplary message may only be interpreted with a focus on the fact-based content, i.e., that the offer is unacceptable, which could leave the negotiator to conclude that this message is rather emotionally neutral. In this case, a negotiator would not be cognitively able, or willing, to deploy enough cognitive resources to read or judge the subtle undertone supplied by the grammatical marker "!!!". Another message that illustrates this issue would be "Your previous offer makes me angry!;)." If negotiators would be highly cognitively taxed by the context, i.e., the usage of the eNS, then they may overlook the appended emoticon ";)", which implies that this message should not be considered as angry. As such, the potential of negotiators to decode a message as intended by its encoder depends on the cognitive resources that negotiators can deploy for this activity, and thus on the cognitive complexity of the current situation, which is shaped or enacted by the eNS.

Although research has established strong evidence on the interplay between emotion, cognition, and information processing (Bower 1981; Forgas 1995, 1998; Schwarz 2000), the impact of e-negotiations on this relationship is still not fully explored. For instance, when conducting an e-negotiation via chat (synchronous) and without decision support, negotiator A has only limited time and cognitive information processing capabilities at her disposal to decode and evaluate the angry response by negotiator B and formulate a reply. As a result, she might not be able to fully digest the arguments and the intention of the message both on a socio-emotional and on a fact-oriented level (Friedman and Currall 2003; Loewenstein et al. 2005). In particular when she blames negotiator B (Weiss et al. 1999; Barclay et al. 2005) and is in a state of high negative arousal in reaction to B's message (Barsade 2002; Friedman et al. 2004; Van Kleef et al. 2004a), negotiator A is likely to act less rationally, react with anger, and consolidate the conflict spiral (Brett et al. 1998; Friedman and Currall 2003). Thus, the negative emotions negotiator A experiences on an intra-personal level are likely to infuse her inter-personal behaviors toward negotiator B (Forgas 1995). If the negotiators would be supplied with decision support and negotiate asynchronously, they would be able to process information more accurately (Swaab et al. 2004; Kersten and Lai 2007) and may avoid irrational behavior and cognitive biases (Anson and Jelassi 1990; Foroughi 1998), since cognitive resources would be freed up (Blascovich 1992; Feldman 1995), and negotiators would have more time to cool down (Friedman and Currall 2003; Pesendorfer and Koeszegi 2006). Thus, by having a decision component available that provides a utility assessment of the exchanged offers, negotiator A may be able to consider B's offer in its entirety, rather than using the salient emotional content of negotiator B's message as central information, to evaluate the offer and understand it accordingly. In doing so, the decision support helps to bring the negotiation back to a rational basis and reduce the detrimental effects of emotional biases (Foroughi 1998). By reducing the cognitive effort required by negotiator A to analyze the factual content of the offer, more cognitive resources can be devoted to judge the emotional meaning of the message and formulate a response that is backed by arguments. Finally, decision support would help negotiator A to identify possible trade-offs and craft a mutually beneficial counteroffer (Kersten and Lai 2007) without provoking further negative emotional reactions by negotiator A. Negotiating asynchronously would moreover give negotiator A the time to cool down and avoid being in a state of negative emotional arousal when formulating the reply (Friedman and Currall 2003; Pesendorfer and Koeszegi 2006). Furthermore, she would have the possibility to review the negotiation protocol in order to identify what led up to the critical moment and review her message in order to formulate a reply that redirects the negotiation to positive grounds (Friedman and Currall 2003).

Conclusion and Outlook

Our review shows that emotions play a very important role in e-negotiations. However, an accurate understanding of the role of emotions in e-negotiations is only beginning to emerge. We add important aspects to the current understanding of emotions in e-negotiations by highlighting that the characteristics and functionalities of e-negotiations and eNS are interconnected with emotions. Research in line with the cues filtered-in perspective shows that emotions are a central part of electronic communication and that emotions are not mitigated but may even be intensified in EMC. In this respect, the social functions of emotions should be considered as important driving forces in and throughout e-negotiation processes. Besides being important at the inter-personal level, emotions are also central factors of influence at the intra-personal level. In line with that, we point out that the cognitive complexity of the negotiation situation, which is enacted and defined by the eNS, has an impact on the negotiators' abilities to encode and decode, or understand and communicate, emotions properly and as intended.

The integration of socio-emotional and rational-economic factors is an emerging field in various disciplines and the knowledge gained can be employed for developing and improving eNS. For instance, Brams (see Chap. 7 in this volume) and Loewenstein (2000) show how emotions can be incorporated in game theoretical approaches and the construction of utility functions, respectively—both are cornerstones of the decision support component of eNS. Similarly, the emerging field of "soft" or Behavioral OR considers socio-emotional aspects in the modeling of decision problems in order to help individuals, groups, and organizations to make and take decisions (cf. Hämäläinen et al. 2013). Recent research in the area of eNS also calls for the need to consider the higher level economic and behavioral goals of all parties involved in negotiations including such aspects as emotions (Vetschera et al. 2013). Initial empirical results directly comparing economic and behavioral support indeed show that effects of both support approaches are not limited to the respective support dimension, but actually show several spillovers (Gettinger et al. 2012a). Furthermore, advances in the fields of automated emotion recognition from text (e.g., Kramer et al. 2014) and facial expressions (e.g., Bailenson et al. 2008) can also be fruitfully used in designing socio-emotionally oriented eNS.

So far, only few attempts have been made to directly integrate such aspects and develop more behaviorally oriented eNS. One example is the Graph Model for Conflict Resolution implemented in the DSS GMCR II supporting decision makers and negotiators in strategic conflicts (Hipel et al. 1997). While originally rooted in metagame theory, the paradigm of the Graph Model for Conflict Resolution was later extended to consider emotions (Obeidi et al. 2005). This extension shows that experienced positive emotions augment the set of potential states and therefore recognized actions and alternatives considered by the parties. Experienced negative emotions, on the other hand, restrict the set of possible actions and alternatives.

Alternatively, Broekens et al. (2010) suggested an "affective" eNS that is designed to aid negotiators in managing their own emotions, comprehending and reacting to the emotions expressed by their counterpart adequately, and guiding negotiators in using emotions strategically. The authors also suggest affective support tailored to different negotiation phases. For the preparation phase, they propose to transfer concepts of analytic support approaches to emotional dimensions. Similar to the way preferences regarding issues are elicited and utility values are assigned to issues and issue values, negotiators may also link emotions to specific issues and issue values. Furthermore, negotiators might even want to explicitly state emotional goals for upcoming negotiations including the relative importance of experiencing or not experiencing specific emotions. In the actual conduct phase, an affective eNS could detect prevalent emotions and make negotiators aware of them and their possible consequences. Furthermore, such an affective eNS may also give suggestions and recommendations on how to handle the current emotional state. Moreover, affective eNS could also give advice on when and which emotions should be expressed to gain a strategic advantage in line with the signaling functions of emotions (Morris and Keltner 2000; Van Kleef et al. 2010b). Such affective eNS could provide feedback about prevalent emotions, or proactively intervene in the process by making suggestions and recommendations

Furthermore, affective eNS could be used for novice or expert training, as well as to prepare for specific negotiations. In such an "emotional training", negotiators could be confronted with counterparts differing in their emotional reactions or offer-related behavior during negotiations. By reviewing and analyzing the negotiation afterwards, trainees receive important feedback about their interactions with emotional patterns. eNS may even be used for emotional training without direct human counterparts, which reduces the costs for human capital. eNS could use predefined sentences or entire text messages transmitting and communicating specific emotions, as is already done for research purposes (Van Kleef et al. 2004a;

e.g., Van Kleef et al. 2004b, 2010a). Related research already shows that virtual negotiators are able to express emotions via facial expressions that are correctly interpreted by their human counterparts (e.g., Qu et al. 2013, 2014). An (emotional) training in such a virtual reality has also been found to increase negotiation knowledge and conversation skills (Broekens et al. 2012) and thus seems to be a promising avenue for educational purposes and the "emotional professionalization" of negotiators.

As indicated in the examples throughout this chapter, e-negotiations are likely to be influenced and driven by a myriad of effects that are interrelated with emotions. On an inter-personal level, emotions and their social functions will influence the negotiators' behaviors toward each other. On an intra-personal level, the interconnection of emotions and cognitive processes will impact whether negotiators are able to read and understand emotions as intended by the sender of a message, as well as how a negotiator (emotionally) responds to the counterpart. While an understanding of both inter-personal and intra-personal effects is important to comprehend or analyze negotiation processes, only a limited amount of research considers both simultaneously (Butt et al. 2005; Liu 2009; Overbeck et al. 2010). In the context of e-negotiations, the links between the social functions of emotions and affect-cognition still remain to be investigated and constitute a fruitful and important area for future research. Media synchronicity theory (Dennis et al. 2008), for example, provides a theoretical framework to examine whether eNS enable negotiators to establish a shared emotional meaning and to what extent eNS may support or hinder the synchronization of emotional behaviors. Similarly, the subtle and implicit ways to communicate emotions in text-based interactions and how they influence the social functions of emotions in e-negotiations are still largely unexplored. Finally, it is crucial to investigate how different users with different backgrounds and knowledge approach restriction and opportunities arising from negotiating in an electronic environment, including socio-emotional aspects. As a result, scholars may be able to gain a more comprehensive understanding of negotiations conducted via eNS and build systems tailored to the requirements of individual users.

References

Adair, W. L., & Brett, J. M. (2005). The negotiation dance: time, culture, and behavioral sequences in negotiation. *Organization Science, 16*, 33–51. doi:10.1287/orsc.1040.0102.

Anson, R. G., & Jelassi, M. T. (1990). A development framework for computer-supported conflict resolution. *European Journal of Operational Research, 46*, 181–199. doi:10.1016/0377-2217(90)90131-T.

Arnott, D., & Pervan, G. (2005). A critical analysis of decision support systems research. *Journal of Information Technology, 20*, 67–87. doi:10.1057/palgrave.jit.2000035.

Arnott, D., & Pervan, G. (2008). Eight key issues for the decision support discipline. *Decision Support Systems, 44*, 657–672. doi:10.1016/j.dss.2007.09.003.

Bailenson, J. N., Pontikakis, E. D., Mauss, I. B., Gross, J. J., Jabon, M. E., Hutcherson, C. A. C., et al. (2008). Real-time classification of evoked emotions using facial feature tracking and physiological responses. *International Journal of Human-Computer Studies, 66*, 303–317. doi:10.1016/j.ijhcs.2007.10.011.

Baltes, B. B., Dickson, M. W., Sherman, M. P., Bauer, C. C., & LaGanke, J. S. (2002). Computer-mediated communication and group decision making: A meta-analysis. *Organizational Behavior and Human Decision Processes, 87*, 156–179. doi:10.1006/obhd.2001.2961.

Barclay, L. J., Skarlicki, D. P., & Pugh, S. D. (2005). Exploring the role of emotions in injustice perceptions and retaliation. *Journal of Applied Psychology, 90*, 629–643. doi:10.1037/0021-9010.90.4.629.

Baron, R. A. (1990). Environmentally induced positive affect: Its impact on self-efficacy, task performance, negotiation, and conflict. *Journal of Applied Social Psychology, 20*, 368–384. doi:10.1111/j.1559-1816.1990.tb00417.x.

Barry, B., & Fulmer, I. S. (2004). The medium and the message: The adaptive use of communication media in dyadic influence. *Academy of Management Review, 29*, 272–292. doi:10.5465/AMR.2004.12736093.

Barry, B., Fulmer, I. S., & van Kleef, G. A. (2004). I laughed, I cried, I settled: The role of emotion in negotiation. In M. J. Gelfand & J. M. Brett (Eds.), *The handbook of negotiation and culture* (pp. 71–94). Stanford, CA: Stanford University Press.

Barsade, S. G. (2002). The ripple effect: Emotional contagion and its influence on group behavior. *Administrative Science Quarterly, 47*, 644–675. doi:10.2307/3094912.

Bartel, C. A., & Saavedra, R. (2000). The collective construction of work group moods. *Administrative Science Quarterly, 45*, 197–231. doi:10.2307/2667070.

Blascovich, J. (1992). A biopsychosocial approach to arousal regulation. *Journal of Social and Clinical Psychology, 11*, 213–237. doi:10.1521/jscp.1992.11.3.213.

Boudourides, M. A. (2001). *E-mail, social structure and networks*. Patras: Greece.

Bower, G. H. (1981). Mood and memory. *American Psychologist, 36*, 129–148. doi:10.1037/0003-066X.36.2.129.

Brett, J. M., Olekalns, M., Friedman, R., Goates, N., Anderson, C., & Lisco, C. C. (2007). Sticks and stones: Language, face, and online dispute resolution. *Academy of Management Journal, 50*, 85–99. doi:10.5465/AMJ.2007.24161853.

Brett, J. M., Shapiro, D. L., & Lytle, A. L. (1998). Breaking the bonds of reciprocity in negotiations. *Academy of Management Journal, 41*, 410–424. doi:10.2307/257081.

Broekens, J., Harbers, M., Brinkman, W.-P., Jonker, C. M., Van den Bosch, K., & Meyer, J.-J. (2012). Virtual reality negotiation training increases negotiation knowledge and skill. In Y. Nakano, M. Neff, A. Paiva, & M. Walker (Eds.), *Intelligent Virtual Agents* (pp. 218–230). Berlin, Heidelberg: Springer.

Broekens, J., Jonker, C. M., & Meyer, J.-J. C. (2010). Affective negotiation support systems. *Journal of Ambient Intelligence and Smart Environments, 2*, 121–144. doi:10.3233/AIS-2010-0065.

Bui, T. X. (1994). Evaluating negotiation support systems: A conceptualization. In *Proceedings of Twenty-Seventh Hawaii International Conference System Science*, pp. 316–324.

Butt, A. N., Choi, J. N., & Jaeger, A. M. (2005). The effects of self-emotion, counterpart emotion, and counterpart behavior on negotiator behavior: A comparison of individual-level and dyad-level dynamics. *Journal of Organizational Behavior, 26*, 681–704. doi:10.1002/job.328.

Byron, K. (2008). Carrying too heavy a load? The communication and miscommunication of emotion by email. *Academy of Management Review, 33*, 309–327. doi:10.5465/AMR.2008.31193163.

Byron, K., & Baldridge, D. C. (2005). Toward a model of nonverbal cues and emotion in email. *Academy of Management Proceedings, 2005*, B1–B6. doi:10.5465/AMBPP.2005.18781269.

Cacioppo, J. T., & Gardner, W. L. (1999). Emotion. *Annual Review of Psychology, 50*, 191–214. doi:10.1146/annurev.psych.50.1.191.

Carlson, J. R., & Zmud, R. W. (1999). Channel Expansion Theory and the experiential nature of media richness perceptions. *Academy of Management Journal, 42*, 153–170. doi:10.2307/257090.

Carnevale, P. J. D. (2008). Positive affect and decision frame in negotiation. *Group Decision and Negotiation, 17*, 51–63. doi:10.1007/s10726-007-9090-x.

Carnevale, P. J. D., O'Connor, K. M., & McCusker, C. (1993). Time pressure in negotiation and mediation. In O. Svenson & A. J. Maule (Eds.), *Time pressure and stress in human judgment and decision making* (pp. 117–127). New York: Springer.

Cheshin, A., Rafaeli, A., & Bos, N. (2011). Anger and happiness in virtual teams: Emotional influences of text and behavior on others' affect in the absence of non-verbal cues. *Organizational Behavior and Human Decision Processes, 116*, 2–16. doi:10.1016/j.obhdp. 2011.06.002.

Clark, H. H., & Brennan, S. E. (1991). Grounding in communication. In L. B. Resnick, J. M. Levine & S. D. Teasley (Eds.), *Perspectives on socially shared cognition* (pp. 127–149). Washington, D.C.: American Psychological Association.

Côté, S. (2005). A social interaction model of the effects of emotion regulation on work strain. *Academy of Management Review, 30*, 509–530. doi:10.5465/AMR.2005.17293692.

Daft, R. L., & Lengel, R. H. (1984). Information richness: A new approach to managerial behavior and organizational design. *Research Organization Behavior, 6*, 191–233.

Daft, R. L., & Lengel, R. H. (1986). Organizational information requirements, media richness and structural design. *Management Science, 32*, 554–571. doi:10.1287/mnsc.32.5.554.

Daft, R. L., Lengel, R. H., & Trevino, L. K. (1987). Message equivocality, media selection, and manager performance: Implications for information systems. *MIS Quarterly, 11*, 354–366. doi:10.2307/248682.

Daly, J. P. (1991). The effects of anger on negotiations over mergers and acquisitions. *Negotiation Journal, 7*, 31–39. doi:10.1007/BF01004935.

Damasio, A. R. (1994). *Descartes' error: Emotions, reason, and the human brain*. New York: Avon Books.

De Dreu, C. K. W., & Carnevale, P. J. D. (2003). Motivational bases of information processing and strategy in conflict and negotiation. *Advances in Experimental Social Psychology, 35*, 235–291. doi:10.1016/S0065-2601(03)01004-9.

Delaney, M. M., Foroughi, A., & Perkins, W. C. (1997). An empirical study of the efficacy of a computerized negotiation support system (NSS). *Decision Support Systems, 20*, 185–197. doi:10.1016/S0167-9236(96)00051-6.

Dennis, A. R., Fuller, R. M., & Valacich, J. S. (2008). Media, tasks, and communication processes: A theory of media synchronicity. *MIS Quarterly, 32*, 575–600.

DePaulo, B. M., & Friedman, H. S. (1998). Nonverbal communication. In D. T. Gilbert, S. T. Fiske, & G. Lindzey, (Eds.), *Handbook social psychology* (4th ed., pp. 3–40). New York, NY: Oxford University Press.

Derks, D., Fischer, A. H., & Bos, A. E. R. (2008). The role of emotion in computer-mediated communication: A review. *Computter Human Behavior, 24*, 766–785. doi:10.1016/j.chb.2007. 04.004.

DeSanctis, G., & Gallupe, R. B. (1987). A foundation for the study of group decision support systems. *Management Science, 33*, 589–609. doi:10.1287/mnsc.33.5.589.

Druckman, D. (1994). Determinants of compromising behavior in negotiation: A meta-analysis. *Journal of Conflict Resolution, 38*, 507–556. doi:10.1177/0022002794038003007.

Ekman, P. (1993). Facial expression and emotion. *American Psychologist, 48*, 384–392. doi:10. 1037/0003-066X.48.4.384.

Feldman, L. A. (1995). Valence focus and arousal focus: Individual differences in the structure of affective experience. *Journal of Personality and Social Psychology, 69*, 153–166. doi:10.1037/ 0022-3514.69.1.153.

Fischer, A. H., & Roseman, I. J. (2007). Beat them or ban them: The characteristics and social functions of anger and contempt. *Journal of Personality and Social Psychology, 93*, 103–115. doi:10.1037/0022-3514.93.1.103.

Fischer, A. H., & van Kleef, G. A. (2010). Where have all the people gone? A plea for including social interaction in emotion research. *Emotion Review, 2*, 208–211. doi:10.1177/ 1754073910361980.

Forgas, J. P. (1995). Mood and judgment: The affect infusion model (AIM). *Psychological Bulletin, 117*, 39–66. doi:10.1037/0033-2909.117.1.39.

Forgas, J. P. (1998). On feeling good and getting your way: Mood effects on negotiator cognition and bargaining strategies. *Journal of Personality and Social Psychology, 74*, 565–577. doi:10.1037/0022-3514.74.3.565.

Forgas, J. P., & George, J. M. (2001). Affective influences on judgments and behavior in organizations: An information processing perspective. *Organizational Behavior and Human Decision Processes, 86*, 3–34. doi:10.1006/obhd.2001.2971.

Foroughi, A. (1998). Minimizing negotiation process losses with computerized negotiation support systems. *Journal of Applied Business Research, 14*, 15–26.

Foroughi, A., Perkins, W. C., & Jelassi, M. T. (1995). An empirical study of an interactive, session-oriented computerized negotiation support system (NSS). *Group Decision and Negotiation, 4*, 485–512. doi:10.1007/BF01409712.

Friedman, R., Anderson, C., Brett, J. M., Olekalns, M., Goates, N., & Lisco, C. C. (2004). The positive and negative effects of anger on dispute resolution: Evidence from electronically mediated disputes. *Journal of Applied Psychology, 89*, 369–376. doi:10.1037/0021-9010.89.2.369.

Friedman, R. A., & Currall, S. C. (2003). Conflict escalation: Dispute exacerbating elements of e-mail communication. *Human Relations, 56*, 1325–1347. doi:10.1177/00187267035611003.

Frijda, N. H. (1986). *The emotions*. Cambridge: Cambridge University Press.

Gettinger, J., Dannenmann, A., Druckman, D., Filzmoser, M., Mitterhofer, R., & Reiser, A. (2012a). Impact of and interaction between behavioral and economic decision support in electronic negotiations. In J. E. Hernández, P. Zarate, F. Dargam, B. Delibasic, S. Liu, & R. Ribeiro. (Eds.), *Decision Support Systems—Collaborative Models and Approaches in Real Environments* (pp. 151–165). Berlin: Springer.

Gettinger, J., Koeszegi, S. T., & Schoop, M. (2012b). Shall we dance?—The effect of information presentations on negotiation processes and outcomes. *Decision Support Systems, 53*, 161–164. doi: 10.1016/j.dss.2012.01.001.

Gettinger, J., & Koeszegi, S. T. (2014). Far from eye, far from heart: Analysis of graphical decision aids in electronic negotiation support. *Group Decision and Negotiation, 23*, 787−817. doi:10.1007/s10726-012-9319-1.

Gibbons, P., Bradac, J. J., & Busch, J. D. (1992). The role of language in negotiations: Threats and promises. In L. L. Putnam, & M. E. Roloff (Eds.), *Communication and negotiation* (pp. 156–175), Newbury Park, California: Sage Annual Sage.

Griessmair, M., & Koeszegi, S. T. (2009). Exploring the cognitive-emotional fugue in electronic negotiations. *Group Decision and Negotiation, 18*, 213–234. doi:10.1007/s10726-009-9155-0.

Hämäläinen, R. P., Luoma, J., & Saarinen, E. (2013). On the importance of behavioral operational research: The case of understanding and communicating about dynamic systems. *European Journal of Operational Research, 228*, 623–634. doi:10.1016/j.ejor.2013.02.001.

Hancock, J. T., Gee, K., Ciaccio, K., & Lin, JM.-H. (2008). I'm sad you're sad: Emotional contagion in CMC. CSCW '08. In *Proceedings 2008 ACM Conference Computer Supportive Cooperative Work* (pp. 295–298). San Diego, California.

Hancock, J. T., Landrigan, C., & Silver, C. (2007). Expressing emotion in text-based communication. In *Proceedings of SIGCHI Conference Human Factors Computer System—CHI* '07 (pp. 929–932). doi: 10.1145/1240624.1240764.

Hatfield, E., Cacioppo, J. T., & Rapson, R. L. (1993). Emotional contagion. *Current Directions in Psychological Science, 2*, 96–99. doi:10.1111/1467-8721.ep10770953.

Hatfield, E., Cacioppo, J. T., & Rapson, R. L. (1994). *Emotional contagion*. Cambridge: Cambridge University Press.

Hedlund, J., Ilgen, D. R., & Hollenbeck, J. R. (1998). Decision accuracy in computer-mediated versus face-to-face decision-making teams. *Organizational Behavior and Human Decision Processes, 76*, 30–47. doi:10.1006/obhd.1998.2796.

Hegtvedt, K. A., & Killian, C. (1999). Fairness and emotions: Reactions to the process and outcomes of negotiations. *Social Forces, 78*, 269–303. doi:10.1093/sf/78.1.269.

Hinds, P., & Kiesler, S. (2002). *Distributed work*. Cambridge, MA: MIT Press.

Hipel, K. W., Kilgour, D. M., Fang, L., & Peng, X. (1997). The decision support system GMCR in environmental conflict management. *Applied Mathematics and Computation, 83*, 117–152.

Holtom, B. C., & Kenworthy-U'Ren, A. L. (2006). Electronic negotiation: A teaching tool for encouraging student self-reflection. *Negotiation Journal, 22*, 303–324. doi:10.1111/j.1571-9979.2006.00103.x.

Isen, A. M. (1985). Asymmetry of happiness and sadness in effects on memory in normal college students: Comment on Hasher, Rose, Zacks, Sanft, and Doren. *Journal of Experimental Psychology: General, 114*, 388–391. doi:10.1037/0096-3445.114.3.388.

Jaffe, M. J., Lee, Y.-E., Huang, L.-N., & Oshagan, H. (1999). Gender identification, interdependence, and pseudonyms in CMC: Language patterns in an electronic conference. *Information Society, 15*, 221–234. doi:10.1080/019722499128385.

Johnson, N. A., & Cooper, R. B. (2009). Media, affect, concession, and agreement in negotiation: IM versus telephone. *Decision Support Systems, 46*, 673–684. doi:10.1016/j.dss.2008.10.007.

Johnson, N. A., Cooper, R. B., & Chin, W. W. (2008). The effect of flaming on computer-mediated negotiations. *European Journal Information System, 17*, 417–434. doi:10.1057/ejis.2008.22.

Johnson, N. A., Cooper, R. B., & Chin, W. W. (2009). Anger and flaming in computer-mediated negotiation among strangers. *Decision Support Systems, 46*, 660–672. doi:10.1016/j.dss.2008.10.008.

Jonassen, D. H., & Kwon, H. (2001). Communication patterns in computer mediated versus face-to-face group problem solving. *Educational Technology Research and Development, 49*, 35–51. doi:10.1007/BF02504505.

Keltner, D., & Haidt, J. (1999). Social functions of emotions at four levels of analysis. *Cognition and Emotion, 13*, 505–521. doi:10.1080/026999399379168.

Keltner, D., & Kring, A. M. (1998). Emotion, social function, and psychopathology. *Review of General Psychology, 2*, 320–342. doi:10.1037/1089-2680.2.3.320.

Keltner, D., Young, R. C., & Buswell, B. N. (1997). Appeasement in human emotion, social practice, and personality. *Aggressive Behavior, 23*, 359–374. doi: 10.1002/(SICI)1098-2337(1997)23:5<359::AID-AB5>3.0.CO;2-D.

Kersten, G. E., & Lai, H. (2007). Negotiation support and e-negotiation systems: An overview. *Group Decision and Negotiation, 16*, 553–586. doi:10.1007/s10726-007-9095-5.

Kersten, G. E., & Lai, H. (2010). Electronic negotiations: Foundations, systems, and processes. In D. M. Kilgour & C. Eden (Eds.), *Handbook group decision and negotiation* (pp. 361–392). Netherlands, Dordrecht: Springer.

Kersten, G. E., & Noronha, S. J. (1999). WWW-based negotiation support: Design, implementation, and use. *Decision Support Systems, 25*, 135–154. doi:10.1016/S0167-9236(99)00012-3.

Kiesler, S., Siegel, J., & McGuire, T. W. (1984). Social psychological aspects of computer-mediated communication. *American Psychologist, 39*, 1123–1134. doi:10.1037/0003-066X.39.10.1123.

Kiesler, S., & Sproull, L. (1992). Group decision making and communication technology. *Organizational Behavior and Human Decision Processes, 52*, 96–123. doi:10.1016/0749-5978(92)90047-B.

Knutson, B. (1996). Facial expressions of emotion influence interpersonal trait inferences. *Journal of Nonverbal Behavior, 20*, 165–182. doi:10.1007/BF02281954.

Kock, N. (2005). Media richness or media naturalness? The evolution of our biological communication apparatus and its influence on our behavior toward e-communication tools. *IEEE Transactions on Professional Communication, 48*, 117–130. doi:10.1109/TPC.2005.849649.

Kock, N. (2007). Media naturalness and compensatory encoding: The burden of electronic media obstacles is on senders. *Decision Support Systems, 44*, 175–187. doi:10.1016/j.dss.2007.03.011.

Koeszegi, S. T., Srnka, K. J., & Pesendorfer, E.-M. (2006). Electronic negotiations—A comparison of different support systems. *Die Betriebswirtschaft, 66*, 441–463.

Kramer, A. D., Guillory, J. E., & Hancock, J. T. (2014). Experimental evidence of massive-scale emotional contagion through social networks. In *Proceedings of the National Academy of Sciences United States, 111*, 8788–8790. doi:10.1073/pnas.1412469111.

Kramer, R. M., Newton, E., & Pommerenke, P. L. (1993). Self-enhancement biases and negotiator judgment: Effects of self-esteem and mood. *Organizational Behavior and Human Decision Processes, 56*, 110–133. doi:10.1006/obhd.1993.1047.

Kruger, J., Epley, N., Parker, J., & Ng, Z.-W. (2005). Egocentrism over e-mail: Can we communicate as well as we think? *Journal of Personality and Social Psychology, 89*, 925–936. doi:10.1037/0022-3514.89.6.925.

Kumar, R. (1997). The role of affect in negotiations: An integrative overview. *Journal of Applied Behavioral Science, 33*, 84–100. doi:10.1177/0021886397331007.

Lazarus, R. S. (1991). *Emotion and adaptation*. Oxford, England: Oxford University Press.

Lazarus, R. S., & Smith, C. A. (1988). Knowledge and appraisal in the cognition-emotion relationship. *Cognition and Emotion, 2*, 281–300. doi:10.1080/02699938808412701.

Lee, A. S. (1994). Electronic mail as a medium for rich communication: An empirical investigation using hermeneutic interpretation. *MIS Quarterly, 18*, 143–157. doi:10.2307/249762.

Lewis, M., Sullivan, M. W., & Michalson, L. (1984). The cognitive-emotional fugue. In C. E. Izard, J. Kagen, R. B. Zajonc (Eds.), *Emotions, cognition, and behavior* (pp. 264–288), New York, Cambridge: University Press.

Lim, L.-H., & Benbasat, I. (1992). A theoretical perspective of negotiation support systems. *Journal of Management Information Systems, 9*, 27–44.

Lim, J., & Yang, Y. P. (2007). Enhancing negotiators' performance with computer support for pre-negotiation preparation and negotiation: An experimental investigation in an east asian context. *Journal of Global Information Management, 15*, 18–42. doi:10.4018/jgim.2007010102.

Liu, M. (2009). The intrapersonal and interpersonal effects of anger on negotiation strategies: A cross-cultural investigation. *Human Communication Research, 35*, 148–169. doi:10.1111/j.1468-2958.2008.01342.x.

Liu, L. A., Chua, C. H., & Stahl, G. K. (2010). Quality of communication experience: Definition, measurement, and implications for intercultural negotiations. *Journal of Applied Psychology, 95*, 469–487. doi:10.1037/a0019094.

Liu, Y., Ginther, D., & Zelhart, P. (2001). How do frequency and duration of messaging affect impression development in computer mediated communication? *Journal of Universal Computer Science, 7*, 893–913. doi:10.3217/jucs-007-10-0893.

Loewenstein, G. (2000). Emotions in economic theory and economic behavior. *American Economic Review, 90*, 426–432. doi:10.1257/aer.90.2.426.

Loewenstein, J., Morris, M. W., Chakravarti, A., Thompson, L., & Kopelman, S. (2005). At a loss for words: Dominating the conversation and the outcome in negotiation as a function of intricate arguments and communication media. *Organizational Behavior and Human Decision Processes, 98*, 28–38. doi:10.1016/j.obhdp.2005.03.007.

Loewenstein, G. F., Weber, E. U., Hsee, C. K., & Welch, N. (2001). Risk as feelings. *Psychological Bulletin, 127*, 267–286. doi:10.1037/0033-2909.127.2.267.

Martinovski, B. (2010). Emotion in negotiation. In D. M. Kilgour, C. Eden (Eds.), *Handbook of Group Decision and Negotiation* (pp. 65–86), Dordrecht: Springer.

Martinovski, B., & Mao, W. (2009). Emotion as an argumentation engine: Modeling the role of emotion in negotiation. *Group Decision Negotiation, 18*, 235–259. doi:10.1007/s10726-008-9153-7.

Martinovski, B., & Marsella, S. C. (2005). Theory of mind and coping in discourse. *AISB'05 Society Intelligence Interactions Animal Robotics Agents. Proceedings Joint Commission Symposium Virtual Social Agents,* (pp. 177–184). UK: Hatfield.

McGuire, T. W., Kiesler, S., & Siegel, J. (1987). Group and computer-mediated discussion effects in risk decision making. *Journal of Personality and Social Psychology, 52*, 917–930. doi:10.1037/0022-3514.52.5.917.

McKenna, K. Y. A., & Bargh, J. A. (2000). Plan 9 from cyberspace: The implications of the internet for personality and social psychology. *Personality and social psychology review, 4*, 57–75. doi:10.1207/S15327957PSPR0401_6.

Moore, D. A., Kurtzberg, T. R., Thompson, L. L., & Morris, M. W. (1999). Long and short routes to success in electronically mediated negotiations: Group affiliations and good vibrations. *Organizational Behavior and Human Decision Processes, 77*, 22–43. doi:10.1006/obhd.1998.2814.

Morris, M. W., & Keltner, D. (2000). How emotions work: The social functions of emotional expression in negotiations. *Research in Organizational Behavior, 22*, 1–50. doi:10.1016/S0191-3085(00)22002-9.

Morris, M. W., Nadler, J., Kurtzberg, T. R., & Thompson, L. L. (2002). Schmooze or lose: Social friction and lubrication in e-mail negotiations. *Group Dynamic Theory, Research Practice, 6*, 89–100. doi:10.1037//1089-2699.6.1.89.

Neale, M. A., & Bazerman, M. H. (1992). Negotiator cognition and rationality: A behavioral decision theory perspective. *Organizational Behavior and Human Decision Processes, 51*, 157–175. doi:10.1016/0749-5978(92)90009-V.

Nielek, R., Wawer, A., & Wierzbicki, A. (2010). Spiral of hatred: Social effects in internet auctions. Between informativity and emotion. *Electronic Commerce Research, 10*, 313–330. doi:10.1007/s10660-010-9058-9.

Obeidi, A., Hipel, K. W., & Kilgour, D. M. (2005). The role of emotions in envisioning outcomes in conflict analysis. *Group Decision and Negotiation, 14*, 481–500. doi:10.1007/s10726-005-9004-8.

Ochsner, K. N., Bunge, S. A., Gross, J. J., & Gabrieli, J. D. E. (2002). Rethinking feelings: An FMRI study of the cognitive regulation of emotion. *Journal of Cognitive Neuroscience, 14*, 1215–1229. doi:10.1162/089892902760807212.

Olekalns, M., & Weingart, L. R. (2003). Think globally, act locally: Towards an adaptive model of dyadic negotiations in organizations. In *16th Annual IACM Conference*, pp. 1–46.

Overbeck, J. R., Neale, M. A., & Govan, C. L. (2010). I feel, therefore you act: Intrapersonal and interpersonal effects of emotion on negotiation as a function of social power. *Organizational Behavior and Human Decision Processes, 112*, 126–139. doi:10.1016/j.obhdp.2010.02.004.

Parkinson, B. (1996). Emotions are social. *British Journal of Psychology, 87*, 663–683. doi:10.1111/j.2044-8295.1996.tb02615.x.

Pesendorfer, E.-M., & Koeszegi, S. T. (2006). Hot versus cool behavioural styles in electronic negotiations: The impact of communication mode. *Group Decision and Negotiation, 15*, 141–155. doi:10.1007/s10726-006-9025-y.

Pietroni, D., Kleef, G. A., & De Dreu, C. K. W. (2007). Response modes in negotiation. *Group Decision and Negotiation, 17*, 31–49. doi:10.1007/s10726-007-9089-3.

Pietroni, D., van Kleef, G. A., & De Dreu, C. K. W. (2008). Response modes in negotiation. *Group Decision and Negotiation, 17*, 31–49. doi:10.1007/s10726-007-9089-3.

Qu, C., Brinkman, W.-P., Ling, Y., & Heynderickx, I. (2013). Human perception of a conversational virtual human: An empirical study on the effect of emotion and culture. *Virtual Reality, 17*, 307–321. doi:10.1007/s10055-013-0231-z.

Qu, C., Brinkman, W.-P., Ling, Y., Ling, Y., Wiggers, P., & Heynderickx, I. (2014). Conversations with a virtual human: Synthetic emotions and human responses. *Computer Human Behavior, 34*, 58–68. doi:10.1016/j.chb.2014.01.033.

Raiffa, H., Richardson, J., & Metcalfe, D. (2002). *Negotiation analysis: The science and art of collaborative decision making*. Cambridge, Massachusetts and London, England: The Belknap Press of Harvard University Press.

Rangaswamy, A., & Shell, G. R. (1997). Using computers to realize joint gains in negotiations: Toward an "electronic bargaining table". *Management Science, 43*, 1147–1163. doi:10.1287/mnsc.43.8.1147.

Rice, R. E., & Love, G. (1987). Electronic emotion: Socioemotional content in a computer-mediated communication network. *Communication Research, 14*, 85–108. doi:10.1177/009365087014001005.

Richards, J. M., & Gross, J. J. (2000). Emotion regulation and memory: The cognitive costs of keeping one's cool. *Journal of Personality and Social Psychology, 79*, 410–424. doi:10.1037//0022-3514.79.3.410.

Rockmann, K. W., & Northcraft, G. B. (2008). To be or not to be trusted: The influence of media richness on defection and deception. *Organizational Behavior and Human Decision Processes, 107*, 106–122. doi:10.1016/j.obhdp.2008.02.002.

Rozin, P., & Royzman, E. B. (2001). Negativity bias, negativity dominance, and contagion. *Personality and Social Psychology Review, 5*, 296–320. doi:10.1207/S15327957PSPR0504_2.

Scaife, M., & Rogers, Y. (1996). External cognition: How do graphical representations work? *International Journal of Human-Computer Studies, 45*, 185–213. doi:10.1006/ijhc.1996.0048.

Scherer, K. R. (1999). Appraisal theory. In T. Dalgleish, & M. Power (Eds.), *Handbook of Cognition and Emotion* (pp. 637–663), Chichester, England: Wiley.

Schoop, M. (2010). Support of complex electronic negotiations. In D. M. Kilgour & C. Eden (Eds.), *Handbook of group decision and negotiation* (pp. 409–423). Netherlands, Dordrecht: Springer.

Schoop, M., Jertila, A., & List, T. (2003). Negoisst: A negotiation support system for electronic business-to-business negotiations in e-commerce. *Data and Knowledge Engineering, 47*, 371–401. doi:10.1016/S0169-023X(03)00065-X.

Schoop, M., Koehne, F., & Ostertag, K. (2010). Communication quality in business negotiations. *Group Decision and Negotiation, 19*, 193–209. doi:10.1007/s10726-008-9128-8.

Schoop, M., van Amelsvoort, M., Gettinger, J., Koerner, M., Koeszegi, S., & van der Wijst, P. (2014). The interplay of communication and decisions in electronic negotiations: Communicative decisions or decisive communication? *Group Decision and Negotiation, 23*, 167–192. doi:10.1007/s10726-013-9357-3.

Schroeder, H. M., Driver, M. J., & Streufert, S. (1967). *Human information processing*. New York: Holt, Rinehart and Winston.

Schroth, H. A., Bain-Chekal, J., & Caldwell, D. F. (2005). Sticks and stones may break bones and words can hurt me: Words and phrases that trigger emotions in negotiations and their effects. *International Journal of Conflict Management, 16*, 102–127. doi:10.1108/eb022925.

Schulz von Thun, F. (1981). *Miteinander reden 1: Störungen und Klärungen. Allgemeine Psychologie der Kommunikation*. Reinbeck bei Hamburg: Rowohlt.

Schwarz, N. N. (1990). Feelings as information: Informational and motivational functions of affective states. In E. T. Higgins & R. M. Sorrentino (Eds.), *Handbook of motivation and cognition: Foundations of social behavior* (pp. 527–561). New York: Guilford Press.

Schwarz, N. N. (2000). Emotion, cognition, and decision making. *Cognition and Emotion, 14*, 433–440. doi:10.1080/026999300402745.

Schwarz, N. N., & Clore, G. L. (1983). Mood, misattribution, and judgments of well-being: Informative and directive functions of affective states. *Journal of Personality and Social Psychology, 45*, 513–523. doi:10.1037/0022-3514.45.3.513.

Sebenius, J. K. (1992). Negotiation analysis: A characterization and review. *Management Science, 38*, 18–38. doi:10.1287/mnsc.38.1.18.

Short, J., Williams, E., & Christie, B. (1976). *The social psychology of telecommunications*. London: Wiley.

Siegel, J., Dubrovsky, V., Kiesler, S., & McGuire, T. W. (1986). Group processes in computer-mediated communication. *Organizational Behavior and Human Decision Processes, 37*, 157–187. doi:10.1016/0749-5978(86)90050-6.

Silver, M. S. (1988). Descriptive analysis for computer-based decision support. *Operations Research, 36*, 904–916. doi:10.1287/opre.36.6.904.

Sinaceur, M., & Tiedens, L. Z. (2006). Get mad and get more than even: When and why anger expression is effective in negotiations. *Journal of Experimental Social Psychology, 42*, 314–322. doi:10.1016/j.jesp.2005.05.002.

Singh, D. T., & Ginzberg, M. J. (1996). An empirical investigation of the impact of process monitoring on computer-mediated decision-making performance. *Organizational Behavior and Human Decision Processes, 67*, 156–169. doi:10.1006/obhd.1996.0071.

Smith, C. A., & Ellsworth, P. C. (1985). Patterns of cognitive appraisal in emotion. *Journal of Personality and Social Psychology, 48*, 813–838. doi:10.1037/0022-3514.48.4.813.

Sokolova, M., & Szpakowicz, S. (2006). Language patterns in the learning of strategies from negotiation texts. In *19th Conference Canada Society Computer Studies Intelligence*. doi: 10.1007/11766247_25.

Sokolova, M., & Szpakowicz, S. (2007). Strategies and language trends in learning success and failure of negotiation. *Group Decision and Negotiation, 16*, 469–484. doi:10.1007/s10726-007-9083-9.

Sokolova, M., Szpakowicz, S., & Nastase, V. (2004). Using language to determine success in negotiations: A preliminary study. In A. Y. Tawfik, & S. D. Goodwin (Eds.), *Advances in artificial intelligence*. 17th *Conference Canada Society Computer Studies Intelligence*, Springer, pp. 449–453.

Solomon, R. C. (1989). The emotions of justice. *Social Justice Research, 3*, 345–374. doi:10.1007/BF01048082.

Sproull, L., & Kiesler, S. (1986). Reducing social context cues: Electronic mail in organizational communication. *Management Science, 32*, 1492–1512. doi:10.1287/mnsc.32.11.1492.

Staw, B. M., & Barsade, S. G. (1993). Affect and managerial performance: A test of the sadder-but-wiser vs. happier-and-smarter hypotheses. *Administrative Science Quarterly, 38*, 304–331. doi:10.2307/2393415.

Ströbel, M., & Weinhardt, C. (2003). The montreal taxonomy for electronic negotiations. *Group Decision Negotiation, 12*, 143–164. doi:10.1023/A:1023072922126.

Swaab, R., Postmes, T., & Neijens, P. (2004). Negotiation support systems: Communication and information as antecedents of negotiation settlement. *International Negotiation, 9*, 59–78. doi:10.1163/1571806041262115.

Tangirala, S., & Alge, B. J. (2006). Reactions to unfair events in computer-mediated groups: A test of uncertainty management theory. *Organizational Behavior and Human Decision Processes, 100*, 1–20. doi:10.1016/j.obhdp.2005.11.002.

Taylor, P. J., & Thomas, S. (2008). Linguistic style matching and negotiation outcome. *Negotiation Conflict Management Research, 1*, 263–281. doi:10.1111/j.1750-4716.2008.00016.x.

Thompson, L. L. (2005). *The mind and the heart of the negotiator*. Upper Saddle River, NJ: Prentice Hall.

Thompson, L. L., & Nadler, J. (2002). Negotiating via information technology: Theory and application. *Journal Society Issues, 58*, 109–124. doi:10.1111/1540-4560.00251.

Tripp, T. M., & Sondak, H. (1992). An evaluation of dependent variables in experimental negotiation studies: Impasse rates and Pareto efficiency. *Organizational Behavior and Human Decision Processes, 51*, 273–295. doi:10.1016/0749-5978(92)90014-X.

Van Kleef, G. A., Anastasopoulou, C., & Nijstad, B. A. (2010a). Can expressions of anger enhance creativity? A test of the emotions as social information (EASI) model. *Journal of Experimental Social Psychology, 46*, 1042–1048. doi:10.1016/j.jesp.2010.05.015.

Van Kleef, G. A., & Côté, S. (2007). Expressing anger in conflict: When it helps and when it hurts. *Journal of Applied Psychology, 92*, 1557–1569. doi:10.1037/0021-9010.92.6.1557.

Van Kleef, G. A., De Dreu, C. K. W., & Manstead, A. S. R. (2004a). The interpersonal effects of anger and happiness in negotiations. *Journal of Personality and Social Psychology, 86*, 57–76. doi:10.1037/0022-3514.86.1.57.

Van Kleef, G. A., De Dreu, C. K. W., & Manstead, A. S. R. (2004b). The interpersonal effects of emotions in negotiations: A motivated information processing approach. *Journal of Personality and Social Psychology, 87*, 510–528. doi:10.1037/0022-3514.87.4.510.

Van Kleef, G. A., De Dreu, C. K. W., & Manstead, A. S. R. (2010b). An interpersonal approach to emotion in social decision making: The emotions as social information model. *Advances in Experimental Social Psychology, 42*, 45–96. doi:10.1016/S0065-2601(10)42002-X.

Vetschera, R., Kersten, G. E., & Koeszegi, S. T. (2006). User assessment of internet-based negotiation support systems: An exploratory study. *Journal Organisations Computer Electronic Commerce, 16*, 123–148. doi:10.1207/s15327744joce1602_3.

Vetschera, R., Koeszegi, S. T., & Schoop, M. (2013). Electronic negotiation systems. In J. J. Cochran (Ed.), *Wiley Encyclopedia operations research management science* (pp. 1–8). London: Wiley.
Wadlinger, H. A., & Isaacowitz, D. M. (2011). Fixing our focus: Training attention to regulate emotion. *Personal Society Psychology Review, 15*, 75–102. doi:10.1177/1088868310365565.
Walther, J. B. (1992). Interpersonal effects in computer-mediated interaction: A relational perspective. *Communication Research, 19*, 52–90. doi:10.1177/009365092019001003.
Walther, J. B. (1994). Anticipated ongoing interaction versus channel effects on relational communication in computer-mediated interaction. *Human Communication Research, 20*, 473–501. doi:10.1111/j.1468-2958.1994.tb00332.x.
Walther, J. B. (1995). Relational aspects of computer-mediated communication: Experimental observations over time. *Organization Science, 6*, 186–203. doi:10.1287/orsc.6.2.186.
Walther, J. B. (1996). Computer-mediated communication: Impersonal, interpersonal, and hyperpersonal interaction. *Communication Research, 23*, 3–43. doi:10.1177/009365096023001001.
Walther, J. B., Anderson, J. F., & Park, D. W. (1994). Interpersonal effects in computer-mediated interaction: A meta-analysis of social and antisocial communication. *Communication Research, 21*, 460–487. doi:10.1177/009365094021004002.
Walther, J. B., & D'Addario, K. P. (2001). The impacts of emoticons on message interpretation in computer-mediated communication. *Society Science Computer Review, 19*, 324–347. doi:10.1177/089443930101900307.
Walther, J. B., & Tidwell, L. C. (1995). Nonverbal cues in computer- mediated communication, and the effect of chronemics on relational communication. *Journal Organizational Computer, 5*, 355–378. doi:10.1080/10919399509540258.
Watzlawick, P., Beavin, J. H., & Jackson, D. D. (1967). *Pragmatics of human communication: A study of interactional patterns, pathologies, and paradoxes*. New York, NY: Norton.
Weber, M., Kersten, G. E., & Hine, M. J. (2006). Visualization in e-negotiations: An inspire ENS graph is worth 334 words, on average. *Electronic Markets, 16*, 186–200. doi:10.1080/10196780600841571.
Weiner, B. (1985). An attributional theory of achievement motivation and emotion. *Psychological Review, 92*, 548–573. doi:10.1037/0033-295X.92.4.548.
Weingart, L. R., & Olekalns, M. (2004). Communication processes in negotiation: Frequencies, sequences, and phases. In M. J. Gelfand & J. M. Brett (Eds.), *Handbook negotiation culture* (pp. 143–157). Stanford, CA: Stanford University Press.
Weiss, H. M., & Cropanzano, R. (1996). Affective events theory: A theoretical discussion of the structure, causes and consequences of affective experiences at work. In B. M. Staw & L. L. Cummings (Eds.), *Research organization behavior an annual series analysis essays critical review* (pp. 1–74). Greenwich, Connecticut: JAI Press Ltd.
Weiss, H. M., Suckow, K., & Cropanzano, R. (1999). Effects of justice conditions on discrete emotions. *Journal of Applied Psychology, 84*, 786–794. doi:10.1037/0021-9010.84.5.786.
Yifeng, N. C., Tjosvold, D., & Peiguan, W. (2008). Effects of warm-heartedness and reward distribution on negotiation. *Group Decision Negotiation, 17*, 79–96. doi:10.1007/s10726-007-9088-4.
Zack, M. H., & McKenney, J. L. (1995). Social context and interaction in ongoing computer-supported management groups. *Organization Science, 6*, 394–422. doi:10.1287/orsc.6.4.394.
Zhang, J. (1997). The nature of external representations in problem solving. *Cognition Science, 21*, 179–217. doi:10.1207/s15516709cog2102_3.

Chapter 6
Discourse Analysis of Emotion in Face-to-Face Group Decision and Negotiation

Bilyana Martinovsky

Introduction

Emotion plays an essential role in many social contexts where group decision taking and negotiation are important, such as jurisdiction, science, politics, business, medical care, etc. Despite that, there are few discourse analysis studies dedicated to the understanding of the discursive function and linguistic realization of emotion in group decision and negotiation (GDN). We often experience number of emotions at the same time or in short sequences, some we are conscious of others—not. This is one of the reasons why emotions are seldom explicitly referred to in interaction. Instead, they are mostly indicated by intonation, tone of voice, choice of words, and nonverbal behaviors. Therefore, face-to-face interaction is the most suitable modality for the analysis of emotions in group decision and negotiation contexts. Since discourse entities are multi-functional, qualitative ethno-methodological analysis of recorded interactions is suitable and necessary. GDN involve argumentation. However, following an ancient dichotomy between the emotional and the rational, argumentation models seldom address and involve emotion.

The present paper explores the relation between emotion and discursive concepts and theories such as Reciprocal Adaptation, Interactive Alignment, and Theory of Theory of Mind (ToM), the definitions of which are discussed in the next section. It studies if and how activity and interaction affect the role of emotion in group problem reframing and group problem solution. For that purpose, it seeks evidence for and against Interactive Alignment theory and theory of ToM by observing Reciprocal Adaptation in authentic data. The importance of ToM-based reasoning affects both understanding of Human–Human interaction and modeling of Virtual Human cognition.

B. Martinovsky (✉)
Department of Computer and Systems Sciences, Stockholm University,
Stockholm, Sweden
e-mail: bilyana@dsv.su.se

B. Martinovsky (ed.), *Emotion in Group Decision and Negotiation*,
Advances in Group Decision and Negotiation 7,
DOI 10.1007/978-94-017-9963-8_6

The study explores the linguistic realization and discursive function of emotions as they occur in authentic GDN. The observed here discursive features and functions aim to contribute to the understanding of face-to-face negotiation as a process and to research on the influence of institutions and activity types on the participants' ability to express, perceive, and elicit emotions. The presented model of emotion in GDN reflects the active role emotions play in decision taking as modifiers of theory-of-mind models, goals and strategies. The model is based on empirical studies of emotion in human interaction in different activities such as plea bargains, simulated negotiations, and doctor–patient consultations. Empathy is used as an example of a complex emotion, which has a natural and powerful function in the shaping and re-contextualization of decision processes.

Theoretical Foundations

Research on emotion relates it more intimately to cognitive processes such as memory and planning. In this section, we explore the current views on emotion, argumentation and ToM.

Theories of Emotion

Three hypothetical descriptions of the relation between emotion and cognition have been discussed through the centuries, which, as Scherer (1993) suggests, could be summarized in the following way:

- Emotion is a separate system related to two other systems in an organism, namely cognition and will (Plato, Kant, Mendelsohn, Leibniz etc.)
- Emotion is a grand system, a coordinator of all developing subsystems in an organism (Freud, Descartes)
- Emotion is one of many components in a complex organism, which are in constant dynamic interaction with each other (Aristotle, Spinoza)

The dichotomy between emotion and cognition as well as this between irrational and rational stems back from Plato's political doctrine in "The Republic" where he claims that human and political well-being depend on the harmony between three separate units of society and soul: cognition (ruling class/thought, reason, rational judgment), "thumos" (warrior class/higher ideal emotions), and motivation (lower class/impulses, instincts, low desires). The Aristotelian tradition questioned this dogma by saying that desire can be found even in motivation and in cognition and that there could be many other components in the soul. In the context of Darwinism, emotion has a roll in adaptation in the course of evolution, emotion is universal, and expression of emotion is found in other species (Cornelius 2000). In Descartes' era, emotions intertwined with cognition of stimuli. Freudians called for exploration of emotion as a basic condition influencing the conscious and unconscious. William James (Myers 2001) introduced the role of the body in the cause and effect chain: The mind perceives the reaction of the body to stimuli, e.g., increased heartbeat; the sensation of the physiological response is a feeling which mental representation is an emotion, e.g., fear. In appraisal theory, which is a form of cognitivism, emotion is seen as something automatic, non-reflective, and immediate and at the same time, cognition leads emotion, i.e., the way we cognize events influences our emotions related to them, not the opposite. In this sense, emotions become and involve coping strategies (Lazarus 1999). According to the social and anthropological constructivist theory it is the sociocultural interpretation, which determines emotions and body reactions, e.g., attitudes to language variations such a dialect (Cornelius 2000).

Contemporary neuroscientists report evidence for the involvement of emotion in so-called rational cognitive processing. Neuroscientists such as Von Uexkull and Kriszat (1934), Fuster (2003), and Arnold Scheibel (personal communication) observe that evolution gave privilege to the limbic system: Emotional feedback is present in lower species, but other cortical cognitive feedback is present only in higher species. In that sense, emotion functions in evolution as a coordinator of other cognitive and non-cognitive functions.

Damasio (1994) suggests that the state of the mind is identical to the state of feeling, which is a reflection of the state of the body. He explores the unusual case of Phineas Gage, a man whose ability to feel emotion was impaired after an accident in which part of his brain was damaged. Damasio finds that, while Gage's intelligence remained intact after the accident, his ability to take rational decisions became severely handicapped because his emotions could no longer be engaged in the process. Based on this case, the neurologist comes to the conclusions that rationality stems from our emotions and that our emotions stem from our bodily senses. Certain body states and postures, e.g., locking of the jaw, would bring about certain feelings, e.g., anger, which in turn will trigger certain thought and interpretations of reality, a thought, traced back to William James.

All approaches to emotion underline the major role emotions play in cognitive processing, yet cognitive models of argumentation and negotiation processes exclude the involvement and the effect of emotions.

Argumentation Theories and Emotion

Historically, one of the most influential accounts of argumentation is called Toulmin's model (1958), which analyzes six features of an argument: data, claim, warrant, backing, qualifier, and rebuttal.

van Eemeren and Grootendorst's argumentation theory (2004), the pragma-dialected approach, is currently most popular. They define argumentation as a verbal, social, and rational activity aimed at convincing a reasonable critic of the acceptability of a standpoint by putting forward a constellation of propositions justifying or refuting the proposition expressed in the standpoint.

Walton (1989, 1996) studies negotiation and argumentation by means of informal logic and critical thinking. He offered an account of argument schemes for presumptive reasoning which constitutes the majority of reasoning and argumentation people engage in. Argument schemes are structures or forms of argument, which are normatively binding kinds of reasoning and are best seen as moves, or speech acts in dialogs (Walton 1996).

In legal argument and legal reasoning, case-based and logic-based approaches (e.g., non-monotonic logic) have been applied to study legal argumentation, supplemented with an argument-scheme approach (McCarty 1997; Prakken and Sartor 2002; Prakken 2005). Meanwhile, in artificial intelligence and multi-agent research community, researchers have built computational models for multi-agent negotiation and argumentation-based systems (Parsons et al. 1998; Kraus 2001; Traum et al. 2003).

With the exception of Walton (1992), these theories did not address the role emotions play in argumentation and negotiation. Gilbert (1995) pointed out that emotional, intuitive (*kisceral*), and physical (*visceral*) arguments ought be considered legitimate and studied just as much as logical arguments. However, neither Walton nor Gilbert has come up with a model of how emotions alter negotiation and decision-making process.

Theory of Mind and Emotion

Cognitive-emotive processes that support group decision making and negotiation require a capacity for understanding and empathizing with others. This capacity involves the understanding of differing beliefs, intentions, emotional and visceral states, ability to react and to draw necessary inferences, to predict and plan given these concerns. The term Theory of Theory of Mind (ToM) was coined by Theory of Theory (Morton 1980) and refers to the abilities humans and other higher species have to perceive and reason on the mental/emotional states of others but also of their own. According to some studies, ToM processes provide a special kind of context: the minds and emotions of others (Martinovski and Marsella 2003; Givón 2005). In interaction, people learn to act within these contexts. Beliefs about age, gender, language, environment, and so on contribute to the models that individuals form and keep of each other's intentions. ToM explanations have importance for the interactive realization of emotion, i.e., the way we understand our own and others' emotions in negotiation.

Three mutually exclusive theories have been suggested to explain how we relate to others: by imitation (e.g., Iacoboni 2005), by simulation (e.g., Gordon 1986; Stich and Nichols 1992), or by representation (e.g., Hobbs and Gordon 2005).

Originally, the main process for establishing and communication of ToM models was and still is thought to be imitation. There is increasing evidence from neurosciences "that the neural mechanisms implementing imitation are also used for other forms of human communication, such as language … Functional similarities between the structure of actions and the structure of language as it unfolds during conversation reinforce this notion … Additional data suggest also that empathy occurs via the minimal neural architecture for imitation interacting with regions of the brain relevant to emotion. All in all, we come to understand others via imitation, and imitation shares functional mechanisms with language and empathy" (Iacoboni 2005; see also Chap. 1 in this Volume).

According to "simulation theory," we think of the other's experiences by use of mental and even somatic simulation of, e.g., our own experience of the same kind (Gordon 1986). Thus, if someone has a stomach ache, instead of imitating his/her experience of a stomach ache one can simulate the psycho-somatic processes related to one's own previous experiences of a stomach ache and that way form an understanding and a reaction to his/her state.

Yet a third idea is that ToM is the application of commonsense inferences about the way people think (Hobbs and Gordon 2005). Here, if someone has a stomach ache one can understand her/his state based on ready-made mental representations, which describe what it is to have a stomach ache, without going through somatic imitation or mental simulation.

The last two explanations seem mutually dependent. In order to simulate a stomach ache, one must have some representation of what that is. In order to make inferences about mental representations, one may have to play "as if" games. Martinovski (2007a, b) has suggested that imitation, simulation, and representation are cognitive-emotive processes developed in evolution, all equally available for homo sapiens sapiens.

Researchers have suggested different mechanisms for dealing with ToM's complex processing. Baron-Cohen talks about "mindreading" or the ability to monitor others' intentions. He goes to an extreme, claiming that successful communication entails a constant feedback-check between communicators to verify whether the listener's interpretation corresponds to the intended interpretation. In discourse analysis, this feedback-checking is reflected in the concepts of grounding and feedback (Allwood 1976). In computer science, the concept of grounding has been used for the design of computational models of dialog (Traum 1994).

In the model developed here, ToM plays an important role, parallel to emotion, as it enables reasoning about own and others' goals and strategies and changes thereof.

Interactive Alignment and Reciprocal Adaptation

Negotiation and group decision making are defined as processes of problem reframing and problem solution. Since negotiation and group decision taking are most often conducted interactively, one needs to redefine the concept of framing by adding the socio-interactive aspect of its meaning. Thus by problem reframing, we mean not only cognitive-affective reframing but also socio-interactive restructuring of a problem through discursive grounding. Prospect theory (Kahneman and Tversky 1986) did not offer understanding on decision taking as socio-interactive reframing, but only as a cognitive-affective process. In order to understand negotiation and group decision taking we need to understand how the socio-interactive framing affects the decision process.

The concept of framing has different definition and application in the fields of decision studies and in social studies. Related to decision taking, framing is defined as a cognitive process, which limits and directs the interpretation of and the emotional relation to the perceived and imagined loss and gain. In other words, here the process is cognitive and emotive. One of the ways in which people frame, for instance, losses and gains, is that losses regularly hurt more than gains feel good (ibid.). The framework or the structure that maintains this state of preferences affects decision taking.

In interaction studies and sociology, the concept of frame is different. Goffman's (1967) original description and understanding of framing is described in short as "organization of experience" in interactive and social order. Frames are not only cognitive but also social interactive constructions, i.e., the frame is set also by the activity and the situation as such, including roles, settings, goals. For instance, in a courtroom, the judge sits in the middle of both parties, independently of how the defendant understands the situation. It follows that in Goffman, a situation is not created by the interactants but a frame is.

Gumpertz (1982: 13) definition of Reciprocal Adaptation is also related to framing: "the procedure … where each participant gradually learns to adapt and to enter into the other's frame of reference." In his view, Reciprocal Adaptation is involved in interactive reframing of situations, knowledge, and arguments and it does not presuppose conscious or less conscious processing of information. This communicative, cultural and learning mechanism is not only cognitive but also linguistic, emotive, and behavioral, i.e., speakers adapt to each other on different levels: lexical and semantic choice, syntax, posture, gaze, proximity, orientation, tone of voice, etc. It is a mechanism behind linguistic phenomena such as creole-like varieties of languages and interactive emotions such as empathy and rapport (Martinovski 2010). Similarly, human users adapt even to the speech and behavior of the Virtual Agent (Bell 2003; Martinovski and Traum 2003). Thus, there are basic interactive mechanisms, which characterize human interaction and affect participants' frames of reference, such as Reciprocal Adaptation. Reciprocal Adaptation can be seen as the discursive correspondent to Moore and Iacoboni's neurological concept of *neural resonance* (see Chap. 1 in this Volume).

According to Pickering and Garrod (2006), communication in discourse is accomplished through an interactive process they call alignment and successful communication through good alignment: "the development of similar representations in the interlocutors … interlocutors align situation models during dialogue." (ibid., p. 1). The main claim of their theory is that "automatic processes play a central role and explicit modeling of one's interlocutor is secondary" in communication (ibid.). The alignment involves situation models and non-situational knowledge such as language knowledge. Interlocutors align their situational knowledge, but they also align knowledge of situation and language (for instance, what they think "right" means with the word "right"). The situation models include notions such as "space, time, causality, intentionality, and reference to main individuals under discussion" (ibid., p. 2). Alignment is based on willingness for cooperation and on mechanistic automatic imitation (of lexical choices, syntax, tone of voice, etc.): "Our underlying conceptualization of conversation is collaborative, in that we treat it as a 'game of pure cooperation' … in which it is in both interlocutors' interest for it to succeed for both interlocutors" (ibid., p. 22) and "the interactive-alignment account proposes that alignment is primitive. It is a form of imitation and drops out of the functional architecture of the system … In these accounts, imitation is an automatic, non-inferential process and is in some sense the default response. Generally, imitation does not appear to require any decision to act" (ibid., p. 18). Thus, alignment does not involve building of entire theory of the other but a primitive turn-to-turn alignment on different linguistic levels of the message: phonetic, syntactic, semantic, etc. Each level is processed and aligned for itself and misalignment on one level enhances alignment on another level. Garrod and Pickering point out also that children cannot inhibit alignment, which speaks for the forcefulness of this interactive mechanism. They base their view on situated interaction where participants have to find interactively each other's position in a maze without being able to see it and assume that the same mechanism works on everyday conversation. "Such models are assumed to capture what people are 'thinking about' while they understand a text, and therefore are in some sense within working memory (they can be contrasted with linguistic representations on the one hand and general knowledge on the other). Successful dialog occurs when interlocutors construct similar situation models to each other" (ibid., pp. 1–2). They point out "that this account differs from Clark (1996), who assumes that speakers carefully track their addressees' mental states throughout conversations" (ibid., p. 10) and that "the important point is that effects of partner specificity do not imply that interlocutors need employ complex reasoning whenever they produce an expression. Instead, they have a strong tendency to employ the form that they have just encountered" (ibid., p. 20).

Interactive Alignment is similar to the concept of Reciprocal Adaptation in that they refer to framing in terms of similar discourse processes and do not demand conscious processing during interaction, although the connection has not been made nor explored yet in the literature.

> Reciprocal Adaptation, developed around 1982:
> "the procedure … where each participant gradually learns to adapt and to enter into the other's frame of reference."

> Interactive Alignment, developed around 2004:
> "the development of similar representations in the interlocutors … interlocutors align situation models during dialogue."

In that sense, Garrod and Pickerings response to Goffman's definition is: Interactants use Interactive Alignment to frame their activities in order to make sense of a situation, where alignment is primitive, automatic, based on imitation and realizes on both production and comprehension level. However, it is hardly the case that alignment is the process through which interactants make sense of a situation since by definition this process is primitive, i.e., does not involve complex reasoning or active long-term memory-based monitoring. Rather it is more likely to see it as a way of preliminary or first layer framing. Gumpez' response to Goffman is then: Interactants gradually learn to frame their activities through Reciprocal Adaptation in order to make sense of a situation because Reciprocal Adaptation is defined as a more general phenomenon than Interactive Alignment which does not pose a condition of automaticity and short-term memory basis.

The mechanistic aspect of communication, of actual meeting between people, does bring changes into negotiation, which is otherwise characterized by pre-set values, preferences and strategies, therefore emotive adaptation in negotiation is of great interest and it has not been studied sufficiently. However, even complex cognitive-emotive processes such as some forms of ToM building can bring changes to negotiation and decision taking. For example, Martinovski (2006) found that empathy and rejection of empathy involve ToM modeling. Martinovski (2011) found that emotions function as engines in conflict management and involve opposite Reciprocal Adaptation.

Empathy

Empathy is a complex emotion defined by Mead (1993) as the "capacity to take the role of the other and to adopt alternative perspectives vis-a-vis oneself"; and by Hogan (1969) as the ability to take "the intellectual or imaginative apprehension of another's condition or state of mind." Reik (1949) describes four stages of the empathy process: (i) identification—projecting self into the other, (ii) incorporation—introjecting the other into self, (iii) reverberation—interplaying of own and other experience, and (iv) detachment—withdrawal from subjective involvement and recourse to use of methods of reason. In that sense, empathy points to an interesting phenomenon of communication, namely uncertainty or rather openness to unknown outcomes, to the possibility of change of goals, needs, and behavior in the course of communication. In the case of negotiation, empathy may contribute to the unpredictability of the planned or desired outcome.

Davis (1994) distinguishes between cognitive and emotional (or emotive) empathy, which refers to empathy as attitude or taking the perspective of the other and empathy as emotional response to the emotions of the other, respectively. He also suggests a distinction between two types of emotional empathy: parallel empathy (PE) or empathy related to the other's feeling directed to a third person and reactive empathy (RE) or empathy to the other's feelings oriented toward it/her/himself.

Under stress people seek what Lazarus (1999) calls problem-focused and emotion-focused social support. Empathy is one of the resources available in the process of seeking and giving social support, whether it is predominantly emotional or predominantly problem-or2005iented. In this sense, empathy is a form of a coping strategy.

Empathy has been studied experimentally and theoretically, with short- and long-term perspectives (Bussman and Muller 1992). Heritage () uses a conversation analysis method in his study of social empathy interplay. Goodwin and Goodwin (1987) use ethno-methodology to study the realization of assessments in talk. Jefferson et al. (1987) examine the pursuit of intimacy. These studies, however, are not oriented toward situations of negotiation per se and are concentrated on certain specific feature rather than looking for descriptive features.

Martinovski et al. (2007) indicate that empathy (elicitation, acceptance, rejection, refusal of empathy) may be seen as a general cognitive-emotive capacity necessary for successful human interaction. This view relates to the Theory of ToM, which claims that interactants consciously or less consciously build theories of each others' and own goals, knowledge, characteristics, social and emotional status, facilitated by specific neural resources and processing. Three competitive theories explain how ToM building occurs: by simulation, by imitation, or by representation. Martinovski (2007a, b) finds manifestation of all three cognitive-emotive processes in discourse.

Definitions of Basic Concepts

Section "Theoretical Foundations" above discussed analytical concepts such as Reciprocal Adaptation, Interactive Alignment, and ToM-based reasoning, which are used in the empirical analysis in the next sections of this chapter. The present section states the choice of working definitions of main concept used in the study such as negotiation, group decision, and emotion. Negotiation is commonly defined as the communication process through which a group of people or agents try to reach a mutually acceptable agreement on some matter (Bussman and Muller 1992). Typical examples are business negotiations, labor negotiations, salary negotiations, negotiation in courtrooms, diplomatic negotiations. Negotiations can be seen as bargaining or as problem solving or as dispute resolution. One may also use negotiation in a broader social sense as the communicative process, through which social values are discussed before and as they are shared in the community. Negotiations thus involve not only problem solving skills but also general communication skills, including management of emotions. The involvement of empathy in the discussion of the process of negotiation may encourage a more collaborative rather than conflict-oriented conceptualization of negotiation. The group decision is defined by its main goal, which is taking a decision, whereas negotiations may not aim nor end up with a decision (see also Meerts and Vukovic in this volume).

I define emotion in a broad sense as a physiological, cognitive, and discursive experience, which is affected by and affects processing and outcome of cognitive and discursive activity, i.e., emotion is defined as recognition of sensory feedback and as coping strategies, which coordinate decision making not only on personal level but also in interaction. Thus I include as emotions not only experiences of joy, sadness, anger, and fear, but also complex emotive-cognitive experiences such as trust and empathy. Emotions are not static. They are processes on a neurological, biological, and expressive level. One and same stimuli can cause a chain of different physiological reactions, emotional sensations, and cognitive appraisals, each of which can influence the other in time.

Data and Method

The present study uses discourse and conversation analysis methodology in order to observe the relation between linguistic and discourse features and functions of emotion in GDN. Conversation analysis uses detailed analysis of specific and representative dialog to isolate generalizable or not generalizable features and processes. Before conducting any meaningful statistical analysis or modeling we need to understand the phenomena we are dealing with and one way to do that is through a sufficiently rich analysis, which will help us to extract the focal features, their function and organization (Martinovski 2000). The aim of such analysis is to observe the small-scale and local interactive events and processes, which cause social change rather than to infer how institutions determine the interaction. Certainly, many factors shape the emotion episodes and their linguistic realizations, e.g., institutions, biological states, temperaments, cultures, etc. Institutional settings structure the roles of the speakers with respect to their rights and obligation to elicit, give, and respond to emotion. For instance, in courts, emotion elicitation is less successful and welcome; in the doctor's office and between friends all functions of empathy are quite expected; on a war field the wounded may have the advantage of empathy, etc.

The present study uses data from several different genres of negotiation dialog, including Talkbank, Role Play, an informal conversation, and a plea bargain. The Talkbank Clinical data involve interactions between a healthcare provider and a patient: http://xml.talkbank.org.:8888/talkbank/file/talkbank/Clinical/Holland/. The nurse tried to negotiate with the patient to participate in the scheduled treatments without creating conflict.

The other set of data consists of transcriptions of role-playing dialogs between a US captain and a lay-person playing the role of a Spanish doctor from a non-governmental medical organization in Iraq. The captain has been instructed to negotiate with the doctor to move his clinic without exposing secret information and the doctor has been instructed that in his negotiation he must care mainly about his patients and that he is representing an independent non-militant organization.

The audio-recorded and transcribed informal conversation comes from John Heritage's corpus. The audio-recorded and transcribed plea bargain is a part of Douglas Maynard's corpus.

Transcription Standards

The utilized transcription conventions are: "[]" stands for overlapped speech; ":" stands for prolonged vowel; "=" stands for latching speech; "/" indicates pause; capital letters indicate emphatic speech; "+" indicates cutoff; "()" stands for inaudible speech; "?" stands for rising intonation; "." stands for falling intonation; "," stands for continuing intonation; "=" stands for latching; "_" stands for emphasis; "{0.9}" stands for seconds of pause. Each line in the transcription indicates an intonation unit.

Structure of the Plea Bargain

The plea bargain has a particular sequential structure. Sitting in a room with a judge, we have a defense attorney and a district attorney. The discussion is whether the accused should get jail and for how long or a fine and in that case of what amount. In general, the parties have to agree first that they are willing to settle the case, then to establish the Penal Code provision that applies of the crime and at last, agree on the settlement value. This particular instance of a negotiation involves sequences and phases of main activities and different kinds of subactivities and topics:

Main activities and subactivities/topics and their initiators (*subactivities in italics;* ***major negotiation accomplishments in bold***):

1. Brings up Frank Bryan's case—Judge (Jge)
2. *Inserted talk about a different case procedure referring back to a topic discussed before line 1 where the judge brings up Frank Bryan's case—Prosecutor (Prs)*
3. Return to the case topic—Jge

    Parties present their interpretation of events
    Defense offers settlement and reference to Penal code, insists that this is a case of disorderly conduct (CPC: 647f) rather than Arrest Resistance case (CPC: 148).

4. A meta-comment on the origin of his settlement strategy—Defense (Def) to Jge
5. **Agrees to settle, suggest a type of crime, 148 rather than 647f—Prs**
6. Discussion on events, type of crime, and arrest period—Def and Prs
7. *Didactic instruction—Jge to Prs*

8. Aggressive refusal to involve defendant's prior criminal history—Def
9. *Side talk about rain—Jge*
10. **Plea Bargain Agreement—Prs, Def**

Each one of the phases in the negotiation has particular initiation signals and initiators. The order of the phases provides context and grounding for the rest of the phases, i.e., this sequential order provides the organic structure of the interaction. Phases are defined as larger units of talk distinguished by topic, activity, and location in the conversation. Sequences are units of talk, which involve at least an adjacency pair and which build up phases in conversation. They are often used to jointly accomplish a communicative act/project.

There are number of concrete facts, which are considered by the parties in order to apply relevant provisions, establish settlement value, provide substantial justice, and eventually reach a plea bargain agreement:

1. Did the defendant resist arrest?—yes/no
2. Did the defendant strike an officer?—yes/no
3. Did the defendant cause disorder?—yes/no
4. Did the defendant spent time in jail already?—yes/no/how long
5. Does the defendant have prior convictions?—yes/no/what kind

The defense counsel's arguments mitigate each stance based on the above questions:

> Defendant did not resist arrest other than verbally and if he did it just looked like resistance but it was not because he was drunk;
> Defendant's character when not drunk is a very peaceful and sweet;
> There is no evidence that he stroke an officer;
> Defendant caused disorder but it is a minor family thing thus trivial, in fact he was probably even justifiably angry since "what kind of mom calls the police on her son";
> Defendant was drunk and if he was not he would not do what he did;
> Defendant is black and if he was not it is less likely someone would call the police, even his mother.

Prosecutor's arguments refer to police report and legal provisions texts:

> Defendant resisted arrest but not only verbally: he tried to escape;
> There is not evidence he stroke an offices but the report is not full;
> Defendant caused serious disorder to this extent that his own mother called the police, which points to 647f provision related to disorder conduct;
> Defendant has spent time in jail justly since he did resist arrest although not clear for how long;
> Defendant has prior convictions related to disorder conduct and violent resistance to arrest, including striking an officer, thus the most relevant and urgent provision is CPC: 148, which provides jail in order to reach substantial justice.

Linguistics Manifestation and Functions of Emotions in GDN

Emotion occurs spontaneously, but in negotiation it can be used strategically as argumentation and it can be manifested in various ways. This section studies linguistic manifestations and functions of emotion and their relation to cognitive appraisal and coping processes, which go parallel with interaction.

The first 7 subsections use examples from a plea-bargain conversation in chronological order, followed by a subsection which concentrates on linguistic realization of empathy using friendly conversation between two women and role-play negotiations between a Doctor and a Captain (see also Section "Data and Method" above).

Entertainment

The prosecutor expresses intention to settle rather than continue to trial, what needs to be decided is the settlement price. Instead of acknowledging that the defense attorney (Def) initiates one side talk as a form of entertainment and a show (*italized*) of his experience and friendship with famous and successful lawyers.

Prs: Well I'd li[ke to settle (it)
Jge: [Yo(h)u ha(h)lwa(h)ays s(h)ay tha(h)a(h)at
[˙i h h][˙ihh][h u h][h u h]
Def: [Well as- I][I lea][rned that (t][rade) from Harr]y Moberg,
Jge: ˙uhh[hOh:] hah [hah][h a h ˙h h] (   )=
Def: [uh:] [hee][cuz with Harry], (0.2) >you=
Jge: =[((thrt clr))]
Def: =[start talkin'] to each other through clenched< teeth.
[And after about] five] minutes of (.) challenging each=
Jge: [ah hih!hihhih] ( )]
Def: =other to go [to trial, and I know 'at 'e doesn't try any=
[((sound of small item dropped on table))
Def: =ca(h)ses see(h)ee, [˙hh o(h)nly r(h)eason's I g(h)otta go to=
Jge: [( )
Def: =trial a[gainst one'a his new kids, r(h)ight?=
Jge: [˙hhh
Jge: =Huh!=
Def: = ˙hh Or [(hi)his (n- old pro like) mister Franklin, ˙hhh=
( ): [(   )
Def: =And so I finally tried to get the conversation around t(h)a what we were talkin' about. like sett'lin' the ca(h)ase ˙hhh It ˆworks.<Harry and I cuddo a lot of business that wa(h)ayhh [wu-
Jge: [(hih) hih huh huh ˙hh=
Prs: =Uh- (0.2) I- I think it's a case that oughta be i- uh settled. It's a=
Def: =°Okay.=

In this embedded sequence, the Def manages to entertain both the Judge, who often laughs, and his opponent with a subnarrative. He also points out that he behaves within a context and with a strategy, that he is playing a role as prescribed by the best in his business. The linguistic means he uses to accomplish emotional experience such as entertainment are:

Narrative
Slang imitation
Feedback elicitors ("right?")
Lexical choices ("new kid," "old pro," "that trade")
Tone of voice
Intonation

There are many and different kinds of communicative acts involved in this narrative, all carrying a joyful emotion but the context changes illocutionary force of these acts into mitigated forms of threat, i.e., expressing and evoking emotions of fear and humiliation.

Empathy Evocation

Number of the defense' arguments build on and aim to evoke empathy: Being black is a disadvantage therefore an excuse; being drunk provides an excuse too, as well as having one's "mom" call the "cops."

Def: [Well. lemme ask 'im. I assume 'is mumma bailed 'im out after
she called the c(h)ops on 'i(h)m f(h)in' ou(h)t what
[(i'was) all ab(h)out.]

Empathy evocation is signaled by number of linguistic devices, which remind of adolescent speech style thus pointing to the person's immaturity, reaches also to personal association with own family history such as:

Tone of voice
Intonation
Lexical choices ("mom," "cops")
Gesture

Anger

The entertaining and ridiculing style is interchanged with demonstrations of helpfulness and claimed agreeability, which later develop into aggression and disgust (*italized*). The reaction of the prosecutor (Prs) is again self-explanation presented in an even weaker manner as he stutters and has a problem formulating a sentence.

The Def continues his ridicule by use of mocking back channels, initial interruptions, latching, ridiculing mocking repetitions, etc. In this manner, the Def gains a dominant emotional role in the conversation, wins the floor, and presents his personal hypothetical interpretations as arguments.

Prs: He has ub a: one prior. (0.3) conviction in this jurisdiction
with thee uhm (0.8) sheriff's office, of of interestinly
enough. u:v striking a public officer and of disturbing peace.
Def: *Will you knock it off. ((disgusted tone)) (0.5) You wanna make*
a federal case out of this¿
Prs: N:o, [I I just] think [that that i]t's it's not uh this uh=
Def: *[˙h h h] [h h m]*
Prs: =happy go lucky chap's uh first (1.0) encounter with uh um (1.8)
Def: [Statistic]ly if ya got black skin:. you ar (0.2) you ar (.)=
Prs: [( )]
Def: =hhighly likely to contact the police. I think
uh:substantially more likely than if you're white.<*Now come*
on.<Whadda want from 'im. (0.6) He's got a prior.
(1.8)
Jge: Well we know he spent ten ho:urs, ehhem (1.0) end
uh:: [we know he's been down here fer] mo:re
Def: *[(He) o: n l y s p e n t ten] ((mock shock))*
(0.8)
( ): *((throat clear))=*

Emotionally loaded imperative expressions such as "knock it off" and "come on" and throat clearing act as more powerful persuasion devices than the arguments, which are inferential and unmotivated:

Tone of voice
Intonation
Sentence modality
Turn taking—interruption, latching
Lexical expressions
Sequential timing of aggression

It is the interplay between context and emotion that changes the illocutionary force of Def's communicative acts, i.e., the question "You wanna make a federal case of this" in combination with the underlying emotion of anger and aggression carried out by tone of voice, intonation and context turn the interrogative illocutionary force into a threat, evoking fear.

Ridicule, Sarcasm

As the prosecutor has agreed to settle he proposes a settlement value. He is joining the Def in his playful colloquial style of speech, which is evident in lexical choices such as "dandy," "wanna," "probably." Def objects to the suggestion starting with an interruption and an initial "wull" discourse particle. Def has no good argument other than reasoning based on his personal hypothetical interpretation of events. Def interrupts again this time the very beginning of the Prs attempt to take the floor and present his own objection. Def objection is again underlying his personal view in a categorical manner, which involves even sounds such as garbling, signaling ridicule or his personal view of discontent. In response to the Prs is defensive and presents an explanation of his initial settlement suggestion which more or less cancels it and expresses his own uncertainty. When he tries to present his view of the situation, starting with a Theory-of-Mind expression such as "I think" the Prs is again interrupted by the Def. This time the Def continues the ridiculing strategy vocalizing a mocking reaction (*italized*) of surprise with a single discourse particle or exclamation "oh."

Prs: =Strikes me as a dandy one forty eight uh- (1.0) >probably
better one fortyeight than a six fortyseven ef< if you wanna
be very stric[t about it.
Def: [Wull I- thu- I see it as a six forty seven ef.
uh: 'e didn' lay hands on any officers, ˙hh if he 'adn't been
so ˇdrunk I assume nothing none'uh this woulda ha:ppened.
˙hh[h
Prs: [W[ell I-
Def: [I don't think it's worth any jail time no matter what it
is. (("no" is garbled))
Prs: I was being academic when I said that. [I]uh: I I think=
Def: *[°Oh,]*

Having put the Prs in a discursive corner, made him abandon his own judgments and after vocalizing ridicule of the Prs the Def suggests his own version of a settlement value which is of completely different kind, not jail but a very low fine. He does that by following the entertainment line of argument, where he invents a new word and then playfully offers a mocking apology. In that sense, he combines entertainment and ridicule of the Prs by playfully and subtly suggesting that he is too narrow-minded and works only with aid of books, laws, and dictionaries.

Repetitions
Turn-taking—interruption, latching
Rhetorical questions
Throat clearing
Tone of voice

Intonation

The feedback utterance "oh" serves often as expression of surprise, thus in combination with its context and the emotions expressed by its intonation the illocutionary force changes into expression of ridicule and evocation of shame.

Apology

The apology is a communicative act with emotional content and function. It aims to express emotions such as sadness, disappointment, and shame directed toward one-self not others. It intends to evoke satisfaction and empathy. In the example below, we have an explicit linguistic reference to this communicative act, "I'm sorry," but its intent and effect is changed by the lack of the expected emotions, which is indicated by tone of voice and intonation. Playfully sweet and charmingly apologetic (*italized*), Def is playing with words ("justicy," "justiciabe") used earlier by the Prs thus diminishing his importance and in effect mitigating the effect of his claims for justice.

Def: *[Okay, uh: twenny fi dollar fine?<does*
that so:und [justicy?][justici]able?
Prs: [W e: ll,][u m :]
Prs: Um: (0.4) i- hh (0.4)[( )
Def: *[>I made it up.[I'm sor]ry.I didn't=*
Prs: [Yih got-]
Def: *=look at the diction-I made up a [°w o rd.<]*

Thus instead of expressing sadness the apology is used to express joy, fun and this is how we get ridicule of the opponent. Locally, it follows the argumentation line directed toward the judge, namely the line of entertainment.

Flattery

By emphasizing his own professionalism (see Section "Empathy Evocation" above) Def is also using professionalism as a compliment to his opponents.

Def: [He doe:]s (.) take a menacing sta:nce, ˙hh but
on the other hand he doesn't attempt ta strike an officer.<I
assume that the officer's highl- high- degree of
prufessionalism: pruvents my client from getting himself into
further tr(h)ouble. ˙hhh[hh

Flattery is a well-known communicative emotion elicitor, presented here in a more serious and structured language, in difference from other moments of entertainment, sprinkled with casual colloquial mannerisms.

Agreeable and Helpfulness

The Def presents himself as helpful when the Prs lacks information on important issue such as how long the defendant spent in jail already. In parallel with the entertainment and ridicule, Def presents himself also as an agreeable negotiation who does what the Prs wants. This agreeable persona is expressed with a reference to the personal name of the Prs who was just made fun of and put in a corner.

Def: Well what are you asking for.<>Lemme I mean I always usually go along with whatever Jerry says.<

This helpfulness is again dominated by the playful entertaining tone, which mitigates the seriousness of the offense and thus works toward minimal judgment. The contrast between this emotion and the aggression and ridicule expressed earlier illuminates the manipulative character of the expressed emotion.

Empathy

Empathy does not always smooth over negotiations. It may also be rejected and thus complicate negotiations. Most of the research on empathy is focused on the ability or skill of giving empathy, but reception of empathy can also be described as a skill and ability since both acceptance and rejection of empathy function as coping strategies.

In this section I explore the linguistic and discursive realizations of empathy with a special emphasis on rejection of given empathy in order to understand its mechanisms and functions in negotiations and thus contribute to the planning and design of empathy training.

Before we examine the function of rejection of empathy giving in negotiations, we will observe shortly the general realization of empathy in a casual conversation between friends who do not have conflicting interests and use that in comparison with negotiation situations where the parties try to overcome differences in interest.

Like any other communicative act, the act of empathy can be elicited (E), given (G), and received (R). The reception may be either acceptance or rejection. One may reject an act of giving of empathy or reject an act of elicitation of empathy. We will study the first case. These functions of the empathy signs may be realized in phases and different degrees. For instance, one may expect the default formulation of a "fulfilled" empathy episode to start with elicitation of empathy, continue with empathy giving followed by empathy receiving (see example 1). One and the same utterance can have all three functions at the same time: It could be an elicitation, an expression, and a response (e.g., line 35 in example 1).

Ritualistic Exchange of Empathy

The following example illustrates the above mentioned distinctions as well as a situation of successful "empathic moments" (Heritage 2005).

(1) [Holt Xmas 85:1:4]

1. Joy: ye-:s I'm alright,
2. Les: oh:. hh yi-m- you know I-I- I'm boiling about something hhhheh [1 heh hhhh]
3. Joy: [1 wha::t.]
4. Les: well that sa:le. {0.2} at- at . the vicarag {0.6}
5. Joy: oh ye[2 :s],
6. Les: [2 t] {0.6} u ih your friend 'n mi:ne wz the:re {0.2}
7. (): (h[3 h hh)]
8. Les: [3 mmis] ter: R:,
9. Joy: (oh ye:s hheh) {0.4}
10. Les: and em: we really didn't have a lot'v cha:nge that day becuz we'd been to bath 'n we'd been: christmas shoppin:g, {0.5} but we thought we'd better go along t'th'sale 'n do what we could, {0.2} we hadn't got a lot . of s:e- ready cash t'spe:nd. {0.3} t[4 hh]
11. Joy: [4 Mh].=
12. Les: =In any case we thought th'things were very expensive.
13. Joy: oh did you. {0.9}
14. Les: AND uh we were looking rou-nd the sta:lls 'n poking about 'n he came up t'me 'n be said Oh: hhello leslie, . still trying to buy something f'nothing,
15. Joy: PEG-> .hhhahhhhhh! {0.8 } oo[5 : : :: LESLI E]
16. Les: PEE-> [5 oo:.ehh heh heh] {0.2}
17. Joy: PEG-> i:s [6 n ' t he]
18. Les: REE-> [6 what] do you sa:y. {0.3}
19. Joy: PEG-> oh isn't he drea:dful.
20. Les: PEE-> eye-:-:s: {0.6}
21. Joy: PEG-> what'n aw::f'l ma::[7:::n]
22. Les: PEE-> [7 ehh] heh-heh-heh
23. Joy: PEG-> oh:: honestly, I cannot stand the man it's \ just {no[8 :}]
24. Les: RPEE-> [8 I] bought well I'm gon' tell Joyce
   that,ehh[7 heh]=
25. Joy: [9 ( )]=
26. Les: RPEE=[9 heh-heh he-e] uh: eh [10 eh hhhhh]
27. Joy: PEG-> =[10 O H : : : :.] I do think he's dreadful
28. Les: PEE-> tch oh: dea-r

29. Joy: PEG-> oh: he r[11 eally i]:s,
30. Les: RPEE-> [11 he dra-]ih-he (.) took the win' out'v
my sails c'mpletel(h)y .
31. Joy: REG-> I know the awkward thing is you've never
got a ready a:n[12 swer have you. that's
ri:ght,]
32. Les: REE-> [12 no: I thought'v lots'v ready a]nswers
a:fterward[13 s],
33. Joy: REG-> [13 yes] that's ri::gh[14 t].
34. Les: RER-> [14 yes] .
35. Joy: REG-> but you c'n never think of them at the
ti:[15 me a:fterwards I always think. oh I
should've said that. or I should've said
thi]s.
36. Les: RER-> [15 no:.no:. oh y e s e h- r i : g h t.] {0.7}
37. Joy: REGE-> b[16 ut] I do:'nt think a'th'm at the ti:me
38. Les: RERG-> [16 mm:]. ehh huh huh {0.8}
39. Joy: oh:: g-oh 'n I think carol is going, t'the
[17 meeting t'ni g h t,]

The empathy episode starts with an announcement of trouble on line 2. It is welcomed and elicited on line 3. This is followed by a narrative background on lines 4–13. Turn 14 gives the punch line, which elicits empathy, both parallel and reactive, cognitive and emotional. Joy gives her rather emotional empathy on line 15, and Les implicitly accepts it on line 16. Then starts the separation of parallel and reactive empathy. On line 17, 19, 21, 23, 27, and 29 Joy gives a clear example of what is meant by parallel empathy, i.e., she expresses a disapproval of the person by whom Les feels hurt in that way mirroring Les' dislike of this person's actions. These expressions of parallel empathy have also degrees; first it starts with a rhetorical question on lines 17 and 19, then the degree rises to clear assessments such as on line 21, and at last we have a assertive (e.g., "honestly," "I do think") and explicit formulations of subjective opinion, e.g., lines 23 and 27. Joy's parallel empathy is predictable and predicted by Les, in fact she motivates (line 24) her expression of a need of emotional support by pointing to Joy's disposition to the negative feelings they both share against mister R. At that point it is not even clear who gives the empathy, Joy or Les. On line 30 Les expresses her internal distress, which changes the character of the elicited empathy:

On the next line 31 Joy performs a good example of the so called reactive empathy. This empathy type is realized here by the use of the generalizing pronoun "you" and by a tag question followed by a confirmative assessment. The tag question is an elicitor of consent, which again turns the roles around: Joy is supposed to be the empathy giver but she often becomes the empathy elicitor as a form of empathy giving. Thus, being both the "empathizer" and the "empathee" is an important capacity in the process of informal discussion of social values and attitudes, all intertwined with associated and even negotiated emotions. On line 32 Joy exchanges the general "you" with a reference to herself, which in a sense functions as voicing Les' internal discomfort and embarrassment for which she seeks empathy. This voicing is expressed as a quotation of internal dialog. Thus Joy internalizes Les' inner state, i.e., she displays reactive emotive empathy. On line 37 Joy has completely taken Les' internal position and talks about her own experiences of the same state of mind Les complains from. Les now functions both as a receiver and a giver of empathy, the process has reached its climax and suddenly on line 39 Joy announces a completely new topic.

The empathy process in example 1 is fulfilled: There was elicitation, giving, and acceptance of empathy, and there was also identification (e.g., line 31), incorporation (e.g., line 35), reverberation (e.g., line 37), and finally detachment (line 39). The verbalizations are at first more emotional and then become more cognitive as they turn to comparisons of experiences. In this empathy process both speakers verify, confirm, and reconfirm for each other the legitimacy of their experiences, values, and attitudes. The sudden change of topic at the end of example (1) and the repetitive turning of the roles in the process of empathizing suggest that the empathy process is rather ritualistic.

Rejecting Empathy

One may expect empathy to always be as successful as in example 1, but empathy is not always accepted which may be as much a source of trouble as lack of empathy. The next three examples illustrate different ways of rejecting empathy in negotiation. In the first example, we have a role-play, in which an US captain is in negotiation with a Spanish-speaking doctor representing a non-governmental medical organization. The captain has to convince the doctor to move his clinic. The captain (C) has introduced the request and now he has to deal with the reaction of the doctor (D).

(2) RPSASO'04.1b

14. C: we have , we have [1 (xx)]
15. D: [1 and WHERE] am i going to GO ?
16. C: we have [2 definite+]
17. D: [2 and HOW] am i going to GET there .
18. C: i certainly understand your concerns sir ,
[3 but we have+]
19. D: [3 all of a sudden] now you want
me to MOVE , and now you're willing to
give me HELP to move me out of here ,
when YOU wouldn't come here in the last year . //
you understand the position i'm in .
20. C: i do understand your position [4 sir ,]
21. D: [4 i i]
22. C: [5 but (xxx)]
23. D: [5 i i have to get back .]
24. C: [6 (xxxx)]
25. D: [6 i have to get back to my patients .]
I have to get back to my patients .
26. C: [7 i understand that sir ,]
27. D: [7 because I care] about my patients .
all YOU care about is GIVING me more patients . /
and i am NOT gonna gonna deal with this.
if you want to send your commander back here ,
he can come in here , and he can take me by FORCE.
and i will make SURE every camera see
this .
now instead of coming in and telling me to MOVE / MY PATIENTS out of here ,
WHY can't you come in here to tell me that you're bringing me SUPPLIES .
ANTIBIOTICS .
BANDAGES .

In utterances 15, 17, and 19 the doctor repeatedly takes the turn without waiting for the captain to finish his turn; he verbalizes a list of issues and questions which need to be addressed and/or which make a decision difficult for him. At first, on line 14 and 16 the captain tries to address the questions, but in utterance 18 he signals understanding of the function of the questions without awaited answer as a call for display of empathy which he verbalizes in utterance 18. However, even this display of problem-focused (cognitive) empathy is ignored. In 19 the doctor starts right after the captain's continuous intonation and overlaps with the captain's continuation. Does the doctor react to the attempt to add a qualification ("but") or does he react to the expression of empathy? He might anticipate an argument and try to cancel it before it even starts. His utterance on line 19 expresses reasons to mistrust the captain's empathy giving expressions by pointing to inconsistency of behavior. Also, in the same utterance the doctor himself elicits empathy by reformulating the captain at the end of his utterance "you understand the position I'm in." This elicitation is more of a response to or a reception of the empathy given on 18 because it is formulated as a declarative sentence with falling intonation. It functions as an argument in the negotiation, as a motivation of reluctance to accept suggestion. In that sense it is a way of facilitating negotiation because it displays desire to be understood. Thus we may tend to believe that the overlap in utterance 19 is a reaction to the display of empathy rather than to the anticipation of an argument. On line 20 the captain responds to the elicited empathy by repeating the elicitation expression of the doctor and reformulating his own formulation in utterance 18. In this way, he attempts to create greater similarity of positions on the negotiation floor. However, he is again overlapped and in utterances 22, 23, 24, and 25 we have simultaneous speech: The captain most probably continues his argument (this part not audible) whereas the doctor signals desire to walk out from the negotiation in utterance 25 by repeating the same utterance twice, once as simultaneous speech and once after winning the turn. This rapid removal from the negotiation is met by the captain with continued display of empathy, which is again completely overlapped by the doctor's expression of lack of trust and direct criticism in utterance 26. This last utterance is complex because it contains change of strategy and change of phase in the negotiation. The doctor rejected empathy (utterances 15, 17, 19, 21, 23, 25, 27), motivated why (19, 27), displayed desire to walk out (25, 27), threatened with intentions to refuse cooperation and damage planned operation (27) and at last, staring with a topic initiating "now" he stated conditions for further negotiation (27). In this sequence the rejection of empathy functions as a display of lack of trust, as a display of lack of desire to be locked in a disadvantageous negotiation and as a bargaining method.

Eliciting, giving, accepting, and rejecting empathy are thus strategic resources in a negotiation. The actual realization or style of empathy exchange can be part of the strategy as such. In the above example (2) we had a rather aggressive doctor who used time pressure, listing of issues, interruptions etc. to realize his strategy of rejection of empathy which would give him stronger positions in negotiating benefits for his party, because he has no interest in moving unless he manages to gain something substantial for his patients.

Polite Rejection of Empathy

In the next example (3) we have another pair of role-playing doctor and captain, where the doctor is realizing the same strategy (i.e., rejection of given empathy) for the same reasons (namely, increase own benefits and avoid being locked in a disadvantageous agreement). However, here the doctor realizes the strategy in a more polite and evasive manner with even high degree of success because the captain is now truly anxious to satisfy the doctor's needs.

(3) RPSASO'04.1a

C: 38 we can certainly i can certainly get some supplies ,
39 i imagine in this area you're in you would have some difficulty getting supplies ,
40 how+ how are you doing with supplies .
D: 41 well to be honest uh captain ,
42 our situation is very very difficult .
43 we're low on bandages ,
44 low on penicillin , ...
49 um if you have access to to medical supplies we are in great need of things like that .
C: 50 yes i i think i have some avenues where i could i could get some supplies for you , ...
52 and quite frankly it would be much easier for us to KEEP you supplied if you were in a safer area among our troops .
53 uh it's [3 a little (difficult)]3
D: 54 [3 i i i SEE]3 captain
55 but uh ...
<phone continues to ring>
60 excuse me .
C: 61 we're we're we're all busy .
62 yeah that that's perfectly fine . ...
66 but REALLY my major concern is is the safety of YOU and your STAFF . ...
D: 69 well i i uh ,
70 i APPRECIATE your concern captain ,
71 but you must understand that we are an independent organization , ...
75 to tell you the truth i was in the middle of dealing with a patient ,
76 and i have a very very busy patient schedule today .
77 uh if if you don't MIND , ...
81 we will uh consider whether this is in the best interest of our patients .
C: 82 well i can CERTAINLY understand your concerns ,

83 and i'm sure you're a very busy man ,
84 there's been a lot of casualties here …
D: 87 [4 you must]4
88 you must understand captain that we we uh we cannot be connected too closely with the united states army . …
C: 93 we we don't want to get involved at ALL in ANY of the operations of your clinic .
…
D: 108 well thank you captain for your concern um ,
109 i'm i'm afraid i must uh get back to my patient now …
C: 115 oh that's that's very understandable .
116 i i think this is a very difficult decision for you and uh know certainly
117 i i certainly know that you probably don't want to TELL your staff what to do ,
118 you want to get some consensus from them ,
119 um ,
120 i the only thing i'd like to urge is is to keep in mind that time is of the essence here .
121 a a as you know [5 from]5
D: 122 [5 i am]5 aware of the situation .
C: 123 as you know from your casualty rate ,
124 the fighting is only getting worse and , …
D: 130 well to
131 i i again i appreciate your CONCERN captain , …
135 so i will look forward to meeting you again .
136 now uh if if you will excuse me ,
137 i have a very sick little girl who needs my attention .
C: 138 wh+ wh+ when do you think the best time to talk would be ?

The captain is not in a position to get empathy whereas the doctor is. These positions are reflected in the dynamic of the negotiation: The captain gives repetitive displays of empathy and the doctor politely acknowledges them and rejects them at the same time. The captain repeats with increasing intensity the claim that he has "concerns" (line 66, 82, 131). His first concern about accessibility to supplies is performed first by a form of reactive empathy starting with a self-report "I imagine" and guessing the other's situation utterance and ending with a wh-question which shows care. This first concern and proposal is accepted by the doctor. The next expression of concern occurs after a weak promise to do a personal favor to the doctor: The captain refers to "i i think I have some avenues"; also on line 38 the captain rephrases his utterance from "we can certainly" to "I can certainly" which shows that he is in fact not so certain how he can get supplies and that this proposal is his personal strategy for establishing trust before presenting the real cause of his visit, the mission to remove the clinic. Line 52 presents his purpose and request staring with an expression which mirrors the doctor's formulation of his needs "well to be honest captain …" namely "and quite frankly." Thus the captain formulates a bargain in which even the linguistic expressions are even: I can find you supplies if you move close to us. However, if the promise of supplies is formulated as a personal favor the demand to move and "keep save" is formulated as a collective gain: "much easier for us to KEEP you supplied if you were in a safer area among our troops": The personal pronoun "I" is changed to plural "us" and "our." At that point, line 54 above the doctor performs the first interruption by voicing with emphatic idiomatic expression

"I SEE" his realization of the captain's negotiation strategy, i.e., realizing that the supplies he agreed to accept at the beginning are conditional and the expressed concern and empathy were strategic, not authentic. At that same point the doctor starts to walk out of the negotiation. His initial trust signaled by acceptance of empathy and offer for help has been broken; from now on every following utterance by the doctor expressed his need to remove himself from the conversation. The captain realizes the lost trust with respect to his real purpose, and he tries to fight for it by explicitly stating his concern and emphasizing the authenticity of his intentions and empathic feelings on line 66 "but REALLY my major concern is is the safety of YOU and your STAFF." This effort is acknowledged by the doctor in the following way: he does not interrupt; he also explicitly states his acknowledgement and also emphasizes his feelings "APPRECIATE"; he gives authentic reasons why the captain's demands are problematic by demanding reactive cognitive empathy using strong deontic modal verb expressions such as "you must understand," after which he implicitly points out what was missing in the captain's concern, namely the condition of the patients (on line 66 the captain emphasized concern for the staff and the doctor but not the patients, who are the doctor's main concern and purpose) and in that way again appealing for empathy toward the patients; at last he opens the possibility of future negotiation by promising to discuss the issue with others.

As a response to that on line 82–3 and 115–18 the captain starts to display reactive and parallel empathy (which reminds of Joy's empathy giver on line 31, example 1) after a sequence of unsuccessful problem-solution-oriented empathic displays (e.g., line 38, 50, 66, etc.). The emphatic "i CERTAINLY understand" on line 82 is a response in strength to the doctor's deontic appeal "you must understand." The captain again states cognitive empathy for the doctor's situation, but he exchanges the term "patients" for the more militant and mitigated term "casualties." This time he is met by a repetition of the deontic appeal for cognitive empathy presented in an interruption (line 87) followed by a reformulation of the previously stated reasons (line 88). When the captain does not show more empathy but gives promises the doctor evades the negotiation by an implicit rebuttal through the initial "well" followed by a polite dismissal: An expression of gratitude (line 108) and a polite need to leave (line 109). The captain again perceives a need to express empathy, and his following lines are tribute to that: he starts with impersonal formulations of understanding which are lexically emphasized with qualifiers such as "very," then uses self-report formulations to voice the other's mental states thus expressing reactive empathy: "I think … that you," "I certainly know that you probably …." The modally strong adverb "certainly" and verb "know" here seem not to be meant to state certainty in the other's state because they are followed by a modally weak adverb "probably," but they seem to be meant to amplify the expression of empathy as such. These are followed by declarative guessings of the other's private desires (line 118) which function as invitations for confirmation of the guessing which is given space in a separate intonation unit on line 119 and filled with a hesitation sound. The doctor does not join this expression of empathy as Les did in line 32, example 1 thus the captain continued by stating new conditions of negotiation. This is met by a next repetition of polite acknowledgment of empathy ("I i again appreciate your CONCERN"), polite dismissal ("so I will look forward to meeting you again"), and polite expression of desire to leave the negotiation ("now uh if you excuse me") with a new implicit lexical emphasis elicitation of empathy ("very sick little girl") toward the patients and the time pressure.

Thus in this dialog, the doctor practiced the strategy of politeness, elicitation of empathy and walking out whereas the captain was using the strategy of giving empathy, presenting demands, deadlines, extending his authority, and at the end urging for caucusing.

Antagonistic Style of Giving and Rejecting Empathy

Empathy can be rejected in a more explicit way. In the following example (4) we have an excerpt from a conversation between a patient (P) who suffered a stroke and a nurse (N). The patient has demonstrated anger especially before doing therapy, which he refuses to do. The patient suffers loss of memory, general discomfort, worry for his life, and quality of life. The nurse deals with the patient's uncooperative behavior. She intends to ensure the patient's cooperation with the medical personal in the future which she explicitly states in a few occasions during the long conversation. She has introduced the issue after an initial polite empathic chat and on line 65 below we see part of the patient's explanatory response.

(4) Whocares.TALKBANK'04

65. P: mhm forget all about it because it don't
make no difference.
I mean it sounds silly to me and it don't matter what kind of methods I get
anyhow.
66. N: you know what ?
67. P : hmm .
68. N: they do have a reason .
but I have a feeling + .
69. P : I don't even want to know about it .
70. N: you don't even care, huh ?
71. P : uhuh no .
72. N: ok .
73. P : I got enough problems on my shoulders
tonight.
I try a little bit I got shoulders by / day by day shoulder to shoulder day .
take it now I don't have time for that bull shit .
74. N: I think probably all they want to do is keep
track of your improvement .
75. P : mhm honey who cares ?
76. N: well I know a couple people that care .

The nurse is faced with an angry avoidance and rejection of empathy. The rejection here is not realized with interruptions and cutoffs, but it is verbalized as cutoff and explicit rejection (utterance 69 above), confirmations of rejections (71), imperative orders and swear words (73), and rhetorical questions (75) and ironic signals of elicitation of empathy (e.g., initial reference "honey" preceding rhetorical question). The nurse is not offering emotional empathy, and she is not giving cognitive empathy as the captain in example (2). She does not use any of the parallel or reactive empathy expressions we observed in example (1) above. Instead, she uses devices such as ritualistic questions (utterance 66 is an question which promises introduction of news or surprise, prepares the mind of the listeners to something unexpected or undesired but still true), guessing of mental state ("I have a feeling," "you don't care," "I think probably all they want …"), acceptance (utterance 72), personal formats and modal expressions ("I think," "I know"), mitigators or "softeners" (such as "probably," initial "well," final feedback requests such as "huh") and even rebuts (76). The initial "well" in utterance 76 is typically used preceding partial disagreement and qualification of statement, which has been provoked by other's utterance and/or understanding of an attitude. Thus the nurse's display of empathy is antagonistic which reflects her position as a caregiver: she needs to display empathy with the patient's state but also needs to display commitment to the patient's medical treatment. The patient's rejections of empathy are also antagonistic and at first seem to have no bargaining purpose. The patient displays lack of desire to negotiate but also lack of belief in sincerity and true care or at least lack of desire to display trust. In contrast to the previous negotiation where the doctor takes over control of the negotiation, here the patient rejects empathy as a rebuttal but does continue to engage in the conversation (the continuation is not displayed above) and does not interrupt the nurse, which contradicts his linguistic display of no desire to talk. In fact, this conversation continues for quite a while despite the explicit refusals, which suggests that the rejections of empathy do have some strategic value for the patient (which might be the reason why the nurse is reluctant to engage in a more emotive empathy episode).

Linguistic Manifestations of Empathy

Giving empathy is not sufficient to realize empathy. There must be also willingness, ability, and even skill in receiving empathy. In the analyzed examples, rejection of empathy is associated with lack of trust, lack of desire to engage in negotiation and/or with desire to gain control over the negotiation conditions, i.e., as a bargaining strategy. The less trust there is between the negotiating parties, the more unreceptive they are to expressions of empathy and the more strategic for the negotiation the functions of empathy become, as observed in examples (2), (3) and (4). And the opposite, the more receptive the speaker is to empathy the more trustful and smooth the negotiation is, as we could see in example (1).

As a discourse phenomena empathy is complex: It is hard to pick one linguistic feature and tie it uniquely to one function only, but one can observe co-occurrences and patterns, in which multiple linguistic features realize multiple functions in particular sequences.

Rejection of given empathy is realized linguistically by discursive features such as refusal to release the turn, overlaps, interruptions, cutoffs, and simultaneous speech as well as by communicative acts such as explicit rejections, confirmations of rejections, rhetorical questions, imperative orders, irony, swearing, "walking out" moves but also display of reception of given empathy followed by rejection.

Giving empathy, on the other hand, is realized by communicative acts such as answering questions, display of non-elicited empathy, repetitions of elicited empathy, ritualistic rhetorical questions, guessing of mental state, acceptance, rebuts. All these are realized with the help of discourse devices such as personal formulations of modal expressions, quoting, and mitigators or "softeners." In our data exclamations, extra-linguistic emotional expressions, rhetorical question, assertions, and assessments realize the displays of parallel empathy. Reactive empathy is verbalized as voicing of other's mental states, comparing inner experiences, and exchanges of generic and personal pronouns.

Elicitations of empathy are realized by narratives, "walking out" moves, repetitive deontic declaratives, quoting, exclamations, laughter, rhetorical questions with prolonged such as "what do you say."

We may observe sequences of features such as:

> Rejection of empathy = final – initial overlaps + enumeration of questions → contrastive narrative of other behavior → topicalized declarative descriptions of other's actions (see example 2)

There are also degrees for realization of empathy in, e.g., giving of parallel empathy:

> 1st degree: rhetorical question (line 17 and 19, example (1))
> 2nd degree: assessment (line 21, example (1))
> 3rd degree: assertive with self-report (line 23 and 27, example (1))

References to authenticity of feeling or intention such as "well to be honest uh" (line 41, ex. 3) and "and quite frankly" (line 5, ex. 3) produced one after the other by both negotiators contribute greatly to the ritualistic proximity searched in negotiation which takes even linguistic expression, i.e., the negotiators tend to repeat each others expressions and even communicative acts, which is one way of signaling closeness or similarity. This proximity would then become a basis for more trust between the parties and thus facilitate acceptance of both empathy and propositions.

Reciprocal Adaptation, ToM Vs AI, and Cooperation Versus Collaboration

This section explores the way in which activity and interaction affect the decision process. In particular, I seek evidence for and against Interactive Alignment Theory and Theory of ToM by observing authentic data. I use again two types of activity, one is an everyday interactive sharing between two friends and the other is an example of strategic interaction, namely a plea bargain negotiation, both from Heritage's and Maynard's corpora.

Reciprocal Adaptation in Empathy Exchanges

Emotive Reciprocal Adaptation is manifested linguistically most expressively when Joy offers elicited empathy on line 15 and Les implicitly accepts it on line 16. The example is quoted again for the sake of clarity.

Example (1) [Holt Xmas 85:1:4]

1. Joy: ye-:s I'm alright,
2. Les: oh:. hh yi-m- you know I-I- I'm boiling about something hhhheh [1 heh hhhh]
3. Joy: [1 wha::t.]
4. Les: well that sa:le. {0.2} at- at . the vicarag {0.6}
5. Joy: oh ye[2 :s],
6. Les: [2 t] {0.6} u ih your friend 'n mi:ne wz the:re {0.2}
7. ( ): (h[3 h hh)]
8. Les: [3 mmis] ter: R:,
9. Joy: (oh ye:s hheh) {0.4}
10. Les: and em: we really didn't have a lot'v cha:nge that day becuz we'd been to
    bath 'n we'd been: christmas shoppin:g, {0.5} but we thought we'd better go along t'th'sale 'n do
    what we could, {0.2} we hadn't got a lot . of s:e- ready cash t'spe:nd. {0.3} t[4 hh]
11. Joy: [4 Mh].=
12. Les: =In any case we thought th'things were very expensive.
13. Joy: oh did you. {0.9}
14. Les: AND uh we were looking rou-nd the sta:lls 'n poking about 'n he came up
    t'me 'n be said Oh: hhello leslie, . still trying to buy something f'nothing,
15. Joy: PEG-> .hhhahhhhhh! {0.8 } oo[5 : : :: LESLI E]
16. Les: PEE-> [5 oo:.ehh heh heh] {0.2}
17. Joy: PEG-> i:s [6 n ' t he]
18. Les: REE-> [6 what] do you sa:y. {0.3}
19. Joy: PEG-> oh isn't he drea:dful.
20. Les: PEE-> eye-:-:s: {0.6}
21. Joy: PEG-> what'n aw::f'l ma::[7:::n]
22. Les: PEE-> [7 ehh] heh-heh-heh
23. Joy: PEG-> oh:: honestly, I cannot stand the man it's \ just {no[8 :}]
24. Les: RPEE-> [8 I] bought well I'm gon' tell Joyce
    that,ehh[7 heh]=
25. Joy: [9 ( )]=
26. Les: RPEE=[9 heh-heh he-e] uh: eh [10 eh hhhhh]
27. Joy: PEG-> =[10 O H : : : :.] I do think he's dreadful

28. Les: PEE-> tch oh: dea-r
29. Joy: PEG-> oh: he r[11 eally i]:s,
30. Les: RPEE-> [11 he dra-]ih-he (.) took the win' out'v
my sails c'mpletel(h)y .
31. Joy: REG-> I know the awkward thing is you've never
got a ready a:n[12 swer have you. that's
ri:ght,]
32. Les: REE-> [12 no: I thought'v lots'v ready a]nswers
a:fterward[13 s],
33. Joy: REG-> [13 yes] that's ri::gh[14 t].
34. Les: REG-> [14 yes] .
35. Joy: REG-> but you c'n never think of them at the
ti:[15 me a:fterwards I always think. oh I
should've said that. or I should've said
thi]s.
36. Les: REG-> [15 no:.no:. oh y e s e h- r i : g h t.] {0.7}
37. Joy: REGE-> b[16 ut] I do:'nt think a'th'm at the ti:me
38. Les: REG-> [16 mm:]. ehh huh huh {0.8}
39. Joy: oh:: g-oh 'n I think carol is going, t'the
[17 meeting t'ni g h t,]

The exclamations on lines 15 and 16 are similar; Les starts her exclamation with a similar sound to this of Joy "oo" and continues with a slight differentiation. In that sense, the speakers align with each other in tone and sound, starting with an imitation, although the functions of the utterances are different. On lines 17, 19, 21, 23, 27, and 29 Joy expresses a mirrored feeling of disapproval of the person by whose actions Les feels hurt, i.e., this is a parallel form of entering into each other's frame of reference, i.e., of Reciprocal Adaptation through emotional alignment. Line 31 illustrates role-play simulation, which is another linguistic formulation of the Reciprocal Adaptation mechanism. Exchange of roles and positions is part of the reciprocity ritual (see Section "Linguistic Manifestations of Empathy" above).

Line 35, however, is an example of verbalized simulation process, which is in the lines of theory of ToM rather than Interactive Alignment theory. On line 37 Joy has taken Les' internal position and talks about her own experiences, which is another example of cognitive Reciprocal Adaptation.

The adaptation is at first more somatic, uncontrollable and then becomes more cognitive as they turn to comparisons of experiences and mental representations of experiences. In this empathy process both speakers verify, confirm, and reconfirm for each other the legitimacy of their experiences, values, and attitudes and in the processes they often mirror each other's verbal actions. We observe Interactive Alignment but also ToM building processes during empathy exchange. Interactive Alignment has diverse linguistic manifestation, e.g., exclamations, tone of voice, tag-questions, parallel and reactive empathy forms. Interactive ToM building manifests at the incorporation and reverberation empathy stages and take the form of explicit reasoning from the other's point of view through generalized pronouns. Thus, Reciprocal Adaptation in ritualistic informal empathy exchange is realized by frequent Interactive Alignment and a few final more complex interactive ToM processes. The next section studies if the same format of Reciprocal Adaptation takes place in a more strategic and formal activity such as a plea bargain.

Interactive Alignment Versus Complex ToM Reasoning

In comparison with friendly sharing and empathy exchange, a plea bargain is a more formal activity, which involves strategic and tactical interaction. It is a negotiation where participants have conflictual roles and goals. Garrod and Pickering predict manifestations of misalignment in such activities. Would there also be ToM building processes? To answer this question I first outline the structure of the plea bargain and then analyze manifestations of both alignment and ToM processes.

I have studied this plea bargain earlier. Here I will concentrate on the occurrences of Interactive Alignment and interactive ToM reasoning in relation to Reciprocal Adaptation and emotion in negotiation.

Introduction Phase

Already at the very start of the plea bargain the incompatibility of Interactive Alignment theory or theory of ToM is questioned. The judge introduces the topic, asks about the identity of the defendant (line 3) and the defense attorney responds (line 4–6). The prosecutor is not joining the topic yet and throws in another topic, as a subtopic (lines 7, 8).

Example (2) [Frank Bryan]

Jge: A:n now that brings us to Frank Bryan.
(): ˙hhh[h hhhh
Jge: [Is he the poor chap sitting out there all by h[imself,
Def: [Ye:ah he's
the sweet man with the nice smile, (0.5) a:nd this is ay six
forty seven ef an' a one forty eight. ((throat clear))=
Prs: =(thi-) these (Wednesday) specials by the way are on: th- the
date set for trial one eleven¿

The question of the judge expresses abundance of empathy: "poor chap," "all by himself," light tone of voice, positive rhetorical intonation. The response of the defense counsel aligns with this choice of description by adding sympathy and kindness to the character of his client: "sweet man," "nice smile," mild tone of voice. (It is possible and common that perpetrators of crime do not look aggressive, thus how the defendant looks is the least important evidence related to the case.) This is a clear Interactive Alignment and interactive framing of the case, but it is hardly likely that this alignment is primitive, unconscious, mechanistic, and imitative. Just the opposite, if the defense attorney aligns so obviously to the judge's formulation, it is a clear indication of their ToM of the case and its outcome. Utterance on line 6 topicalizes the preferable "disorderly conduct" ("six forty-seven ef") interpretation instead of the "arrest resistance" ("one forty-eight") interpretation and adds a throat clear, which function seems to be to nonverbally mark or problematize the "arrest resistance" story. On the surface, this is grounding though Interactive Alignment using a question–answer pair, semantically similar lexical choices producing cooperatively achieved orientation in the case. However, the emotionally charged formulations by the judge and the defense counsel and the similarity of their descriptions manifest a case-theory-building intentionality or intentionally synchronized framing of the case. Each formulation directs the outcome of the plea bargain, together they are even stronger. The prosecutor is met from the start with two opposing parties, and he is 1:2. This explains the fact that the prosecutor does not align at first, but he does not misalign either; later (see Example (6) below) he monitors the story told by the defense and only at the end of the plea bargain clearly aligns but negatively (on line 211 below) and addresses issues of importance to law, namely that the defendant has a prior related to both resistance to arrest and disorderly conduct. In that sense, already at the start of the plea bargain, we see manifestations of both

Interactive Alignment and complex ToM reasoning at the same time, which in their combination express the strategic character of the activity.

Interactive Story Telling and Leading Questions

Story telling is an interactive way of framing, of making sense of a situation or a case. Interrogation is another. In a plea bargain, there is no interrogation of witnesses, but the defense takes the opportunity to frame the problem at hand by telling a story. Below I give the entire phase of the story telling which ends with the decision to settle the case rather than go to a trial. On line 31 below the defense counsel opens the plea bargain with a yes–no question, initiated by a lip parting gesture, emphasizing "s" in "strike", pronounces "actually" rather informally, and ends with a rising intonation. Then he waits for an answer for a long time, even after the prosecutor's "hmm:" on line 33, which is not a sign of misalignment; of its tone we understand it expresses lack of knowledge. Since one is asking and the other has no answer, both align in lack of knowledge, interactively. However, when the defense attorney establishes that the prosecutor is not prepared to answer this crucial for the final verdict question the defense attorney takes the privileged opportunity to frame the case through a story, the way he wants to see it, i.e., suitable for his client. Now, did the defense counsel ask an honest question or did he trigger on purpose the fact that there is no violence? The fact is that he repeats the same question one more time on lines 58–59. There the question is formulated as a leading tag-question, it starts with a volume escalation, rather colloquial humoristic lexical choice, it is uttered in overlap, and this time it does not allow or await an answer. This indicates that the defense counsel did not ask a question he did not already have an answer to. On the surface we have alignment of "no knowledge," but actually we have a planned and explicit modeling of the interlocutor and case framing. The defense uses such a leading question again on line 71, with a tag question and ample time for a response, thus emphasizing it. The fact that the defendant has been in jail already is an important fact for the defense, because it claims that time has been served already although crime is not clearly established. It is important for the judge to memorize that fact as well, i.e., it informs the judge that the man he found to be a "poor chap" has already sat in jail for unknown amount of time, increasing the reasons for empathy. That is, again we see that Interactive Alignment realizes complex reasoning rather than automatic processing, i.e., this question does not seek information, it seeks to strategically show and influence a ToM process, not just Interactive Alignment of information.

Example (3) [Frank Bryan]

29 Jge: Now on Frank Bryan?

30 (2.0)

31 Def: ˙hh ((lips parting)) Did he acshually strike an officer¿

32 (2.0)

33 Prs: Hmm:, ((not sure, high pitch))

34 (1.0)

35 Def: ˙hh See this tu- i- he's comes he's drunk. and he comes home

36 to his own house at wh-whe- where e'd have a fight with 'is

37 family, ˙hhh an' he's out in front of 'is in 'is own front yard

38 with 'is (0.2) parently: havin' such a fight er[: least]

39 Prs: [His mu-] his

40 mother having called the police.

41 Def: M(h)oth(h)er h(h)aving c(h)alled thu(h) c(h)ops, ˙hhh i- it's

42 a fa:mily thing.<He's screamin' an' an' ish then sayin' fuck.

43 an' all that kinda stuff. ˙hh or motherfuck. I assume, a:nd

44 u:m

45 ( ): [˙hh shh °huh(huh)

46 (J): [hihhihhihhihhihhihhihhihhihhihhihhihhihhihhihihihhihh=

47 Def: [yih kno:w, ˙hh getting into what=

48 (J): =[hihhihhihhihhih ih hh ih hh ˙hh hh ˙hh hh ˙hh ih hih]ih hih=

49 Def: =[(°>i- trans i-<) happening there, (.) and he's drunk.]

50 (J) =ih [˙hh ( )]

51 Def: [And this] is I mean the same i- a very happy golucky

52 good natured guy, as you can tell for sitteen out in the

53 courtroom, ˙hh £an' when the °police come onto his own home,

54 his ca(h)stle (h)he dec(h)ides (h)he ai(h)n't go(h)in'°

55 w(h)ithout makin' some trouble.£ ˙hhh=

56 ((° = volume escalation)),

57 (J): =He[:

58 Def: [°An' I don't think he swings° on anybody

59 [does he?]

60 ( ): [(No i)]( )[( )] ((garbled))

61 Def: [He doe:]s (.) take a menacing sta:nce, ˙hh but

62 on the other hand he doesn't attempt ta strike an officer.<I

63 assume that the officer's highl- high- degree of

64 prufessionalism: pruvents my client from getting himself into

65 further tr(h)ouble. ˙hhh[hh

Prs: [Yeah, thee he (slipped and fell) of
[uh: the (court) apparently >[which's caused< that uh:: a:=
Def: [Yeah hhhh [h h h h h h
Prs: =laceration above his uh: (0.4) on i- [on i- ( )]
Def: [He's terr]ibly sorry
he did this.<I believe they took him to jail. did they not?
(0.3)
Prs: They did. and it was somewhere in the- in thee=
Def: =˙hh hhhm=
Prs: =process of being uh:b (0.5)
Def: ˙hh hh[m
Prs: [he did resist being[handcuffed. and resist wa:lking=
Def: [˙hh-
Prs: =from the residence and in the process of that resistance he:
(1.5) quote collapsed. and str[uck his head on the floor. end=
Def: [˙hhh
Prs: =q[uote,]
Jge: [Hh:]hih[(hih)
Def: [Y(h)e(h)ah well e-[he mighta had a certain=
Prs: [(and)
Def: =amount 'a justice a(h)r(h)ead(h)y hea hI (h)on't th(h)ink
th(h)e puhlice w(h)ere puhttin' up w(h)ith 'im. ˙hh[hhhh.]
Prs: [Wu- one]
senses thet u:m u::h i: other than that it was a lot of talk.
o:f u- assuming fighting stances an' then ru[nning] away.
Def: [Y e a]h
Prs: U[h:
Def: [It's a verbal:. w:: one forty eight. and a real six forty
seven ef. Now u: >if you< I would like to settle this case.
Prs: Well I'd li[ke to settle (it)

The defense attorney's story telling is not a monolog. It involves: intonation shifts, style shifts, volume escalations, laughter, lexical jokes, rich adjectives, pointed reformulations, other repetitions, emphasis and repetition of crucial for the story aspects ("own house," "own front yard," own home, "his castle"), interruptions, latching, initial feedback givers and elicitors, etc. All these are linguistic-discursive means for framing or reframing a problem. The prosecutor adds and corrects, contributing to the interactive framing of the case, which ends up with agreement to settle. However, the moments of clear alignment, such as this on lines 40 and 41 do not support the primary role of mechanic alignment. On these lines, the defense repeats literally the prosecutor's addition that it is the mother who called the police. He does not do such an other repetition before or after during the framing of the case. He chooses to align there and uses that as a support of his framing, but this is not simply because it is easier to imitate but because it fits his framing of the story, his goal, after explicit modeling of the interlocutors and the effect of the fact, not only the prosecutor but also the judge. He makes a joke out of this fact, which entertains the judge, makes him laugh, thus mitigates the severity of his client's actions. Thus alignment here realizes a complex strategy using ToM modeling, not automatic processing. The final lines above 94 and 95 exhibit alignment and also realize agreement through other repetition, but again the decision of agreement has come first and then the decision of alignment through repetition, not the other way around.

Meta-Comments as Interactive Manifestations of ToM Processes

Evidence for the interactive ToM building is the "intermission," the subjectivity directly after the agreement to settle:

Example (4) [Frank Bryan]

96 Jge: [Yo(h)u ha(h)lwa(h)ays s(h)ay tha(h)a(h)at
97 [˙i h h][˙ihh][h u h][h u h]
98 Def: [Well as- I][I lea][rned that (t][rade) from Harr]y Moberg,
99 Jge: ˙uhh[hOh:] hah [hah][h a h ˙h h] ( )=
100 Def: [uh:] [hee][cuz with Harry], (0.2) >you=
101 Jge: =[((thrt clr))]
102 Def: =[start talkin'] to each other through clenched< teeth.
103 [And after about] five] minutes of (.) challenging each=
104 Jge: [ah hih!hihhih] ( )]
105 Def: =other to go [to trial, and I know 'at 'e doesn't try any=
106 [((sound of small item dropped on table))
107 Def: =ca(h)ses see(h)ee, [˙hh o(h)nly r(h)eason's I g(h)otta go to=
108 Jge: [( )
109 Def: =trial a[gainst one'a his new kids, r(h)ight?=
110 Jge: [˙hhh
111 Jge: =Huh!=
112 Def: = ˙hh Or [(hi)his (n- old pro like) mister Franklin, ˙hhh=
113 ( ): [( )

The subjectivity is initiated by the judge's laughing comment on the settlement, line 96. As a response, the defense lawyer starts a story, which explains and describes what happened in lines 1–95 and what will continue for the rest of the plea bargain. He tells a story of a colleague, a famous lawyer, who strategizes interactively in such a way that he always makes the opponent agree to settle after some time of mutual challenging. This meta-comment reveals that the defense counsel's contributions build on chess game-like premeditated processes, which are often repeated and passed on:

Example (5) [Frank Bryan]

Def: *=And so I finally tried to get the conversation around t(h)a what*
we were talkin' about. like sett'lin' the ca(h)ase ˙hhh It
ˆworks.<Harry and I cuddo a lot of business that wa(h)ayhh
[wu-

In that sense, this meta-explanation grounds the judge's laughing meta-comment, but it also frames the plea bargain as a routine, however, not a routine of automatic alignment but a routine of strategic planning based on complex interactive ToM modeling.

Emotion as Manifestation of ToM-Reasoning-Based Strategies; Positive and Negative Reciprocal Adaptation

Reciprocal Adaptation or the procedure by which participants gradually enter each other's frame of reference may realize in different ways. Rather than claiming that there is resistance to adaptation, the data indicate that there is adaptation even in negative contexts. For instance, in Example 6 below the prosecutor offers facts, which aggravate the guilt of the defendant and indirectly suggest a harsher verdict. He does that after refusing to respond to empathy elicitation by the defense counsel. In effect, the defense counsel interprets the prosecutor's stance taking as a challenge (204–6) and responds with a sudden explosive expression of anger, contempt and a threat (line 207). This emotional Reciprocal Adaptation takes a form of mirroring: A calm and sober threat to his client's interests is met with an emotionally loaded counter threat. On top of that, the defense repeats lexically the prosecutor on lines 216 and 220 with mocking intonation. This is good lexical alignment but no cooperation and no success in communication, in the sense of communication as alignment. In the sense of communication as a meeting with otherness this is good communication, because it expresses otherness. Rather than getting into the other's frame of reference and accepting it the defense counsel gets into the other's frame of reference, rejects it and, with the emotional display, blames the other party. Thus there is adaptation in negative terms, but it is not in the mechanistic alignment format but rather as a well-planned ToM process, predicting and preventing other's interactive moves and reactions (as described by the defense counsel himself in the "intermission" phase).

Example (6) [Frank Bryan]

204 Prs: He has ub a: one prior. (0.3) conviction in this jurisdiction
205 with thee uhm (0.8) sheriff's office, of of interestinly
206 enough. u:v striking a public officer and of disturbing peace.
207 Def: Will you knock it off. ((disgusted tone)) (0.5) You wanna make
208 a federal case out of this¿
209 Prs: N:o, [I I just] think [that that i]t's it's not uh this uh=
210 Def: [˙h h h] [h h m]
211 Prs: =happy go lucky chap's uh first (1.0) encounter with uh um (1.8)
212 Def: [Statistic]ly if ya got black skin:. you ar (0.2) you ar (.)=
213 Prs: [( )]
214 Def: =hhighly likely to contact the police. I think
215 uh:substantially more likely than if you're white.<*Now come*
216 on.<Whadda want from 'im. (0.6) He's got a prior.
217 (1.8)
218 Jge: Well we know he spent ten ho:urs, ehhem (1.0) end
219 uh:: [we know he's been down here fer] mo:re
220 Def: [(He) o: n l y s p e n t ten] ((mock shock))
221 (0.8)
222 ( ): ((throat clear))=

To this explosion of anger, the prosecutor reacts with self-explanation and he stutters and has difficulties formulating a sentence (line 209). The self-explanation on line 209–211 consists of a rejection of the defense counsel's story or ToM of the defendant using a quotation ("happy go lucky chap") of the defense's own formulation on line 51–52, in the beginning of the plea bargain. At the time, the prosecutor did not say much as the defense counsel was telling his view of the story, just answering leading questions and adding details that could change the story but nothing explicit. All of a sudden now, the prosecutor directly rejects the story and the picture the defense counsel drew of the case based on the available evidence. According to Interactive Alignment theory the alignment happens from turn to turn but here we have an Interactive Alignment using negative lexical quotation, which jumps over 100 turns in the conversation. Such instances are rather manifestations of the strategic character of the interaction in this activity, which presupposes conscious ToM building and monitoring. The ToM processing is calculative even on the level of timing: When the relevant evidence if to be mentioned in the conversation appears crucial as to its effect to the goal of the opposing parties.

Locally, on lines 211–213, we do not have adaptation in the form of mirroring but in the form of opposite reaction: The prosecutor adapts to threat and blame by rejection, confusion, defense, reference to contradicting evidence, increase of self-repetitions, pauses, hesitation sounds, and final silencing, i.e., by reframing the problem through an opposite story or ToM frame plus reactive emotional alignment.

The defense counsel continues his ridicule by use of mocking back channels, initial and final interruptions, latching, ridiculing, mocking repetitions, etc. (lines, 207, 208, 216, 220). In this manner, he gains once again a dominant role in the conversation. Emotionally loaded imperative expressions such as "knock it off," "come on" and vocal gestures such as throat clearing act as more powerful persuasion devices than the arguments. Defense's sudden and timely anger display on line 207–219 has a successful strategic effect because 10 turns later on line 239 the opponent himself suggests to settle on terms preferred and suggested by the defense.

The linguistic manifestations of the ToM models as minds-of-others context (Martinovski and Marsella 2003; Givón 2005) in this plea bargain are summarized as follows (Table 6.1):

Similarly to the finding in Chap. 3 in this Volume the juxtaposition of the discursive manifestations of the ToM contexts of the two main participants shows that there is emotional coherence in the performance and experience of each party and that this need of emotional coherence leads argumentation and negotiation, which may go through distortions. While the defense counsel is staging an entertainment performance relying on prior contact with the judge, the prosecutor reacts to this emotional domineering by bringing in the external context of the law. The linguistic features clearly exhibit this ToM contextual contrast. The negotiation goes through number of stages, which are driven by dynamic re-contexualizing of the other's mind: As the defense attorney presents his client as "a good guy in trouble," the prosecutor refers to previous record; as the previous record is mentioned, the defense counsel ridicules the idea of a jury trial for "such as small thing," etc. After a few cycles of strategically emotionally loaded interactive duel the parties end in silence with no resolution:

Table 6.1 Linguistic manifestations of interactive contexts as minds-of-others in a plea bargain

ToM context/expression type	Defense counsel	Prosecutor
Lexical	Positive client descriptions "sweet," "nice," "a very good go lucky good natured guy" Mitigating expressions "swing" (instead of "hit"), "slipped and fell" (instead of "collapsing due to resistance to arrest") ToM modal expressions: "actually," "apparently," "i assume" Entertaining: playful imitation of US African slang, yih know, overlap with other's laughter Negatively framed Q + final positive or negative Q Colloquialisms: "mighta," "wanna," "woulda" Thrown in comments, compliments: "i wanna have to add" Apologies	Approximating expressions "somewhere" Declarative questions and clarification requests; latching Downplaying expressions such as "just," "by the way," "possible," "probably better 148" "I see" and "alright" as backchannels Impersonal expressions "one senses that"
Prosodic	"Feel sorry for him"—prosody Emphasis on "jail" and "strike" as contrast to innocent description of client Fun intonations: higher volume at ending of preferred narrative, as escalation in the fun story Stress initial contra "i don't think …"	Lower voice, professional, even intonation
Paralinguistic	Throat clearing signaling ridicule Lip parting in questions of doubt Laughing through words Garbled self-confirming "no" Breath in at end of defense speech	Hesitations, self-repetitions, pause in own speech, self cutoffs, hesitation sounds
Behavioral	Thrown-in sarcastic empathy + laughter; telling the frame of the story not the actual reason of accusation; not reading evidence but ad hoc story compilation; references to and reformulations of judges previous; sarcastic apologies; entertaining	Quoting, uncertainty, filling in the opponents story, impersonal agreements on story, allows to be interrupted line 163

Jge: *Do I hear it raining again? Is it [( )]*
Def:: *[°Oh my] god.*
(1.2)
(D): *˙h[h*
Jge: *[I think that's rain [isn' it?*
Def: *[It only does it for spite.*
(0.5)
Prs: *I think it is too.=*
Def: *=The suit's made of sugar.<It melt[s.*
Prs: *[( ) out of (.)*
of (0.7) top on it. °It's a firebird. It's a- (0.5) ((clicking sound: chair?)) ( ).
( ): *((audible breathing))*
(J): *˙hhh*
Prs: Is a seventy ˆfive dollar (fine)?
Jge: Hh Heh huh. ˙hh-
Def: Why don't we compromise and make it fifty.
Prs: That's done.
Def: Ar[ri(h)ght.]

This sudden interruption brings an unexpected reframing of the situation outside of the judicial and personal/emotive context. Instead of directing attention to the other's mind as a context, the participants are asked to shift mental attention to a larger context, in which they are all embedded. The explicit shifting of attention from contexts of other's minds and emotions to larger inclusive contexts offers relief in face-to-face negotiation, which brings out collaborative re-interpretations of the situation at hand.

Based on the empirical observations presented in this section, this chapter continues with a formulation of a model for dynamic re-interpretation and re-contextualization of emotion in GDN.

Model of Emotion in Negotiation and Decision Taking

The Model of Emotion in Negotiation and Decision Taking (MEND) developed here suggests a process-based representation of emotion in decision taking and negotiation and offers operationalization of the process components. Following the definition of emotion presented in Section "Definitions of Basic Concepts" above, physiological reactions may bring about an emotion, which can influence cognitive

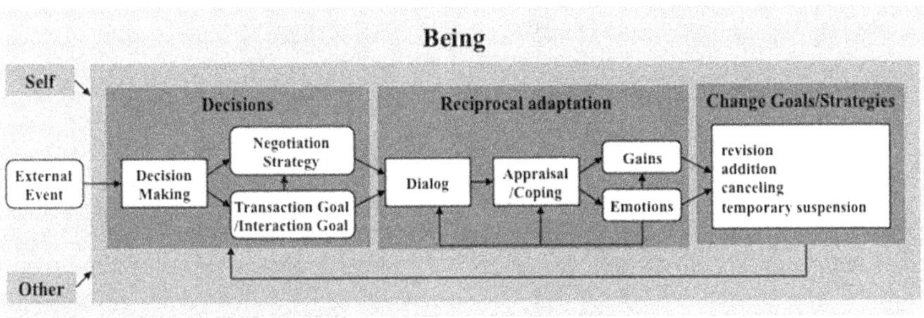

Fig. 6.1 A model of emotion in negotiation and decision making

appraisal, but this appraisal can in turn bring about coping strategies, which generate other emotions.

In this model (see Fig. 6.1) emotions and ToM beliefs (the later summarized as "self" and "other") can be instrumental in alteration of goals and strategies in the decision-taking process. Their importance is a derivate not only of visceral reactions but also of planning and ToM processing. Each negotiation situation starts with some set of ToM beliefs and goals associated with Self and Other, which relate to a choice of negotiation strategy and tactics realized in the conversation. The decision making is analyzed into negotiation strategies and transaction and interaction goals. These influence the communication process, which is lead by Reciprocal Adaptation, which, as suggested by the theoretical analysis in Section "Theoretical Foundations" and the empirical analysis in Sections "Linguistics Manifestation and Functions of Emotions in GDN" and "Reciprocal Adaptation, ToM Versus AI, and Cooperation Versus Collaboration" above, comprise both Interactive Alignment and complex ToM-based reasoning.

During communication feelings and appraisal of gains and emotion bring about coping strategies. These trigger re-evaluation of ToM models (ToMM), goals, beliefs, and strategies, which might be changed. Besides the particular goals, ToMM and beliefs, each negotiation is embedded in a larger existential context, which wraps in all human and other activity. Studies suggest (e.g., Martinovski 2007a, b) that awareness of and reference to co-existence in a larger context facilitate group decision making and negotiation.

Goal Structure

The goals can be interactional, i.e., related to ethics, face saving, ego (see also Chap. 7 in this Volume), and transactional, i.e., related to issues at stake. The interactional and transactional goals can be subdivided into cooperative (win–win), combative (win–loose), and non-cooperative (loose–loose). The negotiation strategies are designed for accomplishing goals and could be avoidance, demand and

Table 6.2 Types of goals and subgoals: functional, strategic and tactical

Goal type	Subgoals		
Functional	Transactional	Interactional	Neither
Tactical	Power	Bonding	Credibility
Strategic	Attack	Consent	Avoid

consent (the Dual Model of Negotiation adds even other goals such as conceding and compromising). The goals are communicated and in the process gains and emotions arise and are appraised, consciously or subconsciously, followed by coping with gains in status and emotions. Coping may result in evaluation of need to change goals and/or negotiation strategies. In the following turn we show how one can distribute goals, tactics, and strategies within MEND (I use as an example of Doctor/Captain negotiation, see Section "Data and Method" and Example (2) RPSASO'04.1b above) (Table 6.2).

Example 0:
A: you have to move the clinic, it is too dangerous here.

The MEND analysis is as follows:
interactive goal: show desire to help someone or/and help someone
transactive goal: move the clinic
tactics: bonding
negotiation strategy: direct demand
emotion: empathy giving

Each speaker has a particular set of interactive and transactive goals, which might change during communication. Since the interactive goals often determine the choice of tactics, they are not always stated. In addition, in certain utterances, the transactive goals are more salient (ex. move the clinic), in other's it is the interactive goals, which are more prominent (ex. it is too dangerous here). There are different types of goals. We choose to model functional, tactical, and strategic goals each of which can acquire different values, i.e., different types of subgoals.

In each interaction, one is dealing with the model of the other's goals one has rather than with the actual goals of the other. This is true not only for the cognitive organization of a virtual human but also for interaction between humans. The communicative exchange and feedback system involved in it serves to resolve mismatches due to this ToM character of communication. According to MEND emotions can be instrumental in alteration of goals and strategies in the decision-taking process. Here are a few examples of how the model can play out in relation to empathy in an artificial intelligence simulation of a negotiation between a virtual human doctor and a human captain. In that sense, what is available during decision making is only the internal "mental" and "emotional" process of the modeled agent, including its represented interpretations of the other. The ToM goal model is dynamic, i.e., it is generated and created via and during interaction.

Operationalization of the Model of Emotion in Negotiation: Empathy

This section goes through an operationalization of the model of emotion in negotiation in terms of preparation of a rule-based system. Different emotions have different effect on the decision-making process. This operationalization takes as its object empathy because it stimulates negotiation and has great importance for social harmony (Stephan and Finlay 1999; Davis 1994; see also Chaps. 1 and 3 in this Volume), and as it is one of the complex cognitive processes that involve emotion, rational reasoning, understanding, and feeling of the other also on a visceral and somatic level. Similar to other discursive phenomena empathy realizes under certain conditions and has three main functions in discourse: giving, eliciting, and reception, as well as their negative counterparts, namely, refusal to give and rejection to accept empathy.

Conditions for Realization of Empathy

Empathy is realized under certain conditions, which involve factors such as power, credibility, and bonding. Even in the weakest form of credibility, trust is a necessary condition for empathy. Others' empathy is empowering; this is expressed by the power condition—an aspect of communication, which is not necessarily determined by social status but by general human co-being.

POWER:

POWER:
A has power over B iff A can cause pain or joy to B and
A can change B's ToMMs (including goals), location, etc.

If A feels empathy for B then B has power over A
If A feels empathy for B then A has power over B

CREDIBILITY:
A finds B credible iff A beliefs that B says the truth and A beliefs B is competent.
If A feels empathy for B then A finds B credible.

CLOSENESS, BONDING:
A is close to B iff A shares N values, goals, interest, and/or experiences with B.
If A feels empathy for B then A feels close to B.
In the following example, A exercises power over B, displays closeness and credibility to B by expressing empathic feelings on personal matters. By accepting them B allows the exercise of power and closeness and implicitly confirms the credibility of the communicated state of affairs:

A: I am sorry you could not meet your mother before she died.
B: Thank you, dear.

Power, credibility, and bonding are disjunctive conditions for empathy, but they are also results of realized empathy. By giving and accepting empathy one increases power, credibility, and closeness.

Functions of Empathy in Interaction

Empathy has different functions in discourse. It can be experienced, given, elicited, accepted, rejected, and refused. Having in mind Allwood's (1997) conditions for ideal cooperation, namely cognitive and ethical consideration and trust, and the conditions for realization of empathy described below, one may conclude that according to a wider definition, empathy or lack of it may be characteristic of any interactive situation. In the present analysis, one may feel empathy without communicating it intentionally. Lack of empathy does not imply lack of cognitive consideration, but it does signal a lower level of cognitive consideration.

EMPATHY:
A feels empathy for B iff A adopts B's ToMM (emotions, goals, feeling, mental states, beliefs) and A feels close to B and/or A finds B credible and/or B allows A to exercise power over B.
Giving (EG): When one feels and appraises empathy for the other that may mean that if the goals were combative, one may re-evaluate to change, e.g., permanently or temporarily suspend some or all transactional goals, which are not aligned with the good of the other and change or not some or all interactional goals in such a way that they benefit the other. Empathy giving could be displayed insincerely in case it has a strategic value.
GIVE EMPATHY:

A gives empathy to B iff A feels what B feels
A intends to communicate empathy to B
and/or A feels close to B and/or A finds B credible and/or
B has power over A (i.e. B allows A to exercise power over B)

Acceptance (EA): When during communication phase one feels and appraises that one is accepting empathy, one may also go through goal and strategy revision in such a way that they benefit the other.
ACCEPT EMPATHY:

B accepts A's empathy iff B believes that A feels empathy for B
B allows A to exercise power over B
and/or A feels close to B and/or A finds B credible and/or
B has power over A (i.e. B allows A to exercise power over B)

Eliciting (EE): When in communication one appraises and feels the need to elicit empathy by the other, if this was not a goal from the start, that means that one changes interactional goals, negotiation strategies and may be even transaction goals in order to receive empathy.
ELICIT EMPATHY:

A elicits empathy by B iff A desires B to feel empathy for A
A intends to communicate desire for empathy to B
and/or A wants to feel close to B and/or A wants to find B credible
and/or B has power over A

Rejection when given (ER): When during communication one appraises and feels empathy one may choose to cope with it by rejecting it which ultimately means that one has added a new interactional and may be even new transactional goals and negotiation strategies and that one is going to keep some or all combative goals. Empathy can be rejected for local reasons but the main causes for rejection of empathy in this model are lack of desire to give power to others over ones self, lack of credibility and/or lack of closeness.
REJECT EMPATHY:

B rejects empathy given by A iff B does not desire that A feels empathy for B,
B intends to communicate rejection of empathy to B,
and/or B does not feel close to A and/or B does not find A credible
and/or B does not allows A to exercise power over B

Refuse to give (RefE): When during coping one rejects to give empathy, one may go through goal and strategy revision in such a way that they combat the other or may keep goals combative.
REFUSE EMPATHY:

A refuses to give empathy to B iff A does not feel empathy for B,
A intends to communicate refusal of empathy to B
and/or A does not feel close to B and/or A does not find B credible
and/or A exercises power over B.

Levels of Consciousness for Realization of Empathy

Any of emotional process may happen on different levels of consciousness and be realized in interaction on different levels of consciousness: display, signal, and indication (Allwood 1996).

Sender:
DISPLAY EMPATHY:

A intends to communicate and communicates empathy to B.

SIGNAL EMPATHY:

A intends to appear as if A intends to and communicates empathy to B.

INDICATE EMPATHY:

A does not intend to communicate but communicates empathy to B.

Signal is a premeditated level of consciousness in interaction, display is involved in interaction on most common daily level of consciousness, and indication is communication on the lowest level of consciousness.

Summary and Conclusions

Emotion is a complex phenomenon with cognitive and behavioral aspects and manifestations. This chapter studied the role of emotion in negotiation and demonstrated in different ways how discourse analysis can contribute to the understanding of emotion in GDN and how emotion can be an engine of argumentation, driving the wagons of rational thought (Martinovski and Mao 2009). Specific linguistic manifestations of emotional dominance (flattery, sarcasm, ridicule, aggression etc.) function as strategic means for negotiation with different levels of awareness—from lexical choices to tones of voice and paralinguistic expressions. The study suggests that communicative acts can be defined not only in terms of pragmatic meaning but also in terms of emotion, because changes in emotional state bring changes of illocutionary force and the opposite. Analysis of grammatical-pragmatic concepts in term of emotion will facilitate the study of emotion in Negotiation Support Systems, which for the moment do not involve systematic relation between emotion and communicative acts (see Chap. 5 in this Volume).

Problem reframing or negotiation is described as a process affected by interactivity and led by discursive mechanisms such as Reciprocal Adaptation, which can realize as Interactive Alignment or/and complex processing. The type of activity interlocutors involved in predicts the functionality of Reciprocal Adaptation. We noticed that in plea bargains Interactive Alignment realizes complex ToM reasoning rather than automatic processing. We also saw that in the case of empathy we have automatic alignment in the early phase of empathy process and ToM reasoning in the later phase. Discourse features such as other repetition cannot be classified simply as alignment because they can realize complex ToM processes, i.e., understanding of alignment cannot be based on statistical occurrences.

Based on such observations, the paper presents a model of dynamic re-interpretation and re-contextualization of negotiation, MEND (Modeling Emotion in Negotiation and Decision making), according to which emotions contribute to the changes of goals and strategies during negotiation. The purpose of the model is to aid understanding of the role of emotion in negotiation but also to assist artificial intelligence models of negotiation. The operationalization of the model relates adjacent turns and utterances to updates of ToM strategies, transactive and interactive goals, tactics, and interpretations of emotion, either on primary or on appraisal and coping level. A typical example of an emotion, which requires adoption of other's goals is empathy. Following the empiria, the model suggests that explicit shifting of attention from contexts of other's minds to larger inclusive contexts offers relief in face-to-face negotiation, which brings out collaborative re-interpretations of the situation at hand. In the MEND model, emotion is a process that regulates Interactive Alignment and the ToM models, which interactants build of each other's goals, states, tactics, and strategies.

If offered and accepted, empathy may cause adoption of others' assumed goals or change of own goals and thus enhance decision making (Thagard 2000, see also Chap. 3 in this Volume). The traditional idea of win–win, win–lose, and lose–lose negotiation types is thus put into perspective where these processes are seen as dynamic re-conditioning of negotiation by changes of ToM models driven by emotions. The realization that each negotiation is embedded in a larger context of co-being invites empathy and awareness of common goal/condition. Besides being a cognitive and neural process, empathy is a joint interactive effort in which speakers verify, confirm, and reconfirm for each other the legitimacy of their experiences, values, and attitudes. This verification is of great importance for the development and the function of the individual in the social and discursive world. Being able to take the role of the "empathizer" and the "empathee" is an essential characteristic of the empathic communication. Rejection of empathy may be due to failed recognition of the rejector's needs and desires, it may have strategic functions gaining momentum in the negotiation or it may be a combination of both. In any case, it is a phase in the negotiation not a breakdown. Elicitation, giving, acceptance, and rejection are functions of empathy any of which could be eliminated of the dialog with consequences. The style of empathy exchange, e.g., antagonistic or polite can also be a strategy in negotiation.

Future applications of discourse analysis of GDN would benefit the understanding of emotion in GDN if they include rich information about nonverbal aspects of face-to-face GDN.

Acknowledgments The author of this chapter wishes to thank Douglas Maynard and John Heritage for kindly providing data, Wenji Mao, David Traum, and Stacy Marsella for allowing the use of common research results, Rudolf Vetschera for invaluable comments, and Melvin Shakun for confident support.

References

Allwood, J. (1976). *Linguistic communication as action and cooperation.* Gothenburg Monographs in Linguistics 2. Department of Linguistics, University of Göteborg.

Allwood, J. (1996). Some comments on Wallace Chafe's "How consciousness shapes language". *Pragmatics and Cognition, 4*(1).

Allwood, J. (1997). Notes on dialogue and cooperation. In K. Jokinen, D. Sadek & D. Traum (Eds.), *Collaboration, cooperation and conflict in dialogue systems. Proceedings of the IjCAI-97 Workshop on Collaboration, Cooperation and Conflict in Dialogue Systems*, Nagoya.

Bell, L. (2003). *Linguistic adaptation in spoken human–computer dialogues.* Doctoral Thesis, Kungliga Tekniska Högskolan, Stockholm.

Bussman, S., & Muller, J. (1992). A negotiation framework for co-operating agents. In S. M. Deen (Ed.), *Proceedings of CKBS-SIG* (pp. 1–17). Dake Centre, University of Keele.

Clark, H. H. (1996). *Using Language.* Cambridge: Cambridge University Press.

Cornelius, R. R. (2000). Theoretical approaches to emotion. In *Proceedings from ISCA Workshop on Speech and Emotion: A Conceptual Framework for Research.*

Damasio, A. (1994). *Descartes' error: Emotion, reason, and the human brain.* New York: Putnam Publishing.

Davis, M. H. (1994). *Empathy: A social psychological approach.* Madison, WI: Brown and Benchmark.

Dohonue, W. A., & Roberto, A. J. (1993). Relational development as negotiated order in hostage negotiation. *Human Communication Research, 20*, 175–198.

Donohue, W. A. (2001). Resolving relational paradox: The language of conflict in relationships. In W. F. Eadie & P. E. Nelson (Eds.), *The language of conflict resolution* (pp. 21–46). Thousand Oaks, CA: Sage.

Erikson, E. H. (1968). *Identity: Youth and crisis.* New York: Norton.

Eysenck, S. B. G. (1981). Impulsive and antisocial behavior in children. *Current Psychological Research, 1*, 31–37.

Fuslier, G. D. (1988). Hostage negotiation consultant: Emerging role for the clinical psychologist. *Professional Psychology: Research and Practice, 19*, 175–179.

Fuster, J. M. (2003). *Cortex and mind: Unifying cognition.* New York: Oxford University Press.

Gilbert, M. A. (1995). Emotional argumentation, or, why do argumentation rheorists argue with their mates? In *Analysis and Evaluation: Proceedings of the Third ISSA Conference on Argumentation* (Vol. II).

Givón, T. (2005). *Context as other minds: The pragmatics of sociality, cognition and communication.* Amsterdam: John Benjamins.

Goffman, E. (1967). *Interaction rituals: Essays on face-to-face behavior.* New York: Pantheon.

Goodwin, C., & Goodwin, M. (1987). Concurrent operations on talk: Notes on the interactive organization of assessments. *IPrA Papers in Pragmatics, 1*(1), 1–52.

Gordon, R. (1986). Folk psychology as simulation. *Mind and Language, 1*, 158–170.

Gumpertz, J. J. (1982). *Discoursive Strategies.* Cambridge: Cambridge University Press.

Heritage, J. (2005). *Empathic moments.* California: Talk at UCLA.

Hobbs, J., & Gordon, A. (2005). Encoding knowledge of commonsense psychology. In *7th International Symposium on Logical Formalizations of Commonsense Reasoning, 22–24 May 2005*, Corfu, Greece.

Hogan, R. T. (1969). Development of an empathy scale. *Journal of Consulting Psychology, 33*, 307–316.

Iacoboni, M. (2005). Understanding others: Imitation, language, empathy. In S. Hurley & N. Chater (Eds.), *Perspectives on imitation: From cognitive neuroscience to social science.* Cambridge, MA: MIT Press.

Jefferson, G., Sacks, H., & Schegloff, E. (1987). Notes on laughter in the pursuit of intimacy. In G. Button & J. R. E. Lee (Eds.), *Talk and social organisation* (pp. 152–205). Clevedon, England: Multilingual Matters.

Kahneman, D., & Tversky, A. (1986). Rational choice and the framing of decisions. *The Journal of Business, 59*(4). Part 2: The behavioral foundations of economic theory (October, 1986, pp. S251–S278).

Kraus, S. (2001). *Strategic negotiation in multiagent environment*. Cambridge, MA: The MIT Press.

Lazarus, R. (1999). *Stress and emotion*. New York: Springer.

Martinovski, B. (2000). *Repetitions and reformulations in court proceedings—a comparison of Sweden and Bulgaria*. Gothenburg Monographs in Linguistics. Department of Linguistics. Goteborg University, Goteborg.

Martinovski, B. (2006). Cognitive and emotive empathy in discourse. In *Proceedings of CogSci 2006*, Vancouver, Canada.

Martinovski, B. (2007). Empathy and theory of mind and body in evolution. In E. Ahlsén, et al. (Eds.), *Communication—action—meaning. A festschrift to Jens Allwood* (pp. 343–361). Department of Linguistics, University of Gothenburg.

Martinovski, B. (2007). Shifting attention as re-contextualization in negotiation. In *Proceedings of GDN*, Montreal.

Martinovski, B. (2010). Emotion in negotiation. In M. Kilgour & C. Eden (Eds.), *Handbook on group decision and negotiation*. Amsterdam: Springer.

Martinovski, B. (2011). Reciprocal adaptation and emotion in conflict transformation. In *Proceedings of International Conference in Conflict Resolution*, Istanbul, Turkey.

Martinovski, B., & Mao, W. (2009). Emotion as an argumentation engine: Modeling the role of emotion in negotiation. *Journal of Group Decision and Negotiation, 18*(3).

Martinovski, B., & Marsella, S. (2003), Dynamic reconstruction of selfhood: Coping processes in discourse. In *Proceedings of Joint International Conference on Cognitive Science*, Sydney.

Martinovski, B., & Traum, D. (2003). The error is the clue: Breakdown in human–machine interaction. In *Proceedings of ISCA Tutorial and Research Workshop International Speech Communication Association*, Switzerland.

Martinovski, B., Traum, D., & Marsella, S. (2007). Rejection of empathy in negotiation. *Journal of Group Decision and Negotiation, 16*(1).

McCarty, L. T. (1997). Some arguments about legal arguments. In *Proceedings of the Sixth International Conference on Artificial Intelligence and Law*.

Mead, G. H. (1993). *Mind, self, and society*. Chicago: University of Chicago Press.

Morton, A. (1980). *Frames of mind*. Oxford: Oxford University Press.

Myers, G. E. (2001). *William James: His life and thought*. London: Yale University Press.

Parsons, S., Sierra, C., & Jennings, N. R. (1998). Agents that reason and negotiate by arguing. *Journal of Logic and Computation, 8*(3), 261–292.

Pickering, M. J., & Garrod, S. (2006). Alignment as the basis for successful communication. *Research on Language and Computation, 4*, 203–228.

Powell, J. O. (1989). *Negotiation processes in hostage and barricaded incidents*. Unpublished doctoral thesis, University of Iowa.

Prakken, H. (2005). AI & Law, logic and argument schemes. *Argumentation, 19*, 303–320. (special issue on *The Toulmin Model Today*).

Prakken, H., & Sartor, G. (2002). The role of logic in computational models of legal argument. In A. Kakas & F. Sadri (Eds.), *Computational logic: Logic programming and beyond, essays in honor of Robert A. Kowalski* (Part II, pp. 342–380). Berlin: Springer.

Reik, T. (1949). *Listening with the third ear: The inner experience of the psychoanalyst*. New York: Grove.

Rogan, R.G. (1999). F.I.R.E.: A communication-based approach for understanding crisis negotiation. In O. Adang & E. Giebels (Eds.), *To save lives: Proceedings of the first European conference on hostage negotiations* (pp. 25–42). Amsterdam: Elsevier.

Salem, R. (1982). Community dispute resolution through outside intervention. *Peace and Change Journal, VIII*(2/3).

Scherer, K. R. (1993). Neuroscience projections to current debates in emotion psychology. *Cognition and Emotion, 7*, 1–41.

Stephan, W. G., & Finlay, K. (1999). The role of empathy in improving intergroup relations. *Journal of Social Issues, 55*(4), 729–743.

Stich, S., & Nichols, S. (1992), Folk psychology: Simulation or tacit theory? *Mind and Language, 7*, 35–71.

Taylor, P. (2002). A cylindrical model of communication behavior in crisis negotiation. *Human Communication Research, 28*, 7–48.

Thagard, P. (2000). *Coherence in thought and action*. Cambridge: The MIT Press.

Toris, C. (1994). A negotiation model of empathy. In *9th International Balint Federation Congress, November 9–13*, Charleston, South Carolina.

Toulmin, S. E. (1958). *The uses of argument*. London: Cambridge University Press.

Traum, D. (1994). *A computational theory of grounding in natural language conversation*. PhD thesis, Department of Computer Science, University of Rochester.

Traum, D., Rickel, J., Gratch, J., & Stacy, M. (2003). Negotiation over tasks in hybrid human–agent teams for simulation-based training. In *Proceedings of the Second International Joint Conference on Autonomous Agents and Multiagent Systems*.

van Eemeren, F. H., & Grootendorst, R. (2004). *A systematic theory of argumentation: The pragma-dialected approach*. Cambridge: Cambridge University Press.

Von Uexkull, J., & Kriszat, G. (1934). *Streifzuge durch die Umwelten Von Tieren und Menschen*. Ein Bilderbuch unsichtbarer Welten. Berlin: Springer.

Walton, D. N. (1989). *Informal logic: A handbook for critical argumentation*. New York: Cambridge University Press.

Walton, D. N. (1992). *The place of emotion in argument*. The Pennsylvania State U.P., University Park, PA.

Walton, D. N. (1996). *Argumentation schemes for presumptive reasoning*. Mahwah, NJ: Lawrence Erlbaum Associates.

Chapter 7
Game Theory and Emotions

Steven J. Brams

Introduction

Emotions like anger, jealousy, and love are spontaneous feelings that practically all of us experience at one time or another. Although there may be good reasons for us to be angry, jealous, or fall in love, these feelings, especially when they overtake us suddenly, seem not to be the product of rational calculation. Rather, they overpower us, so to speak, which seems the antithesis of the careful means-ends analysis that we normally associate with rational choice. Indeed, Gerlernter (1994, p. 29) argues that "you cannot choose your emotions. Emotions choose themselves," which suggests that emotions have no rational basis.[1]

I thank Eva Brams, Ben D. Mor, and anonymous reviewers for valuable comments on an earlier draft and the C.V. Starr Center for Applied Economics at New York University for its support. This article originally appeared in Brams (1997a) and is reprinted with permission. It was republished in somewhat modified form as Chap. 7 in Brams (2011). To say that the bulk of social activity consists of playing games does not necessarily mean that it is mostly "fun" or that the parties are not seriously engaged in the relationship (Berne 1964, p. 17).

[1]Gerlenter (1994, pp. 27–28) defines an emotion to be "a mental state with physical correlates; it is a *felt* state of mind, where 'felt' means that signals reach the brain that are interpreted as bodily sensations," creating an "affect link" to thought. Recent research, however, challenges "bodily states as the central feature of emotions" (Parrott and Harré 1996, p. 14), arguing instead that emotions have strong cultural and social, as well as biological, roots. In the later formal analysis, I will show how emotions enable a person to move to an inferior state, if only temporarily, in order to effect a better final state, thereby rendering them rational "expressions of judgement" (Parrott and Harré 1996, p. 1).

S.J. Brams (✉)
Department of Politics, New York University, New York, USA
e-mail: steven.brams@nyu.edu

B. Martinovsky (ed.), *Emotion in Group Decision and Negotiation*, Advances in Group Decision and Negotiation 7,
DOI 10.1007/978-94-017-9963-8_7

In a spate of books and articles, economists and game theorists such as Hirshleifer (1987, 1994), Frank (1988), Gilboa and Schmeidler (1988), Geanakoplos et al. (1989), Huang and Wu (1992), Rabin (1993), Howard et al. (1993), and Howard (1994), philosophers such as de Sousa (1987) and Solomon (1993), a political scientist (Elster 1991, 1994), a neurologist (Damasio 1994), and sociologists and other social scientists (Emotions and Rational Choice 1993) have argued that expressing emotions is compatible with acting rationally. Our goals, according to some of these analysts, are not always the narrow ones postulated by economic theory but broader, if somewhat inchoate and ineffable, ends (e.g., about living meaningful lives). Moreover, we are often passionate in our pursuit of these ends, which may undermine the achievement of more commonplace goals, such as ensuring our personal safety or economic security.

How can we explain these passions and the sudden welling up of emotions that give rise to them? In this Chapter, I focus on the emotion of *frustration*, which arises from being "prevent[ed] from accomplishing a purpose or fulfilling a desire" (American Heritage Dictionary 1980). Although frustration may arise from impersonal forces (e.g., the weather) and not the actions of others, it is often aggravated by a "freely acting agent" (Frijda 1986, p. 198) who blocks one's preferred choices.

It is these interpersonal situations of frustration that I will analyze here. I hypothesize that *people become frustrated when they are in an unsatisfying situation and feel an inability to escape it because of the control of others.* This lack of control is especially frustrating when the others who could help have no interest in changing the situation.

Put another way, when a person cannot help himself or herself but must depend on the actions of others who are not helpful, this person will tend to react emotionally, suddenly becoming aroused. Feeling hemmed in, without room to maneuver, he or she explodes in *anger*—the most common behavioral response to frustration—to try to escape.

One might reasonably argue that anger is the emotion being described, not the frustration that gives rise to it and may be unobservable. However, since I will be analyzing interpersonal situations that cause frustration, I find it convenient to use "frustration" as a shorthand for "frustration and the anger it evokes."

Psychological theories of frustration, as well as other emotions, say little if anything about the *structural features* of a situation that incite people to become emotional. By contrast, game theory provides powerful tools for identifying situations in which people experience a lack of control—and those in which they can regain it.[2]

---

[2]Here I am concerned with emotions that arise in interpersonal situations rather than "existential" (Lazarus and Bernice 1994, pp. 41–66) or "self-conscious" (Lewis 1995) emotions, like anxiety, guilt, or shame. The latter, which concern the way we see ourselves, are often independent of the actions of others in a game (though not in *Macbeth*, as discussed later).

By definition, a game is an interdependent decision situation, with the outcome depending on what all so-called players do. Although measures of the degree of interdependence of player choices in a game have been proposed (Thibaut and Kelly 1959; Kroll 1993), they are quantitative and cannot be applied to the strict ordinal games that I analyze here, in which players are assumed only to be able to rank outcomes from best to worst but not attach numerical values, or cardinal utilities, to them.

I limit the analysis to strict ordinal games in which there are just two players, each of whom has two strategies, which defines a 2 × 2 normal-form, or matrix, game. Although there are 78 distinct 2 × 2 strict ordinal games (1966), 21 are games in which there is a mutually best outcome, which are unlikely to create frustration for the players.

Of the remaining 57 games, which I call *conflict games*, I distinguish two classes, the first of which subsumes 12 "frustration" games and the second of which subsumes six "self-frustration" games. Altogether, there are 17 different games (one game is common to both classes), which is 30 % of all conflict games.

In frustration games, a player's lack of control takes the form of an "advantaged" player's having a dominant strategy that inflicts the two worst outcomes on the "frustrated" player. In the self-frustration games, it is the "self-frustrated" player who has the dominant strategy; the advantaged player does not, but this player's best response to the self-frustrated player's dominant strategy induces the self-frustrated player's next-worst outcome.

I consider whether, based on the "theory of moves" (Brams 1993, 1994b; Brams and Mattli 1993), there is any escape from an inferior outcome for the frustrated or self-frustrated player.[3] It turns out that if the frustrated player has "threat power," then he or she can induce a better outcome with a "deterrent threat" in four of the 12 frustration games.

The situation is easier for the self-frustrated player in the six self-frustration games. Although threat power is effective in these games, the self-frustrated player can always induce a better outcome for himself or herself, and sometimes for the other player as well, without resort to such power. This outcome, which is called a "nonmyopic equilibrium (NME)," requires only that players think ahead about their moves and countermoves, based on rules of play (to be described) that are different from those postulated by standard game theory.

To illustrate the role that emotions play in the frustration and self-frustration games, I turn to two works of literature (Brams 1994a), each of which has strong political overtones. *Lysistrata,* Aristophanes' most popular play, describes how women in ancient Greece, immensely frustrated when their men went off to war—leaving them lonely and with little support for their children—were moved to use

[3]For other applications of the theory of moves, see Brams and Mor (1993), Mor (1993, 1995), Colomer (1995a, b), Maoz and Mor (1996), Brams and Togman (1996), Simon (1996), Lax (1996), Massoud (1998), and Brams (1997b).

abstinence from sex as a weapon to induce the men to stop fighting. In *Macbeth*, Shakespeare describes how Lady Macbeth, seething at Macbeth's initial hesitation to seek his prophesied royal destiny, flew into a rage, belittling Macbeth's manhood, to incite Macbeth into killing King Duncan.

In both games, the frustrated and self-frustrated players, stuck at inferior outcomes, initially moved to still worse outcomes, exploding in anger to try to effect an ultimately better outcome. By linking the theory of moves to emotions expressed *along the path to equilibria*, one can identify conditions, in the dynamic play of a game, when it is rational to express emotions like frustration.

I emphasize the *process* by which a stable outcome is achieved, rather than the outcome itself, because once a game has stabilized at an equilibrium outcome, emotions are much less likely to be expressed. Although emotions may be feigned, I take them to be genuine in the analysis that follows, which is plausible in games in which players have little recourse but to escalate a conflict in order to try to escape their frustration and gain some relief.

The Frustration Game

The "generic" Frustration Game, which is shown at the top of Fig. 7.1, is a 2 × 2 game in which the row player, Advantaged (A), has two strategies, s_1 and s_2, and the column player, Frustrated (F), has two strategies, t_1 and t_2. The payoffs to the players at the resulting four possible outcomes are given by ordered pairs (x_{ij}, y_{ij}), where x_{ij} is the payoff to A, and y_{ij} the payoff to F, when A chooses strategy s_i and F chooses strategy t_j $(i, j = 1 \text{ or } 2)$.

"Advantaged" does not mean that A has any special prerogatives or privileges; rather, he has a dominant strategy.[4] Associated with his dominant strategy is a Nash equilibrium, which in a 2 × 2 strict ordinal game is unique (Hamilton and Slutsky 1993, p. 50, Lemma 1).[5]

F, who may or may not have a dominant strategy, is "frustrated": Her two worst outcomes are associated with A's dominant strategy, which he would presumably choose.[6] By contrast, I will show shortly that, with one exception, A never suffers his two worst outcomes when F chooses a dominant strategy (if she has one).

---

[4]Henceforth, I assume that A is male and F (and later SF in the Self-Frustration Game) is female.

[5]I could have called the row player simply "Dominant," but this would not have distinguished him from the column player, who sometimes has a dominant strategy, too. Moreover, in the Self-Frustration Game, it is column, the self-frustrated player, who has the dominant strategy—row does not—so calling the row player in the Frustration Game "Dominant" would create confusion.

[6]I will discuss shortly under what circumstances A would *not* choose his dominant strategy, enabling F to escape her lack of control in this game.

Generic Game

Frustrated (F)

		t_1	t_2	
Advantaged (A)	s_1	$\underline{(x_{11}, y_{11})}$ 2	(x_{12}, y_{12}) 1	← Dominant strategy for A ($x_{11} > x_{21}$ and $x_{12} > x_{22}$), containing the two worst outcomes for F (1 and 2).
	s_2	(x_{21}, y_{21})	(x_{22}, y_{22})	

12 Specific Games Subsumed by Generic Game

Class I (8 games): No relief for F from Nash equilibrium of (x_{11}, y_{11})

5 (17)		6 (18)		10 (10)		11 (11)	
(4,2)	(3,1)	(4,2)	(3,1)	(3,2)	(4,1)	(3,2)	(4,1)
(2,4) ↑	(1,3)	(1,4) ↑	(2,3)	(2,4) ↑	(1,3)	(1,4) ↑	(2,3)

18 (35)		19 (36)		25 (45)		26 (46)	
(4,2)	(3,1)	(4,2)	(3,1)	(3,2)	(4,1)	(3,2)	(4,1)
(2,3)	(1,4)	(1,3)	(2,4)	(2,3)	(1,4)	(1,3)	(2,4)

Class II (4 games): Relief through the exercise of deterrent threat power

22 (39)		28 (48)		32 (12)		35 (21)	
(4,2)	(2,1)	(2,2)	(4,1)	(2,2)	(4,1)	(4,2)	(2,1)
(3,3)′	(1,4)	(1,3)	(3,4)′*	(1,4) ↑	(3,3)′*	(3,4)′ ↑	(1,3)

Key: (*x*, *y*) = (pay-off to A, pay-off to F)
4 = best; 3 = next best; 2 = next worst; 1 = worst
Nash equilibrium underscored
t/*t** = deterrent threat outcome for F/both players
↑ = dominant strategy for F

Fig. 7.1 Frustration game

More formally, the Frustration Game satisfies the following three conditions:

1. *Dominance for A*. Without loss of generality, assume that s_1 is A's dominant strategy, so

$$x_{11} > x_{21}; \quad x_{12} > x_{22}. \tag{1}$$

That is, whatever strategy F chooses (t_1 or t_2), A prefers his payoffs associated with s_1 to those associated with s_2, making s_1 A's unconditionally better strategy.

2. *Nash equilibrium*. Without loss of generality, assume that (x_{11}, y_{11}) is the unique Nash equilibrium that is associated with A's dominant strategy of s_1, so

$$y_{11} > y_{12}. \tag{2}$$

That is, F prefers her payoff at (x_{11}, y_{11}) to that which she would receive at (x_{12}, y_{12}) if she switched from t_1 to t_2. Similarly, A prefers (x_{11}, y_{11}) to (x_{21}, y_{21})—and so would not switch from s_1 to s_2—because of the dominance of s_1, assumed in inequalities (1).[7]
3. *Lack of control*. Let 4 indicate the best payoff to a player, 3 the next best, 2 the next worst, and 1 the worst. Thus, the higher the number, the greater the payoff. But because these payoffs are *ordinal*, they indicate only an ordering of outcomes from best to worst, not the degree to which a player prefers one outcome over another.

F's lack of control, and consequent frustration, stems from her two worst outcomes (1 and 2) being associated with A's dominant strategy of s_1. From inequality (2), it follows that

$$y_{11} = 2; \quad y_{12} = 1.$$

Depending on whether $y_{21} = 3$ and $y_{22} = 4$, or $y_{21} = 4$ and $y_{22} = 3$, F may have two different complete orderings of her payoffs.

On the other hand, the dominance of s_1 for A, as given by inequalities (1) that define a partial ordering of his payoffs, admits six different complete orderings:

$$x_{11} > x_{21} > x_{12} > x_{22}; \quad x_{12} > x_{22} > x_{11} > x_{21};$$
$$x_{11} > x_{12} > x_{22} > x_{21}; \quad x_{12} > x_{11} > x_{21} > x_{22};$$
$$x_{11} > x_{12} > x_{21} > x_{22}; \quad x_{12} > x_{11} > x_{22} > x_{11}.$$

The two orderings of F, and the six orderings of A, define a total of 12 different strict ordinal games subsumed by the "generic" Frustration Game, which are divided into two classes in Fig. 7.1.[8]

I summarize properties of these games with three propositions, the last of which distinguishes between the two classes of games:

[7]Technically, a Nash equilibrium is not an outcome like (x_{11}, y_{11}) but the strategies of the players that lead to this outcome. For convenience, however, I will identify equilibria—both Nash and later nonmyopic—by the outcome, or payoffs at this outcome, rather than by the strategy pair that produces this outcome.

[8]The *generic* Frustration Game is the game that satisfies the three conditions, whereas the numbered games are specific instances of the generic game. The numbers shown above each numbered game are those given in the classification schemes of Brams (1994b) and, in parentheses, Rapoport and Guyer (1966).

Proposition 1 *In six of the 12 specific games subsumed by the generic Frustration Game, F has a dominant strategy (indicated by vertical arrows for games 5, 6, 10, 11, 32, and 35 in* Fig. 7.1*), but only in game 32 (Prisoners' Dilemma) does F's choice of this strategy lead to A's two worst outcomes (1 and 2).*

Thus, the apparent frustration that F experiences when A chooses his dominant strategy cannot be duplicated by F when she chooses her dominant strategy (if she has one), except in Prisoners' Dilemma.

Proposition 2 *In the 12 specific games subsumed by the generic Frustration Game, A's ranking of his payoff at the Nash equilibrium is better than F's ranking in 10 games and the same as F's in two games (games 28 and 32).*

Of the 10 games in which A's ranking is better, six are games in which A obtains his best payoff (4) and four are games in which he obtains his next-best payoff (3). In the two games in which the players tie, they both obtain their next-worst payoffs (2).

So far the picture looks pretty grim for F: She always obtains only her next-worst payoff (2) at the unique Nash equilibrium in the 12 games, whereas A does better than F—at least in terms of comparative rankings (I do not assume interpersonal comparison of utilities)—in 83 % of the games. Because A obtains a higher-ranked payoff in these games, F might not only be frustrated but also envious of A. But I leave for another paper a game-theoretic explication of envy as an emotion.

Fortunately for F, there is a way out of her plight in four of the 12 games if she possesses "threat power" of the "deterrent" kind (Brams and Hessel 1984; Brams 1994b, Chap. 5).

Proposition 3 *The exercise of deterrent threat power by F in the class II games in* Fig. 7.1 *induces an outcome [i.e., either (3,3) or (3,4)] for F at least as good as and sometimes better than that which A obtains at this outcome (in terms of comparative rankings).*

In a 2 × 2 strict ordinal game, a necessary condition for a player to have a *deterrent threat* is that he or she can threaten the choice of a strategy that leads to the other player's two worst outcomes. For example, in game 22 in Fig. 7.1, F can threaten the choice of t_2, which inflicts upon A a payoff of either 1 or 2; if F carried out her threat, A would presumably choose s_1, which yields (2,1), which is called the *breakdown outcome*, rather than choose s_2, which yields (1,4). If there is another outcome, associated with F's other strategy (t_1), that is better for both players (i.e., Pareto superior) than the breakdown outcome, then this is the *threat outcome* F can induce if she has "threat power."

Threat power is the ability of the threatener (F in this case) to withstand the Pareto-inferior breakdown outcome [(2,1) in game 22]—if she is forced to carry out her threat—and therefore induce the other player (A) to accept a Pareto-superior threat outcome.[9] In fact, both (4,2) and (3,3), associated with t_1, are Pareto superior to (2,1). But because F prefers (3,3), this is the threat outcome she can induce with threat power, which would supersede the Nash equilibrium of (4,2).

A similar analysis shows (3,4) to be the threat outcome that F can induce in game 35, with (2,1) again the breakdown outcome. In games 28 and 32, the breakdown outcome is (2,2), which is also the Nash equilibrium. Consequently, it is in *both* players' interest that F be able to induce, with threat power, (3,4) in game 28 and (3,3) in game 32.

In fact, if A has threat power, he, too, can induce (3,4) or (3,3), respectively, in these games by threatening, with the choice of s_1, F's two worst outcomes. Clearly, each player's exercise of threat power in games 28 and 32 would have a salutary effect, leading to an outcome preferred by both players. By contrast, in games 22 and 35, there is a conflict of interest between the players, with A's preferring to induce (4,2), which he can do with a "compellent threat" if he has threat power, and F's preferring to induce (3,3) or (3,4) with a deterrent threat.[10]

The possession of threat power enables F to relieve her frustration in all the class II games, making these games, in a sense, *controllable* (recall that it is a *lack* of control that leads to frustration). By comparison, F's lack of control in the class I games may turn her frustration into *despair*, or a feeling of helplessness. Of course, A, too, will be frustrated by the choice of (2,2) in games 28 and 32; but he, also, can help the players escape this Pareto-inferior outcome if he is able to exercise threat power. Like F's deterrent threat to choose t_1, A's threat involves threatening to choose s_1—and inflicting on F one of her two worst outcomes—in order to induce the Pareto-superior (3,4) outcome in game 28 and (3,3) in game 32.

[9]A threat may be communicated before the players choose strategies, or it may be communicated if players are at a state that F considers unsatisfactory. In game 22, for example, assume that the players are at (4,2). F's *threat* is to switch to t_2 if A is unavailing and continues to choose his first strategy. This would cause the game to move from (4,2) to the Pareto-inferior breakdown state of (2,1)—at which, presumably, the emotional temperature of the conflict would rise—from which F can induce (3,3) with threat power (for reasons given next in the text).

[10]A *compellent threat* is one that involves not just the threat of choice, but the actual choice, of a strategy. In making this choice, the threatener compels the threatened player to choose between a Pareto-inferior breakdown outcome and a Pareto-superior threat outcome. For example, in game 22, by choosing s_1 and refusing to budge from it, A can force F to choose between (4,2) and (2,1); if A has threat power, F will choose t_1, which in this game simply reinforces the choice of the Nash equilibrium. In both this game and game 35, threat power is *effective* in the sense that the player who possesses it does better than if the other player possessed it. By comparison, in games 28 and 32, threat power is *irrelevant*, because the outcome induced is the same whichever player possesses it. (However, it is not irrelevant in the sense that one player's possession of it enables both players to escape the Pareto-inferior Nash equilibrium in these games.) The distinction between "compellence" and "deterrence" was first made, informally, in Schelling (1966). Brams and Hessel (1984) formalized this distinction in terms of threat power; Aumann and Kurz (1977) incorporate the power to hurt others into a different game-theoretic model. For a detailed formal analysis, with examples, of the somewhat informal discussion here, see Brams (1994b, Chap. 5).

The frustration of players caught in real Prisoners' Dilemmas (game 32) is well known. What is less appreciated is that a deterrent threat on the part of one or both players in this game, as well as game 28, offers both an escape from (2,2), but it must be *credible*: The threatener must be able and willing to carry out the threat; emotions can reinforce the commitment to do so (Hirshleifer 1987; Frank 1988).

To be sure, a threat will not be credible unless a game is likely to be repeated, because a threat that leads to a breakdown outcome is, by definition, irrational to carry out in any single play. But if the game is a continuing one, it may be rational to suffer this outcome in early play in order to build up one's reputation for "toughness" in the future.[11] With one's reputation established, the need to carry out threats will be obviated, rendering the earlier suffering at breakdown outcomes worthwhile.

Overcoming Frustration with a Credible Threat: The Case of *Lysistrata*[12]

Aristophanes' comic yet biting anti-war play, *Lysistrata* (411 B.C.E/1973), was written in one of the Athens's darkest hours, after the total destruction of her expeditionary force in Sicily, the threat of invasion from Sparta and Syracuse, and the defections of some of her allies. It is a "dream about peace" by a playwright who believed "any peace must be satisfactory to both sides, and the women of both sides have to cooperate in bringing it about" (Sommerstein 1973, pp. 177–178).

While *Lysistrata* is part of the Old Comedy of Athens, the dream of Aristophanes is not pure fantasy. For one thing, the calculations of its characters are unremittingly strategic, as in real life. For another, powerful emotions, especially frustration, fuel the central action of the play, which gives *Lysistrata* some of the weight of the Greek tragedies of Aeschylus, Euripedes, and Sophocles.

The play begins when Lysistrata encounters her neighbor, Calonice, who recognizes that Lysistrata is "bothered." In fact, Lysistrata admits to being "furious," having "called a meeting [of women] to discuss a very important matter [while] our husbands … are all still fast asleep" (p. 180). She has hatched a plan, after "many sleepless nights," to "save Greece" from a never-ending battle between Athens and Sparta, which had left the lives of women of both city-states lonesome and desolate, and their male children prospective soldiers who might be killed like their husbands.

---

[11]This argument is made in the literature on repeated games, but its assumption of repeated play of a single game, without alteration, is highly unrealistic (Brams 1994b, p. 23). On the other hand, moves *within* a game (to different states), as allowed by the theory of moves, seem more plausible.

[12]This section is adapted, with significant changes, from a student paper of a former NYU undergraduate, Elana Zaas.

But Calonice mocks her:

> The women!—what could they ever do that was any use? Sitting at home putting flowers in their hair, putting on cosmetics and saffron gowns and Cimberian see-through shifts, with slippers on our feet? (p. 181).
> Yet these are exactly the weapons that Lysistrata intends for the women to use in order to get the men to "no longer lift up their spears against one another … nor take up their shields or their swords" (p. 182).

Lysistrata is frustrated, however, because "the ones I was most counting on" haven't shown up (p. 182). Eventually they drift in, and Lysistrata lashes out at their collective plight, with more than a touch of acerbic wit:

> The fathers of your children—don't you miss them when they're away at the war? I know not one of you has a husband at home … There isn't anyone even to have an affair with—not a sausage! (p. 184).

When, after first hesitating, Lysistrata blurts out her plan—"we must give up—sex"—to stop the carnage of war, the stage directions say there are "strong murmers of disapproval, shaking of heads, etc. Several of the company begin to walk off" (p. 184). Indeed, there is a chorus of "I won't do it" from several women, including Calonice, who says she'll "walk through the fire, or anything—but give up sex, never! Lysistrata, darling, there's just nothing like it" (p. 185).

Next there is a discussion of how women, by threatening abstinence, can use their feminine wiles and charm to induce the men to give up fighting. The women, however, worry that the men might divorce them or, worse, "drag us into the bedroom by force." But Lysistrata points out that, even in this case, the women can be as damned unresponsive as possible. There's no pleasure in it if they have to use force and give pain. They'll give up trying soon enough. And no man is ever happy if he can't please his woman (p. 186).

After still more cajoling from Lysistrata, the women take an oath to refrain from sex "with my boyfriend or husband … wearing my best make-up and my most seductive dresses to inflame my husband's ardour" (p. 188).

The women then retire to the Acropolis and close and bar the gates to the men, vowing not to open the gates "except on our terms" (p. 189). In the confrontation that follows, the men are heard to say such things as,

> "Euripides was right! 'There is no beast so shameless as a woman'!" (p. 195); and "Back to your weaving, woman, or you'll have a headache for a month" (p. 201), but their derision is to no avail.

Lysistrata remonstrates to the men that the women will "unravel this war, if you'll let us. Send ambassadors first to Sparta" (p. 204), she says, to negotiate a peace. She adds poignancy to her argument by describing the difficulty women face, which men do not, when the men go off to war:

> Even if we've got husbands, we're war widows just the same. And never mind us—think of the unmarried ones, getting on in years and with never a hope—that's what really pains me … A man comes home—he may be old and grey—but he can get himself a young wife in no time. But a woman's not in bloom for long, and if she doesn't succeed quickly, there's no one will marry her (p. 205).

The second act of Lysistrata occurs five days later, and Lysistrata herself is wavering: She wanders "restless to and fro" from "sex-starvation" (p. 210). Moreover, some women are reneging on their vows. But Lysistrata resolves to continue and prevails over most women, even persuading a woman named Myrrhine, who sees her own unwashed and unfed baby, to rebut the pleas of her husband for companionship by saying, caustically, to him: "I pity him [the baby] all right. His father hasn't looked after him very well" (p. 217).

Ambassadors from Sparta, whose women have followed the Athenian lead and abstained from sex, meet the Athenian negotiators. The men on both sides are distraught, but they take places on either side of Lysistrata, who makes a triumphant entrance ("no need to summon her") "magnificently arrayed" (p. 226).

Lysistrata begins her soliloquy with the brilliantly disarming statement: "I am a woman, but I am not brainless" (p. 227). Laying guilt on both Athens and Sparta, she helps them reconcile their differences, evoking from one impatient negotiator exactly the connection she wanted to make: "Peace! Peace! Bed! Bed!" (p. 229). The play ends with rejoicing and dancing at a banquet: The women have won.

How did they do it? To begin with, "winning" is not really an accurate characterization of the outcome, because the men and women have strong common interests, as depicted in the game in Fig. 7.2a (game 35 in Fig. 7.1).[13] The women, led by Lysistrata, can either refrain (R) from sex or not refrain ($\bar{R}$), and the men can continue to fight (F) or not fight ($\bar{F}$), giving rise to the four outcomes. Starting in the upper-left cell of the matrix, and moving clockwise, I rank them from best (4) to worst (1) for (women, men) as follows:

RF—Frustration: (1,2) The women suffer greatly (1), because their strategy of abstention fails to stop the fighting and, in addition, they are deprived of sex, which makes the men unhappy (2), too.

R$\bar{F}$—Partial success for women: (3,1) Abstention results in an end to fighting, which is good for the women (3)—but not as good as if they had continued sex—whereas the men are extremely upset (1) because, despite their not fighting, sex is withheld.

$\bar{R}$F—Success for men: (2,4) The women are unhappy (2), even though they have sex, because the fighting continues, whereas the men not only enjoy sex but are also able to fight without repercussions (4).

$\overline{RF}$—Resolution: (4,3) The women succeed completely (4), resuming their sex after the fighting ends, and the men benefit from sex but must desist from fighting (3).

While the benefits of fighting for the men may not be readily apparent today, the perspective I offer is that of the characters in the play.

[13]This game, like the game used to model the story in the next section, is purely illustrative. Other situations of frustration might be modeled by one of the 11 other specific games subsumed by the generic Frustration Game in Fig. 1.

(a) Frustration Game 35 (of *Lysistrata*)

Women \ *Men*	Fight (F)	Don't fight ($\bar{F}$)	
Refrain (R)	Frustration (1,2)	Partial success for women (3,1)	← Deterrent threat
Don't refrain ($\bar{R}$)	Success for men (2,4) (underscored)	Resolution $(4,3)^{td}$	← Dominant strategy
	↑ Dominant strategy		

(b) Self-Frustration Game 56 (of *Macbeth*)

Lady Macbeth \ *Macbeth*	Kill (K)	Don't kill ($\bar{K}$)	
Incite (I)	Murder motivated $(3,3)^{tc}$ (circled) [2,4]	Extreme frustration (1,1) [3,3]/[2,4]	← Compellent threat
Don't incite ($\bar{I}$)	Murder unmotivated (4,2) (circled) [4,2]	Status quo $(2,4)^{tc}$ (underscored, circled) [3,3] (underscored)	← Dominant strategy
		↑ Compellent threat	

Key: (x, y) = (pay-off to R, pay-off to C)
$[x, y]$ = [pay-off to R, pay-off to C] in anticipation game
4 = best; 3 = next best; 2 = next worst; 1 = worst
t = state induced by compellent (c) or deterrent (d) threat power
Nash equilibria underscored
Non-myopic equilibria (NMEs) circled in original game 56

Fig. 7.2 A frustration (**a**) and a self-frustration game (**b**)

The reason that game 35 in Fig. 7.2a looks different from the game in Fig. 7.1 is that I have interchanged the row and column players, and their strategies, in Fig. 7.2a. Structurally, however, these games are the same, with the women having a dominant strategy of $\bar{R}$ and the men having a dominant strategy of F, which yields (2,4) in Fig. 7.2a game.

Frustrated at this outcome, and being able by themselves only to move to the breakdown (and worse) outcome of (1,2), the women rebel. They not only threaten the men with R but also carry out this threat, which leaves the men the choice of their two worst outcomes. Between (1,2) and (3,1), they would choose (1,2), except that the threat outcome of (4,3) that the women offer entices them. With apparently few regrets, they choose it.

What is most relevant, from the viewpoint of this Chapter, is the emotional head of steam Lysistrata worked up to get the men to capitulate. First, she realized that her threat had to be carried out to be real. Using an artful combination of logic and zeal, she rallied the women, and later the men, to her side. Furthermore, she expressed her heartfelt anger with clarity and force, as I have already noted, and often with ribaldry, sometimes referring explicitly to male and female sex organs.

What invests this comedy with a sharp edge is the serious nature of the choices the characters face. Both the men and the women are torn by conflicting feelings and do not make their choices frivolously, justifying a game-theoretic view of their situation. At the same time, the characters do not confine themselves purely to an intellectual plane, which gives the women's threats, especially, credibility. Indeed, the characters are variously infused with feelings of sadness, despair, frustration, anger, and betrayal (e.g., when some women desert Lysistrata). In the end, though, even the men seem pleased by the reconciliation between Athens and Sparta.

The Self-Frustration Game

It is one thing for F to experience a lack of control when it is A's dominant strategy that leads to her (i.e., F's) two worst outcomes. But what if it is F, not A, who has the dominant strategy, and—anticipating F's choice of this strategy—A's best response is to choose the one of his nondominant strategies that leads to F's two worst outcomes?

Then, F's grief at A's choice seems as much attributable to her as to A: It is F's preferences—and dominant strategy—that induce A to frustrate her, rather than A's preferences and dominant strategy. (Recall in the Frustration Game that it is A who always has a dominant strategy.) If F is at least partially to blame for her grief in this situation, is escape from frustrating herself any easier than escape from being frustrated by A?

In order to answer this question, I define a new generic game, which I call the Self-Frustration Game (see Fig. 7.3). In this game, the row player, Advantaged (A), is, as before, male. The column player, whom I call Self-Frustrated (SF), is assumed to be female. The Self-Frustration Game satisfies the following four conditions:

1. *Dominance for SF.* Without loss of generality, assume that t_1 is SF's dominant strategy, so

$$y_{11} > y_{12}; \quad y_{21} > y_{22}. \tag{3}$$

   That is, whatever strategy A chooses (s_1 or s_2), SF prefers his payoffs associated with t_1 to those associated with t_2, making t_1 SF's unconditionally better strategy.
2. *Nash equilibrium.* Without loss of generality, assume that (x_{11}, y_{11}) is the unique Nash equilibrium that is associated with SF's dominant strategy of t_1, so

$$x_{11} > x_{21}. \tag{4}$$

That is, A prefers her payoff at (x_{11}, y_{11}) to that which she would receive at (x_{21}, y_{21}) if she switched from s_1 to s_2. Similarly, F prefers (x_{11}, y_{11}) to (x_{12}, y_{12})—and so would not switch from t_1 to t_2—because of the dominance of t_1, assumed in inequalities (3).

3. *Nondominance for A.* Given (4), to prevent s_1 from being dominant requires that

$$x_{22} > x_{12}. \tag{5}$$

4. *Lack of control.* F's two worst outcomes (1 and 2) are associated with A's nondominant strategy of s_1. From the first of inequalities (3), it follows that

$$y_{11} = 2; \quad y_{12} = 1.$$

To ensure the dominance of s_1, the second of inequalities (3) requires that

$$y_{21} = 4; \quad y_{22} = 3,$$

which gives a complete ordering of payoffs for SF of

$$y_{21} > y_{22} > y_{11} > y_{12}.$$

On the other hand, the fact that (x_{11}, y_{11}) is a Nash equilibrium but A does not have a dominant strategy associated with it—as given by inequalities (4) and (5)—defines a partial ordering of payoffs for A that admits six different complete orderings:

$$x_{11} > x_{21} > x_{22} > x_{12}; \quad x_{22} > x_{11} > x_{12} > x_{21};$$
$$x_{11} > x_{22} > x_{12} > x_{22}; \quad x_{22} > x_{11} > x_{21} > x_{12};$$
$$x_{11} > x_{22} > x_{21} > x_{12}; \quad x_{22} > x_{12} > x_{11} > x_{21}.$$

The one ordering of SF, and the six orderings of A, defines a total of six different strict ordinal games subsumed by the generic Self-Frustration Game, which are divided into two classes in Fig. 7.3.[14]

I summarize properties of these games with two propositions:

Proposition 4 *In the six specific games subsumed by the generic Self-Frustration Game, A's ranking of his payoff at the Nash equilibrium is better than SF's ranking in five games and the same as SF's in one game (game 28).*

Of the five games in which A's ranking is better, three are games in which A obtains his best payoff (4), and two are games in which he obtains his next-best

[14]The two classes are distinguished in Proposition 5. Ignore for now the bracketed outcomes, shown below the outcomes in parentheses in Fig. 3, in the so-called anticipation game.

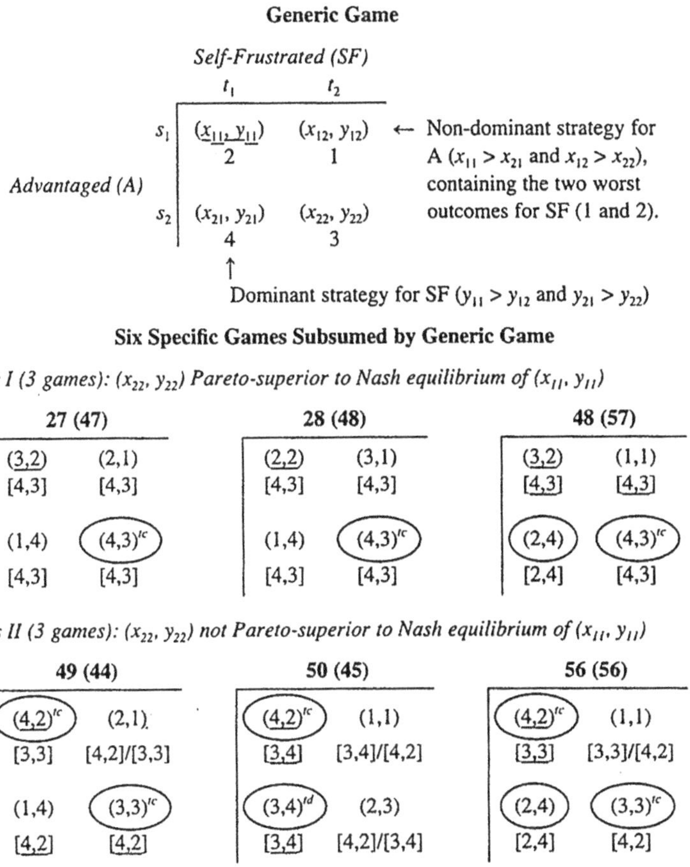

Key: (*x*, *y*) = (pay-off to A, pay-off to SF)
[*x*, *y*] = [pay-off to A, pay-off to SF] in anticipation game
4 = best; 3 = next best; 2 = next worst; 1 = worst
t = state induced by compellent (*c*) or deterrent (*d*) threat power of SF
Nash equilibria underscored (except in anticipation games 27 and 28)
Non-myopic equilibria (NMEs) circled in original game

Fig. 7.3 Self-frustration game

payoff (3). In game 28, which is also a Frustration Game (when the players are interchanged), both players obtain their next-worst payoffs (2).

Like F in the Frustration Game, SF in the Self-Frustration Game always obtains her next-worst payoff (2) at the unique Nash equilibrium in the six games, whereas A does better than SF—at least in terms of comparative rankings—in 83 % of the games. But unlike F, SF can escape her frustration in all six specific Self-Frustration Games, provided she has threat power (which, it will be recalled, offered an escape in only four of the 12 specific Frustration Games):

Proposition 5 *The exercise of either compellent or deterrent threat power by SF always results in a better outcome [i.e., either (3,3) or (3,4)] for her than that which she obtains at the Nash equilibrium. In the class I games, this outcome is, in fact, better for both players; it can also be induced by A's exercise of deterrent threat power.*

But what if the players do not have threat power? And what if the exercise of threat power leads to different outcomes—as it does in the three class II games—depending on which player (if either) possesses it?

Before discussing the class II games in which threat power is effective, I offer a dynamic perspective on the possible play of *all* 2 × 2 games, based on the "theory of moves" (TOM). As I will show, this theory offers SF, in particular, the opportunity to break out of the Nash equilibrium in both the class I and class II Self-Frustration games—without relying on threat power—given that the players are nonmyopic in a sense to be described.

The Theory of Moves (TOM)

The starting point of TOM is a payoff matrix, or *configuration*, in which the order of play is not specified. In fact, players are assumed not even to choose strategies but instead to move and countermove from outcomes, or states, by looking ahead and using "backward induction" to determine the rationality of both their moves and those of an opponent.

Because game theory assumes that players choose strategies simultaneously in games in normal or strategic form,[15] it does not raise questions about the rationality of moving or departing from outcomes—at least beyond an immediate departure, à la Nash. In fact, however, most real-life games do not start with simultaneous strategy choices but commence at outcomes. The question then becomes whether a player, by departing from an outcome, can do better not just in an immediate or myopic sense but, rather, in an extended or nonmyopic sense.

In the case of 2 × 2 games, TOM postulates four *rules of play*, which describe the possible choices of the players at different stages:

[15]Strategies may allow for sequential choices, but game theory models, in general, do not make endogenous who moves first, as TOM does, but instead specify a fixed order of play (i.e., players make either simultaneous or sequential choices). There are some recent exceptions, however, including Hamilton and Slutsky (1990, 1993), Rosenthal (1991), Amir (1995), and van Damme and Hurkens (1996). Typically, these models allow a player in the preplay phase of a game to choose when he or she will move in the play of the game. Yet the choice of when to move applies only to a player's initial strategy choice, whereas the nonmyopic calculations to be described here assume that players, starting at states, make moves and countermoves that depend on thinking several steps ahead. As in the case of threat power, I do not attempt a full technical exposition here, which can be found, with examples, in Brams (1994b, Chaps. 1–3).

1. Play starts at an outcome, called the *initial state,* which is at the intersection of the row and column of a 2 × 2 payoff matrix.
2. Either player can unilaterally switch his or her strategy, and therefore change the initial state into a new state, in the same row or column as the initial state.[16] The player who switches, who may be either row (R) or column (C), is called player 1 (Pl).
3. Player 2 (P2) can respond by unilaterally switching his or her strategy, thereby moving the game to a new state.
4. The alternating responses continue until the player (Pl or P2) whose turn it is to move next chooses not to switch his or her strategy. When this happens, the game terminates in a *final state,* which is the *outcome* of the game.

Note that the sequence of moves and countermoves is strictly alternating: First, say, R moves, then C moves, and so on, until one player stops, at which point the state reached is final and, therefore, the outcome of the game.[17]

The use of the word "state" is meant to convey the temporary nature of an outcome, before players decide to stop switching strategies. I assume that no payoffs accrue to players from being in a state unless it is the final state and, therefore, becomes the outcome (which could be the initial state if the players choose not to move from it). But here I draw attention to the emotions that are evoked before an outcome is reached.

Rule 1 differs radically from the corresponding rule of play in classical game theory, in which players simultaneously choose strategies in a matrix game that determines an outcome. Instead of starting with strategy choices, I assume that players are already in some state at the start of play and receive payoffs from this state if they stay. Based on these payoffs, they decide, individually, whether or not to change this state in order to try to do better.[18]

To be sure, some decisions are made collectively by players, in which case it would be reasonable to say that they choose strategies from scratch, either simultaneously or by coordinating their choices. But if, say, two countries are coordinating their choices, as when they agree to sign a treaty, the most important

---

[16]I do not use "strategy" in the usual sense to mean a complete plan of responses by the players to all possible contingencies allowed by rules 2–4, because this would make the normal form unduly complicated to analyze. Rather, *strategies* refer to the choices made by players that define a state, and *moves and countermoves* to their subsequent strategy switches from an initial state to a final state in an extensive-form game, as allowed by rules 2–4. For another approach to combining the normal and extensive forms, see Mailath et al. (1993).

[17]An emendation in the rules of TOM that allows for backtracking would be most appropriate in games of incomplete information, wherein players make mistakes that they later wish to rectify. Implications of allowing backtracking on "nonmyopic equilibria," which are discussed and illustrated later, are analyzed in Willson (1998).

[18]Alternatively, players may be thought of as choosing strategies initially, after which they perform a thought experiment of where moves will carry them once a state is selected. The concept of an "anticipation game," developed later, advances this idea, which might be considered dynamic thinking about the static play of a matrix game. Generally, however, I assume that "moves" describe actions, not just thoughts, though I readily admit the possibility of a thought interpretation.

strategic question is what individualistic calculations led them to this point. The formality of jointly signing the treaty is the culmination of their negotiations, which does not reveal the move–countermove process that preceded it. This is precisely what TOM is designed to uncover.

In summary, play of a game starts in a state, at which players accrue payoffs only if they remain in that state so that it becomes the outcome of the game. If they do not remain, they still know what payoffs they would have accrued had they stayed; hence, they can make a rational calculation of the advantages of staying versus moving. They move precisely because they calculate that they can do better by switching states, anticipating a better outcome if and when the move–countermove process finally comes to rest.

Rules 1–4 say nothing about what causes a game to end, but only when: Termination occurs when a "player whose turn it is to move next chooses not to switch its strategy" (rule 4). But when is it rational not to continue moving, or not to move in the first place from the initial state?

To answer this question, I posit a rule of *rational termination* (first proposed in Brams 1983, pp. 106–107), which has been called "inertia" by Kilgour and Zagare (1987, p. 94). It prohibits a player from moving from an initial state unless doing so leads to a better (not just the same) final state:

5. A player will not move from an initial state if this move
   - (i) leads to a less preferred final state (i.e., outcome); or
   - (ii) returns play to the initial state (i.e., makes the initial state the outcome).

I will discuss in "From Self-Frustration to Murder in *Macbeth*" how rational players, starting from some initial state, determine by backward induction what the outcome will be.

Condition (i) of rule 5, which precludes moves that result in an inferior state, needs no defense. But condition (ii), which precludes moves to the same state because of cycling back to the initial state, is worth some elaboration. It says that if it is rational for play of the game to cycle back to the initial state after P1 moves, P1 will not move in the first place. After all, what is the point of initiating the move–countermove process if play simply returns to "square one," given that the players receive no payoffs along the way (i.e., before an outcome is reached)?

Not only is there no gain from cycling, but in fact there may be a loss because of so-called transaction costs—including the emotional energy spent—that players suffer by virtue of making moves that, ultimately, do not change the situation.[19] Therefore, it seems sensible to assume that P1 will not trigger a move–countermove process if it only returns the players to the initial state, making it the outcome.

I call rule 5 a *rationality rule,* because it provides the basis for players to determine whether they can do better by moving from a state or remaining in it.

[19]However, other rules of play of TOM allow for cycling; see Brams (Brams 1994b, Chap. 4). In future work, I plan to explore why players might invest emotional energy to prolong conflict through cycling.

Still another rationality rule is needed to ensure that both players take into account each other's calculations before deciding to move from the initial state. I call this rule the *two-sidedness rule*:

6. Given that players have complete information about each other's preferences and act according to the rules of TOM, each takes into account the consequences of the other player's rational choices, as well as his or her own, in deciding whether to move from the initial state or subsequently, based on backward induction. If it is rational for one player to move and the other player not to move from the initial state, then the player who moves takes *precedence*: His or her move overrides the player who stays, so the outcome is that induced by the player who moves.

Because players have complete information, they can look ahead and anticipate the consequences of their moves. I next show how, using backward induction, they do this in the context of an example illustrating the emotions evoked when players make moves, first to inferior states, in order to get to still better states. I will also mention some theoretic tie-ins of the Self-Frustration Game to other generic games.

From Self-Frustration to Murder in *Macbeth*[20]

A central feature of Shakespeare's (1606/1994) great tragedy, *Macbeth*, is the conflict between Lady Macbeth and her husband, Macbeth, over murdering King Duncan. Duncan's demise would facilitate their ascent to the throne as king and queen of Scotland, but there are risks.

Lady Macbeth's ambition is fed by a letter she receives from Macbeth prophesying his greatness, based on his meeting with three "Weird Sisters" (who are considered to be witches). After mentioning in his letter that the Sisters saluted him with "Hail King that shalt be," he writes his wife—"my dearest partner of greatness"—of "what greatness is promised thee" (I, v, 10–12).

But Lady Macbeth worries—with good reason, it turns out—that her husband's "nature is too full o'th' milk of human kindness/To catch the nearest way" (I, iv, 15–17). Consequently, she wishes

> That I may pour my spirits in thine ear,
> And chastise with the valour of my tongue
> All that impedes thee from the golden round (I, iv, 25–27).

The advice she gives to Macbeth that will advance him to the "golden round" (i.e., crown) is preceded by her own musings.

[20]This section is adapted, with significant changes, from a student paper of a former NYU undergraduate, Nancy Wang.

Upon receiving news that King Duncan will be visiting Macbeth at his castle that very evening, Lady Macbeth thinks about his "fatal entrance under my battlements" (I, v, 38–39). She immediately steels herself psychologically for his murder:

> Come, you spirits
> That tend on mortal thoughts, unsex me here,
> And fill me from the crown to the toe, top-full
> Of direst cruelty. Make think my blood,
> Stop up the'access and passage to remorse,
> That no compunctious visitings of nature
> Shake my fell purpose (I, v, 40–45).

As if intending to murder Duncan herself, she says

> Come, thick night,
> And pall thee in the dunnest smoke of Hell,
> That my keen knife see not the wound it makes (I, v, 49–51).

But, in fact, it is not Lady Macbeth—shed of the womanliness in herself that she despises—who wants to carry out the dastardly deed. Instead, she earnestly hopes that her husband, though he looks "like th'innocent flower," is "the serpent under't" (I, v, 63–64). Macbeth, however, has grave doubts, especially that the murder will "return/To plague th'inventor" (I, vii, 9–10), and that King Duncan's "virtues/Will plead like angels" (I, vii, 18–19) if he is assassinated.

While Macbeth confesses to "vaulting ambition, which o'erleaps itself/And falls on the' other" (I, vii, 27–28), assassinating King Duncan to satisfy this ambition is another matter. Indeed, Lady Macbeth is furious when he tells her, while feasting with Duncan at their castle, that "we will proceed no further in this business/He hath honoured me of late" (I, vii, 31–32). She immediately accuses her husband of cowardice, even unmanliness, saying that *she* would, as a mother, have "dashed the brains out [of her baby], had I so sworn/As you have done to this [sworn to murder King Duncan] (I, vii, 57–58).

Still wavering, Macbeth asks, what "if we should fail?" (I, vii, 59). Lady Macbeth brushes him off:

> We fail?
> But screw your courage to the sticking place,
> And we'll not fail (I, vii, 60–62).

Lady Macbeth then indicates how, when Duncan sleeps, the assassination will be carried out. Macbeth finally agrees, but he is haunted by fear—an emotion that even Lady Macbeth's ferocity cannot dispel—of this "terrible feat" (I, vii, 80).[21]

[21]But the murder, Taylor (1996) argues, rids Macbeth of another emotion—the shame he felt in dishonoring his king and house guest—because, once the murder is carried out, Macbeth's feelings of cowardice and inadequacy are replaced by pride in successfully pursuing his overriding ambition to be king. Lady Macbeth's plunge into madness later in the play eventually undoes the couple, but that unanticipated outcome does not bear on the rationality of their current moves.

The game played between Lady Macbeth and Macbeth involves her choosing to incite him to murder (I) or not inciting him ($\bar{I}$), and Macbeth's killing Duncan (K) or not killing him ($\bar{K}$). Starting in the upper-left cell of the matrix in Fig. 7.2b, and moving clockwise, I rank the states from best (4) to worst (1) for (Lady Macbeth, Macbeth) as follows:

IK—Murder motivated: (3,3) Lady Macbeth is pleased that Macbeth carries out the murder—even if she must strenuously prod him to do so (3)—and Macbeth is pleased to satisfy her desire and demonstrate his manliness (3).

$I\bar{K}$—Extreme frustration: (1,1) To the great chagrin of both Lady Macbeth (1) and Macbeth (1), her pleas are ignored and his courage is thrown into question.

$\bar{I}K$—Murder unmotivated: (4,2) Lady Macbeth is most pleased if Macbeth murders King Duncan without her having to prod him (4), but Macbeth is plagued by guilt and self-doubt when not incited by Lady Macbeth (2).

$\overline{IK}$—Status quo: (2,4) Lady Macbeth is angry at Macbeth and disgusted with herself when neither she nor Macbeth acts to change the status quo (2), whereas Macbeth is happy to be honored by King Duncan and not have to act treacherously against him, especially as his host (4).

Structurally, this is game 56 in Fig. 7.3, except that the row and column players, and their strategies are interchanged in its Fig. 7.2b representation.

Play commences at the status quo of (2,4), which is upsetting to Lady Macbeth once she has read the letter from her husband: She realizes that the throne is within their grasp, but her husband may fail her in the clutch. Because her dominant strategy of $\bar{I}$ is associated with this state, however, standard game theory predicts that she will not move from it; neither will Macbeth, because it is a Nash equilibrium. But TOM makes a different prediction.

Nonmyopic Equilibria (NMEs) in *Macbeth*

From the perspective of TOM, Lady Macbeth would calculate the rational consequences of moving from (2,4)—what countermove, on the part of Macbeth, her move from this state would trigger, what counter-countermove she would make, and so on.

Given that players have complete information about each other's preferences, I assume they base their calculations on *backward induction*, which I will next illustrate for game 56 in Fig. 7.2b. Starting from (2,4) and cycling back to this state, I will show where R (Lady Macbeth) and C (Macbeth) will terminate play[22]:

If R moves first, the counterclockwise progression from (2,4) back to (2,4)—with the player (R or C) who makes the next move shown below each state in the alternating sequence—is as follows (see Fig. 7.2b):

	State 1		State 2		State 3		State 4		State 1
	R		C		R		C		
R starts:	(2,4)	→	(1,1)	→	<u>(3,3)</u>	→|	(4,2)	→	(2,4)
Survivor:	(3,3)		(3,3)		(3,3)		(2,4)		

The *survivor* is determined by working backward, after a putative cycle has been completed. Assume that the players' alternating moves have taken them counterclockwise from (2,4) to (1,1) to (3,3) to (4,2), at which point C must decide whether to stop at (4,2) or complete the cycle and return to (2,4). Clearly, C prefers (2,4) to (4,2), so (2,4) is listed as the survivor below (4,2): Because C *would* move the process back to (2,4) should it reach (4,2), the players know that if the move–countermove process reaches this state, the outcome will be (2,4).

Knowing this, would R at the prior state, (3,3), move to (4,2)? Because R prefers (3,3) to the survivor at (4,2)—namely (2,4)—the answer is no. Hence, (3,3) becomes the survivor when R must choose between stopping at (3,3) and moving to (4,2)—which, as I have just shown, would become (2,4) once (4,2) is reached.

At the prior state, (1,1), C would prefer moving to (3,3) than stopping at (1,1), so (3,3) again is the survivor if the process reaches (1,1). Similarly, at the initial state, (2,4), because R prefers the previous survivor, (3,3), to (2,4), (3,3) is the survivor at this state as well.

The fact that (3,3) is the survivor at initial state (2,4) means that it is rational for R initially to move to (1,1), and C subsequently to move to (3,3), where the process will stop, making (3,3) the rational choice if R has the opportunity to move first from initial state (2,4). That is, after working *backward* from C's choice of completing the cycle or not at (4,2), the players can reverse the process and, looking *forward,* determine that it is rational for R to move from (2,4) to (1,1), and C to move from (1,1) to (3,3), at which point R will stop the move–countermove process at (3,3).

---

[22]Where, of course, depends on the endstate, or *anchor,* from which the backward induction proceeds, which I assume here—for reasons given in the previous section—is after one complete cycle. This assumption defines a finite extensive-form game, but it is dropped in other parts of TOM, where alternative rationality rules are applied to "cyclic games," which may cycle until the player without "moving power" quits (Brams 1994b, Chap. 4). In only two of the six cyclic games (28 and 35) subsumed by the Frustration Game does moving power provide relief from the Nash equilibrium for F, and in these games a deterrent threat works as well in game 28 and better in game 35. In the six specific games subsumed by the Self-Frustration Game, the NME (to be defined in the text) from the Nash equilibrium provides SF with at least as much relief as does SF's moving power, except in game 48, in which SF can induce (2,4), rather than the NME of (4,3), with moving power. For more details on the effects of moving power in these six games, see Brams (1994b, 1995).

Notice that R does better at (3,3) than at (2,4), where it could have terminated play at the outset, and C does better at (3,3) than at (1,1), where it could have terminated play, given that R is the first to move. I indicate that (3,3) is the consequence of backward induction by underscoring this state in the progression; it is the state at which *stoppage* of the process occurs. In addition, I indicate that it is not rational for R to move on from (3,3) by the vertical line blocking the arrow emanating from (3,3), which I refer to as *blockage*: A player will always stop at a blocked state, wherever it is in the progression. Stoppage occurs when blockage occurs for the *first* time from some initial state, as I illustrate next.

If C can move first from (2,4), backward induction shows that (2,4) is the last survivor, so (2,4) is underscored when C starts. Consequently, C would *not* move from the initial state, where there is blockage (and stoppage), which is hardly surprising since C receives its best payoff in this state[23]:

	State 1		State 2		State 3		State 4		State 1
	C		R		C		R		
C starts:	(2,4)	→|	(4,2)	→|	(3,3)	→	(1,1)	→	(2,4)
Survivor:	(2,4)		(4,2)		(2,4)		(2,4)		

As when R has the first move, (2,4) is the first survivor, working backward from the end of the progression, and is also preferred by C at (3,3). But then, because R at (4,2) prefers this state to (2,4), (2,4) is temporarily displaced as the survivor. It returns as the last survivor, however, because C at (2,4) prefers it to (4,2).

Thus, the first blockage and, therefore, stoppage occurs at (2,4), but blockage occurs subsequently at (4,2) if, for any reason, stoppage does not terminate moves at the start. In other words, if C moved initially, R would then be blocked. Hence, blockage occurs at two states when C starts the move–countermove process, whereas it occurs only once when R has the first move.

The fact that the rational choice depends on which player has the first move—(3,3) is rational if R starts, (2,4) if C starts—leads to a conflict over what outcome will be selected when the process starts at (2,4). However, because it is not rational for C to move from the initial state, R's move takes precedence, according to rule 6, and overrides C's decision to stay. Consequently, when the initial state is (2,4), the result will be (3,3), which is indicated for game 56 in Fig. 7.3, and in Fig. 7.2b, by placing [3,3]—in brackets—below (2,4).

The outcome into which a state goes is called the *nonmyopic equilibrium* (NME) from that state. NMEs may be viewed as the consequence of both players' looking ahead and making rational calculations of where the move–countermove process will transport them, based on the rules of TOM, from each of the four possible initial states.

[23]But it is rational in several 2 × 2 games for a player to depart from his or her best state (4), because in these games he or she would do worse if the other player departed first (Brams 1994b, Chap. 3).

To take another example, backward-induction analysis from each state in game 27 shows that each state will go into (4,3). Thus, wherever play starts, the players can anticipate that they will end up at (4,3), making it the unique NME in game 27. This is also true of (4,3) in game 28, but not in game 48, the third class I game. Starting at (2,4) in game 48, the players will not depart from this state, making (2,4) as well as (4,3) an NME in this game.

Like game 48, all games in class II contain at least two NMEs. But some of these NMEs are *indeterminate*, because there is a conflict over who will move first. In game 50, for example, if (1,1) is the initial state, [3,4]/[4,2] indicates that when R moves first from (1,1), (3,4) will be outcome, whereas when C moves first, (4,2) will be the outcome.[24]

Because R prefers (4,2) whereas C prefers (3,4), each player will try to hold out longer in order to induce the other player to move first. Who wins in this struggle will depend on which player has "order power"—that is, who can determine the order of moves, starting at (1,1) (Brams 1994b, Chap. 5).

Every 2 × 2 game contains at least one NME, because from each initial state there is an outcome (perhaps indeterminate) of the move–countermove process. If this outcome is both determinate and the same from every initial state, then it is the only NME; otherwise, there is more than one NME.

In game 56 in Figs. 7.2a and 7.3, there are three different NMEs, which is the maximum number that can occur in a 2 × 2 strict ordinal game; the minimum, as already noted, is one. All except two of the 78 2 × 2 games (game 56 and Chicken, which is not shown) have either one or two NMEs.

The four bracketed states of each game in Fig. 7.3 define what I call the *anticipation matrix*, with each state in this matrix an NME. Insofar as players choose strategies as if they were playing a game based on this matrix, one can determine which NMEs are Nash equilibria in the *anticipation game* and therefore likely to be chosen.[25]

[24]Actually, the result of backward induction by R from (1,1) in game 50 is (2,3) rather than (3,4). But, as I argue in Brams (1994b, p. 114, Footnote 20), the players would have a common interest in implementing the Pareto-superior (3,4) to (2,3) when there is clockwise movement from (1,1). However, the implementation of (3,4) would require a binding commitment on the part of R not to move on from (3,4) to (4,2), which is not assumed possible in noncooperative game theory. I conclude (with an interchange of players and their payoffs): "I do not see an airtight case being made for either (2,3) or (3,4) as *the* NME from (1,1) when R moves first, which nicely illustrates the nuances that TOM surfaces that the rules of standard game theory keep well submerged." Incidentally, game 50 is the only game of the 78 2 × 2 strict ordinal games in which this kind of ambiguity about NMEs arises.

[25]Because the NMEs in games 27 and 28 are all the same, the strategies of the players in their anticipation games are indistinguishable, making all four states Nash equilibria. In the four other games, t_1 is C's (weakly) dominant strategy; R's best response leads to a dominant-strategy Nash equilibrium in each anticipation game, some of which contain other Nash equilibria. Only in game 49 is the Nash equilibrium in the anticipation game, (4,2), also the Nash equilibrium, (4,2), in the original game.

To summarize, where players start in the original games in Fig. 7.3—including the unique dominant-strategy Nash equilibria—may not be where they end up, according to TOM. Thus, an original game may mask a good deal of instability when the players can move and countermove from states.[26]

This instability is evident in *Macbeth*. Lady Macbeth relentlessly hounds Macbeth to murder King Duncan, which brings the players temporarily to (1,1) when Macbeth temporizes. Frustrated, Lady Macbeth explodes with anger, which impels Macbeth finally to act, bringing the players to (3,3) after the murder is committed.[27]

The couple is able, for a while, to escape suspicion, placing the blame on the servants, who are also murdered, and King Duncan's sons, who flee. When Banquo, who had with Macbeth heard the prophecy of the Weird Sisters, seems likely to uncover the Macbeths' plot, Macbeth has him killed. In the end, however, the previously indomitable Lady Macbeth comes apart emotionally and commits suicide. Without her formidable presence, Macbeth loses faith and is slain by Macduff, whose entire family he had had murdered.

Remorseless as Lady Macbeth is until the end, she is a character, in my opinion, brimming with emotion. She uses her frustration to great advantage to push her reluctant and vacillating husband over the brink, so to speak, which Delilah did to Samson, on a different matter, in the famous Bible story (also modeled as game 56 in Brams 1980, 1994b).

Characters in real-life self-frustration games have displayed similar emotions, which often caught their opponents off guard (e.g., the USA by the 1941 Japanese attack on Pearl Harbor; Israel by Egyptian President Anwar Sadat's 1977 peace initiative and visit to Jerusalem). Their moves engendered great shock and surprise (Brams 1997a, b), which is an emotional reaction in its own right triggered by the surpriser's (Japan's and Egypt's) unanticipated actions.

TOM, by explicating the rationale of such moves, makes them less surprising. It turns out that the six specific games subsumed by the Self-Frustration Game in Fig. 7.3 are precisely the games subsumed by a so-called generic Surprise Game (Brams 1997a, b) and a generic Freedom Game (Brams 1999), in which the player with the dominant strategy (SF in Fig. 7.3) finds it rational, according to TOM, to switch to her dominated strategy, in turn inducing A to switch his strategy, too.

[26]Even the choice of a state associated with a dominant-strategy Nash equilibrium in the anticipation games offers no assurance that players will stay at this state. Indeed, except for one of the two states associated with the [3,4] Nash equilibria in the anticipation game of game 50, the players will move from *every* such state to some different NME in the six anticipation games in Fig. 3.

[27]By drugging the servants who were supposed to guard Duncan and making sure the door to his chamber was unlocked, Lady Macbeth was certainly an accessory to murder. But this legalistic interpretation glosses over her preeminent role, which she maintained by an implacable display of cold fury and hot anger. In fact, the NME of (3,3) is reinforced by Lady Macbeth's compellent threat of choosing strategy I and sticking with it, but I prefer the NME explanation for (3,3), because it relies only on the farsighted thinking, not any special powers, of the players.

This move and countermove from the unique Nash equilibrium (upper-left states in games in Fig. 7.3) brings both players to the lower-right states. From the latter states, the players would return to the Nash equilibrium (if given the chance). Unfortunately for Macbeth and Lady Macbeth, they met their ends before this could happen, making these subsequent moves infeasible (Brams 1994b, pp. 40–42).

Conclusions

Frustration is expressed, I have argued, when players who are dissatisfied and lack control are forced to make "desperate" choices—choices that hurt them, at least temporarily, because they involve moves from a Nash equilibrium. But they are not unmotivated choices. By erupting with an emotion like anger or rage when they move to their disadvantage, at least initially, these players signal that they want this loss of control to end—in particular, for the other player to respond by helping them.

I have suggested that the theory of moves (TOM), which offers a rationale for players' making dynamic choices in games, can rationally explain these seemingly irrational choices. In the case of the Frustration and Self-Frustration Games, players express frustration when they threaten the other player, or try to induce a nonmyopic equilibrium (NME), that hurts the frustrated or self-frustrated player, but only initially.

I showed that in the Frustration Game, Frustrated (F) can break out of the unique Nash equilibrium, at which she suffers her next-worst outcome, with a deterrent threat in four of the 12 specific games. But this threat is effective only if F can endure the breakdown outcome better than Advantaged (A), who has a dominant strategy. The women (F) in *Lysistrata* had such threat power in the form of withholding sex from the men (A), which induced the men to stop fighting, making the women ecstatic and the men reasonably happy.

The Self-Frustration Game leaves the player with the dominant strategy, Self-Frustrated (SF), dissatisfied at the unique Nash equilibrium. In this game, I assumed that each player considers the consequences of moving from that state, the other player's countermoving, and so on, which eventually brings both players to what I call a nonmyopic equilibrium (NME). This is the outcome that rational players would be expected to migrate to—and from which, I assume, they derive all their payoffs—if it is rational for them to move at all (based on backward induction).

It turns out that in the six specific games subsumed by the Self-Frustration Game, SF can, starting at the Nash equilibrium, induce an NME better for herself, and sometimes for A, than the Nash equilibrium. Threat power of either the compellent or deterrent kind is also effective in these games for one or both players. In *Macbeth*, however, it seemed less that Lady Macbeth could threaten Macbeth with anything—except, perhaps, withdrawal of her love—than switch to her dominated strategy to induce Macbeth in turn to switch his strategy.

This move and countermove led the couple to plot the murder of King Duncan and successfully execute it. The fact that their crime later unraveled, however, does not undermine the rationality of their calculations in the beginning, undergirded, as these calculations were, by Lady Macbeth's logic and the Weird Sisters' prophecy of greatness.

In the past, TOM has been used to interpret the actions, but not the emotional responses, of the players along the path to NMEs. It is *during* the moves along this path, I suggest, when human emotions come into play, even if (long term) payoffs to the players accrue only when an NME is reached.

I believe other emotions besides frustration can be fruitfully studied using TOM. Thus, for example, an Envy Game might be one in which the good fortune of one player is tied to the bad fortune of the other, suggestive of pure-conflict games, but Elster (1991, p. 57) argues this need not be the case.

For the game theorist, unlike the psychologist, it will be the structure of situations that trigger emotions, rather than the emotions themselves, that will be of primary interest. No generic game that mirrors such structures, however, will capture all the subtleties of emotional interactions that people have in literary, as well as real-life, games. But one psychologist has argued that "a necessary first step is to develop a theoretical system that can account successfully for a reasonably large number of 'emotional' phenomena" (Mandler 1994, p. 243).[28]

A dynamic game-theoretic model offers, in my opinion, a promising start on understanding when frustration *cum* anger and other emotions are likely to arise, and how best to cope with them. Nonetheless, the classification of the different possible paths, the assessment of their payoff consequences, and a psychological interpretation of the emotions these different paths are likely to evoke will require considerable investigation and analysis, even for 2 × 2 games.

To further this endeavor, I propose as a working hypothesis that the more players suffer in nonpreferred states along the path to a nonmyopic equilibrium, the more intense will be their emotions. Insofar as the nonmyopic equilibrium offers "relief" to the players—in the sense of providing them with a preferred state—this emotion will, in the end, be positive.

But if one player remains dissatisfied at this equilibrium state, he or she may want to depart, rendering this equilibrium unstable. Therefore, one might analyze the *stability* of nonmyopic equilibria—a major refinement of the current concept—showing how it depends on the nature of the path taken to reach it and the emotions evoked along this path.

A subsidiary hypothesis is the following: The more difficult the path to a nonmyopic equilibrium, the more likely this equilibrium will remain stable. "Difficulty" might be measured by the number of Pareto-inferior states that a 2 × 2 game contains, especially if it is a "cyclic" game (36 of the 78 2 × 2 games) in which both players have a continuing incentive to move.

[28]Mor (1993) indicates other linkages of the psychology literature to the game-theoretic modeling literature, including that based on TOM, especially in international relations.

According to this hypothesis, a resolution of a crisis in cyclic games that contain two Pareto-inferior states (22 games) is more likely to hold than in cyclic games that contain only one such state (12 games) or no such state (two games, both of which are games of pure conflict). The underlying reason for this greater stability is that the players in games with more Pareto-inferior states suffer together when an equilibrium is upset.

As a case in point, the relative stability achieved in the aftermath of the 1962 Cuban missile crisis may stem not only from the fact that a mutually disastrous nuclear war was averted but also—from an emotions viewpoint—that future superpower leaders had no desire to repeat such a traumatic experience.[29] In this sense, the high drama of agreements forged in crises may be an antidote to their later breakdown, compared with agreements reached in noncrisis situations in which there is no possibility of mutual disaster.

But, of course, this is an untested hypothesis. It and related hypotheses can, I believe, successfully be investigated within the dynamic framework developed here.

References

American Heritage Dictionary. (1980). *New college division*. Boston: Houghton Mifflin.

Amir, R. (1995). Endogenous timing in two-player games: A counterexample. *Games and Economic Behavior 9*(2), 234–237.

Aristophanes (411 B.C.E./1973). *Lysistrata* (Allan H. Sommerstein, Trans.). London: Penguin.

Aumann, R. J., & Kurz, M. (1977). Power and taxes. *Econometrica, 45*(5), 522–539.

Berne, E. (1964). *Games people play*. New York: Ballantine.

Brams, S. J. (1980). *Biblical games: Game theory and the Hebrew Bible* (Rev. ed. 2003). Cambridge, MA: MIT Press.

Brams, S. J. (1983). *Superior beings: If they exist, how would we know? Game-theoretic implications of omniscience, omnipotence, immortality, and incomprehensibility* (Rev. ed. 2007). New York: Springer.

Brams, S. J. (1993). Theory of moves. *American Scientist*, 81(6), 562–570.

Brams, S. J. (1994a). Game theory and literature. *Games and Economic Behavior, 6*(1), 32–54.

Brams, S. J. (1994b). *Theory of moves*. Cambridge, UK: Cambridge University Press.

Brams, S. J. (1997a). Game theory and emotions. *Rationality and Society, 9*(1), 93–127.

Brams, S. J. (1997b). The rationality of surprise: Unstable nash equilibria and the theory of moves. In A. Mintz & N. Geva (Eds.), *Decision making on war and peace: The cognitive-rational debate* (pp. 103–109). Lynn Reiner: Boulder, CO.

Brams, S. J. (1999). Modeling free choice in games. In Myrna H. Wooders (Ed.), *Topics in game theory and mathematical economics: Essays in honor of Robert J. Aumann* (pp. 46–62). Providence, RI: American Mathematical Society.

Brams, S. J. (2011). *Game theory and the humanities*. Cambridge, MA: MIT Press.

[29]Nikita Khrushchev's sense of loss of control in this crisis is reflected in the following statement he made in a letter written to John Kennedy: "If people do not show wisdom, then in the final analysis they will come to clash, like blind moles" (Divine 1971, p. 47).

Brams, S. J., & Hessel, M. P. (1984). Threat power in sequential games. *International Studies Quarterly*, *28*(1), 23–44.
Brams, S. J., & Mattli, W. (1993). Theory of moves: Overview and examples. *Conflict Management and Peace Science*, *12*(2), 1–39.
Brams, S. J., & Mor, B. D. (1993). When is it rational to be magnanimous in victory? *Rationality and Society*, *4*(4), 432–454.
Brams, S. J., & Togman, J. M. (1996). The dynamics of the Northern Ireland conflict. *Oxford International Review*, *7*(2), 50–54.
Colomer, J. M. (1995a). *Game theory and the transition to democracy: The Spanish model.* Aldershot, UK: Edward Elgar.
Colomer, J. M. (1995b) Leadership games in collective action. *Rationality and Society*, *7*(2), 225–246.
Damasio, A. R. (1994). *Descartes' error: Emotion, reason, and the human brain.* New York: Grosset/Putnam.
de Sousa, R. (1987). *The rationality of emotion.* Cambridge, MA: MIT Press.
Divine, R. A. (Ed.). (1971). *The cuban missile crisis.* Chicago: Quadrangle.
Elster, J. (1991). Envy in social life. In R. J. Zeckhauser (Ed.), *Strategy and choice* (pp. 49–82). Cambridge, MA: MIT Press.
Elster, J. (1994). Rationality, emotions, and social norms. *Synthese*, 98(1), 21–49.
Emotions and Rational Choice. (1993). *Rationality and society* (special issue), 5(2).
Frank, R. H. (1988). *Passions within reason: The strategic role of the emotions.* New York: W. W. Norton.
Frijda, N. H. (1986). *The emotions.* Cambridge, UK: Cambridge University Press.
Geanakopolos, J., Pearce, D., & Stacchetti, E. (1989). Psychological games and sequential rationality. *Games and Economic Behavior*, 1(1), 60–79.
Gerlernter, D. (1994). *The muse and the machine: Computerizing the poetry of human thought.* New York: Free Press.
Gilboa, I., & Schmeidler, D. (1988). Information dependent games: Can common sense be common knowledge? *Economics Letters, 27*, 215–221.
Hamilton, J. H., & Slutsky, S. M. (1990). Endogenous timing in duopoly games: Stackelberg or Cournot equilibria. *Games and Economic Behavior*, *2*(1), 29–46.
Hamilton, J. H., & Slutsky, S. M. (1993). Endogenizing the order of moves in matrix games. *Theory and Decision*, *34*(1), 47–62.
Hirshleifer, J. (1987). On the emotions as guarantors of threats and promises. In John Dupré (Ed.), *The latest on the best: Essays on evolution and optimality* (pp. 305–326). Cambridge, MA: MIT Press.
Hirshleifer, J. (1994). The dark side of the force. *Economic Inquiry, 32*(January), 1–10.
Howard, N. (1994). Drama theory and its relation to game theory. part 1: Dramatic resolution versus rational solution; part 2: Formal model of the resolution process. *Group Decision and Negotiation*, *3*(2), 187–206; 207–235.
Howard, N., et al. (1993). Manifesto for a theory of drama and irrational choice. *Systems Practice, 6*(4), 429–434.
Huang, P. H., & Wu H. M. (1992). Emotional responses in litigation. *International Review of Law and Economics*, *12*(1), 31–44.
Kilgour, D. M., & Zagare, F. C. (1987). Holding power in sequential games. *International Interactions, 13*(2), 91–114.
Kroll, J. A. (1993). The complexity of interdependence. *International Studies Quarterly*, *37*(3), 321–347.
Lazarus, R. S., & Bernice, N. (1994). *Passion and reason: making sense of our emotions.* Oxford: Oxford University Press.
Lax, J. R. (1996). *Unanimity and dissent in the supreme court: The conflict of consensus.* Preprint: Department of Politics, New York University.
Lewis, M. (1995). Self-conscious emotions. *American Scientist*, *83*(1), 68–78.

Mailath, G. J., Samuelson, L., & Swinkels, J. (1993). Extensive form reasoning in normal form games. *Econometrica, 61*(2), 273–302.
Mandler, G. (1994). Emotions and the psychology of freedom. In S. H. M. van Goozen, N. E. Van de Poll, & J. A. Sergeant (Eds.), *Emotions: essays on emotion theory* (pp. 241–262). Hillsdale, NJ: Lawrence Erlbaum Associates.
Maoz, Z., & Mor, B. D. (1996). Enduring rivalries: The early years. *International Political Science Review, 17*(2), 141–160.
Massoud, T. G. (1998). Theory of moves and the Persian gulf war. In Murray Wolfson (Ed.), *The political economy of war and peace* (pp. 247–265). Amsterdam: Kluwer.
Mor, B. D. (1993). *Decision and interaction in crisis: A model of international crisis behavior.* Westport, CT: Praeger.
Mor, B. D. (1995). Crisis initiation and misperception. *Journal of Theoretical Politics, 7*(3), 351–367.
Rabin, M. (1993). Incorporating fairness into game theory and economics. *American Economic Review, 83*(5), 1281–1302.
Parrott, W. G., & Harré, R. (1996). Overview. In R. Harré & W. G. Parrott (Eds.), *The emotions: Social, cultural and biological dimensions* (pp. 1–20). London: Sage.
Rapoport, A., & Guyer, M. J. (1966). A taxonomy of 2 × 2 games. *General Systems: Yearbook of the Society for General Systems Research, 11*, 203–214.
Rosenthal, R. W. (1991). A note on robustness of equilibria with respect to commitment opportunities. *Games and Economic Behavior, 3*(2), 237–243.
Schelling, T. C. (1966). *Arms and influence.* New Haven, CT: Yale University Press.
Shakespeare, W. (1606/1994). *Macbeth.* In N. Brooke (Ed.). Oxford, UK: Oxford University Press.
Simon, M. V. (1996). When sanctions can work: Economic sanctions and the theory of moves. *International Interactions, 21*(3), 203–228.
Solomon, R. C. (1993). *The passions: Emotions and the meaning of life.* Indianapolis, IN: Hackett.
Sommerstein, A. M. (1973). Introduction. In Aristophanes (Ed.), *Lysistrata* (pp. 9–38). London: Penguin.
Taylor, G. (1996). Guilt and remorse. In R. Harré & W. G. Parrott (Eds.), *The emotions: Social, cultural and biological dimensions* (pp. 57–73). London: Sage.
Thibaut, J. W., & Kelley, J. W. (1959). *The social psychology of groups.* New York: Wiley.
van Damme, E., & Hurkens, S. (1996). Commitment robust equilibria and endogenous timing. *Games and Economic Behavior, 5*(2), 290–311.
Willson, S. J. (1998). Long-term behavior in the theory of moves. *Theory and Decision, 43*(3), 201–240.

GPSR Compliance
The European Union's (EU) General Product Safety Regulation (GPSR) is a set of rules that requires consumer products to be safe and our obligations to ensure this.

If you have any concerns about our products, you can contact us on

ProductSafety@springernature.com

In case Publisher is established outside the EU, the EU authorized representative is:

Springer Nature Customer Service Center GmbH
Europaplatz 3
69115 Heidelberg, Germany

www.ingramcontent.com/pod-product-compliance
Lightning Source LLC
Chambersburg PA
CBHW071440230926
51846CB00001B/298
* 9 7 8 9 4 0 1 7 7 8 6 4 0 *